Competitive Customer Care

A Guide to Keeping Customers

Merlin Stone
and
Laurie Young

Croner Publications Ltd
Croner House
London Road
Kingston upon Thames
Surrey KT2 6SR
Telephone: 081-547 3333

Printed by Whitstable Litho Ltd, Whitstable, Kent

Contents

Foreword

The current emphasis on "quality" as a route to company survival in the 1990s has resulted in a plethora of books on the subject of total quality management – its advantages and how best to gain from its implementation. At Unisys, we have always insisted on the highest standards in the management of our customers. But we have experienced a fundamental change in our market place which has caused us to make a complete review of our approach to customer care. We are intent on taking a market-led approach to our investment in the quality of customer care.

The management processes to achieve quality customer care *must be clearly specified*. This book describes these processes and how to use them in meeting customer needs by applying modern marketing techniques.

It is essential to maintain the focus of the organisation on achieving the highest levels of continued customer satisfaction. I wish the reader success in implementing the approaches described in this book, so as to reach this desirable — indeed essential — goal.

P W Wilcox
Vice President, Customer Services
Unisys Europe

Acknowledgements

This book is the result of many years of experience and thought. Our experience comes from working with a wide range of organisations — in the private, public and voluntary sectors, from discussions with managers on a wide range of training and development programmes with which we have been associated, and from working with our colleagues in management consultancy, education, training and management development.

Our thanks are due to the many companies with which we have worked, whether as employees or consultants, who have allowed us the opportunity to become involved in their efforts to improve customer care.

Our thanks are also due to our employers – Unisys UK and Kingston Polytechnic – for providing the support we needed to complete this enterprise.

Derek Davies of Kingston Polytechnic's Business School provided us with valuable material on customer needs and on the regulatory environment. Stephen Smith of the Polytechnic's School of Social Sciences contributed material on emotional labour. The many staff involved in improving customer care at Kingston Polytechnic have given us valuable insights. John Csaky of Fitch RS contributed material on the role of design in caring for customers. Mike Wallbridge and Adrian Hosford of British Telecom introduced us to the role of direct marketing and customer communications in customer care. Jill

Parker, when she was at British Airways, helped us understand how face to face transactions and marketing communications can work together to improve customer care.

Merlin Stone   Laurie Young
Kingston Polytechnic   Unisys UK

Chapter 1

What is Customer Care?

Caring for customers is a simple idea. It means looking after customers and meeting their needs. In a world where most suppliers need to meet their customers' needs, the experience of many customers is not very happy. When customers do have poor experiences, rather than tell the supplier, they allow the situation to fester. They infect other customers with their attitudes, creating a snowball effect. Meanwhile, the supplier carries on in blissful ignorance, until its overall success starts to falter.

Why do so many suppliers fail in customer care? Why have so many suppliers not worked out how to improve their standards of customer care? Why have so few implemented improved standards? One reason is that customer care is not the only way of meeting customer needs. A well laid-out store, a high quality, well designed new product, a properly targeted and designed direct mail letter — all these are ways of looking after customers and meeting their needs. In an age when marketing has come to the fore, it is on these kinds of factors that most marketing effort has been focused. The special feature of customer care is that it relates to how customers are treated by their supplier's staff. Put more simply, customer care depends upon how people treat people. This is much more difficult to manage.

One reason why suppliers are slow to improve customer care is that many managers who make policy are remote from customers and from those who serve them. These managers may simply be unaware of failings in customer care. Performance problems may be attributed to other elements of the marketing mix.

The aim of this book

The aim of this book is to help managers improve the customer care their organisations deliver. This book shows that:

(a) customer care is critical to competitive success
(b) customer care is the legitimate province of the marketer
(c) professional marketing techniques can be applied to the idea of customer care, using the building blocks of marketing analysis, such as "segmentation" and "hierarchy of needs"
(d) customer care is *the* area where external marketing — to customers — must merge with internal marketing — to staff
(e) a new vocabulary is required to create the right policy focus. This includes terms such as "perceived transaction period", "contact audit", "locus of control", and "parallel industry"
(f) a proper planning process is required to create and sustain customer care, to keep it in step with changing customer needs at optimum cost.

Complaints — or what?

Much of what has been written about customer care focuses on complaint handling. The rightly famous and oft-quoted research by TARP (Technical Assistance and Research Programmes) in the United States and Canada, for the White House Office of Consumer Affairs, helped to create this negative focus. This research, which covered 200 companies, showed that:

(a) the average business does not hear from 96 percent of its unhappy customers
(b) for every complaint received, there are 26 customers with problems and 6 with serious problems

(c) most customers do not think that it is worth complaining. Some do not know how and where to start. Some do not think it is worth investing the time and effort in doing so. Some are sceptical of being dealt with effectively because of considerable past experience of poor problem handling

(d) customers with problems who fail to complain are far less likely to repeat their orders (for the same product or service). They are also far more likely to stop completely their business with the supplier

(e) customers who complain and whose problems are handled well are much more likely to continue doing business

(f) customers with bad experiences are twice as likely to tell others about it as those with good experiences

(g) the average service business loses 10-15 percent of its customers each year through poor service

(h) nearly half of all service problems are caused by failure to read instructions.

(i) over half of all telephone calls to companies are to get information.

It is this last point which provides the key to this book. Customer care is not just about handling complaints. It is about ensuring that customers do not need to complain. Complaint handling is a cost of poor quality — in the relationship between customer and supplier. For example, a system or process which ensures that the customer has the right information is a much better solution that one which provides information to customers only when they complain.

The best demonstration of this is that of the US General Electric's (GE) telephone enquiry centre's roughly two million calls per year, only 10 percent are complaints. 25 percent are from customers seeking information. GE does its best to provide all the information customers might need locally. However, it knows that whatever happens, many customers will not read instructions or notices or listen to sales staff. So what better way to care for their information needs than to provide a highly publicised number which customers know they can call if they have any sales or service enquiry?

More evidence of the positive aspects of customer care comes from the PIMS (Profit Impact of Market Strategy) studies of the Strategic Planning Institute. These show that sustainable high and profitable market shares are most easily achieved when a supplier has better perceived product and service quality than its competitors. There is a clear implication here that good customer service can generate a price premium. In times of recession, good customer service can provide sound protection against losing business through price competition.

There are longer term benefits. In markets for industrial goods and services, many new product ideas are developed and/or refined by customers. But for the required close relationship between customer and supplier to be sustained, good customer service must be delivered.

Who are customers and suppliers?

All organisations have customers. These customers may be private consumers — as individuals or families. They may be trade customers — as individual buyers or users, or whole organisations. They may be voters, members, patients, donors, subscribers, benefit recipients or clients. Put very broadly, a customer is anyone or any group of people who interact with an organisation and whose well-being is important to it. For this reason, the term "supplier" is used throughout this book to refer to any organisation which has customers. It is used even if the main aim of the organisation is not to supply customers with goods or services.

There are often customers within the supplier itself. For example, in a factory, work groups can be customers for each other. One group may supply components for the other to incorporate into a sub-assembly. If the components are defective, the second group suffers.

The group customer

Customers are not always individuals. The idea of the group customer has already been mentioned. For group customers, it can be helpful to identify different individuals within the group and the roles that they play. In organisational marketing, the classic definition of roles is helpful. The buying group is called "the buying centre", in which individuals or sub-groups play particular roles. These roles include:

(a) user — the person actually using the product and whose experiences of customer care can make or break the repeat order
(b) influencer — who influences the buying decision, often someone who works closely with other members of the buying centre, or

whose objectives require the use of the product or service to be successful

(c) decision-maker — who makes the decision, often a budget holder or person in a position of authority

(d) gatekeeper — who brings/allows information about the product into the buying centre, including information about the level of customer care experienced by other customers

(e) buyer — who implements the buying decision using formal procedures

(f) financier — who pays for the product.

These roles may be played formally or informally. Each individual may play a number of roles. Within the family, similar roles are also played. Customer care policy must take these roles into account. Different roles imply different objectives, requirements, levels of influence, and the need for different types of customer care.

For example, a parent buying a complex, expensive toy for a child's birthday, the day before the birthday, may require, as financier, buyer and influencer:

(a) a wide variety of goods on accessible display, so that the child can choose knowing what each product is really like

(b) helpful guidance about the product range

(c) easy payment or credit facilities

(d) immediate replacement if the product proves defective

(e) a competitive price

(f) availability of the product in stock

(g) gift-wrapping

(h) robust packaging, which allows the product to be replaced in it many times when not in use.

The child, as gatekeeper, decision-maker and user, may require:

(a) availability of the product in stock

(b) robust performance, to specification

(c) packaging which can be easily removed.

Of course, the father may be a secret user and have some of these requirements too!

Often, particularly on Saturdays, the family becomes a "mobile buying centre". Shopping is for many families one of the few things they do together as a group. Suppliers have the opportunity of satisfying their requirements as a group, but also the risk of failing to do so. Retailers who make most of their sales on a Saturday should cater for the different members of this group simultaneously (eg by provision of toys for children to play with, chairs for the elderly to sit on, baby changing rooms accessible to both mother and father).

Why is customer care important?

For some organisations, customers' well-being is an explicit objective. This is true of many charities and public sector bodies. However, customer well-being may be a very powerful, if implicit, objective if the organisation is to meet its formal objectives, such as profit, professional satisfaction or election to power. Most people buy, use services or vote according to whether an organisation meets their general needs, what image they have of the organisation, and how the organisation's staff behaves towards them. In such situations, meeting customer needs may be so important that it is elevated to an explicit objective, equalling that of profit for shareholders.

The age of liberalisation

Shareholders must recognise that times have changed and that customers have a greater influence on profits. In a number of countries, the 1980s was a decade of liberalisation of old commercial restrictions. This took a number of forms, including:

(a) more liberal commercial regulations
(b) privatisation of state companies, particularly state monopolies, usually accompanied by the introduction of competition, whether through break-up of the monopoly or entry of new competitors
(c) freer international competition — Europe 1992 and continued multilateral reduction of trade barriers.

In some countries, the 1980s were also a period when the power of the individual against the large organisation (state or private) was used quite dramatically in some cases. Examples include:

(a) the freeing of eastern Europe

(b) the continued power of consumerism

(c) the rise of environmentalism.

Media

These major trends were made more visible by the increased ability of broadcast and published media to obtain and transmit information, from anywhere to anywhere. This had an important effect. It gave confidence to any person in the position of a consumer. It inspired consumers to object when they were treated badly. Any person who is treated badly by an organisation, whether large or small, now feels more confident in objecting. Such people may go the political route, through a local representative. They may use the "approved route", through a formal body set up to represent consumers of the service or directly to the right point in the organisation. They may fumble to find the right route. Or they may go straight to the media. This assertiveness of customers is welcomed by the most customer-oriented companies. It ensures a high quality of feedback, and may even reduce market research budgets!

Education

Changes in education have also enhanced this trend. Children are no longer educated in authoritarian schools. They are taught to question authority in any form. They are taught about their rights as citizens and consumers. They are now happier to question the authority of professionals — teachers, doctors, lawyers and even the police.

Standards of living

Higher standards of living have also led to consumers being able to afford higher quality products and services. Their expectations have risen correspondingly. They are prepared to pay higher prices for better service, but are much more acute at detecting inferior service and quicker to complain.

Legislation

These trends have been reinforced by a battery of consumer legislation, covering everything from pricing, product labelling and product liability to protection from pressure selling (cooling-off periods on contracts).

However, despite all this, some organisations still treat customers poorly and make it difficult for them to express what they want, or their level of satisfaction with what they have received. If they are commercial suppliers, they lose customers to their competition. If they are political organisations, they lose voters. If they are public service organisations, they come under political pressure. Their funding may be reduced. If they are charities, they may lose donors.

Benefits of customer care

Achieving high levels of customer care has obvious benefits for customers. They get better service and often better products. But what are the benefits to suppliers? The answer lies in a very simple statement:

Acquiring customers is much more expensive than keeping them.

This is most obvious in a direct marketing situation, when the costs of acquiring and keeping customers can be accurately quantified. In other marketing environments, estimates show the same.

The benefits of customer care can be shown through accounting techniques which reveal:

(a) costs of acquisition of customers
(b) changes in the number of customers
(c) changes in the amount of business each customer is placing with the supplier.

Figure 1.1 gives an example of the kind of data used.

However, this approach requires a change in the way some companies carry out their marketing calculations. So long as they quantify markets in terms of the volume or value of sales, the connection between customer care and profit is hard to see. But if they also quantify markets in terms of:

(a) the number of customers

8

		Case 1	Case 2	Case 3
1	Cost of customer acquisition — sales force	500000	600000	700000
2	Cost of customer acquisition — advertising	200000	230000	300000
3	Total cost of customer acquisition	700000	830000	1000000
4	Cost of acquiring each customer	500	550	600
5	Number of customers acquired	1400	1509	1667
6	Lifetime contribution per customer (NPV)	1500	1450	1420
7	Lifetime contribution, all customers (NPV)	2100000	2188182	2366667
8	Net surplus through customer acquisition	1400000	1358182	1366667

Figure 1.1 Costs and benefits of customer acquisition

This calculation shows how a supplier might work out the costs and benefits of investing in a combined sales force and advertising campaign to acquire customers.

The values in Row 4 rise because of diminishing returns — it becomes increasingly difficult to attract customers. The values in Row 6 fall because the average quality of customers (measured by their contribution) diminishes as more of them are acquired. The calculation shows that Case 1 is the best combination. However, there is an indication that it might be profitable to run larger campaigns, as the rate at which contribution is diminishing seems to tail off a little (Row 6).

The same argument applies to customer care, except that the main role of customer care is to keep rather than acquire customers. The greater the investment in customer care, the less the additional return. However, if customer care is used as a weapon to undermine the position of a leading competitor, very high investment might be justified to win customers away.

    (b) the value of orders each customer places during their "life" with the company

then the connection becomes clear. Examples of the results of this life-cycle marketing are given in Chapter 15.

Costs of customer care

To the supplier, the costs of increasing levels of customer care relate mainly to possible increased complexity of business process and expenditure on finding out about customers' needs. However, a customer-oriented approach may be cheaper than other approaches in the long run. For example, a customer whose needs are met first time will not return to complain, which would absorb resources. In a technical product market, the number of repeat faults — those which were not dealt with properly the first time — will fall. For this reason, many companies which provide technical service now target a specific proportion of first-time fixes. In this respect, customer care is similar to quality, which comes free when it is planned and implemented properly (see Chapter 10).

However, as with quality, an initial investment is often necessary. This is because procedures may need to be changed, staff may need to be trained, outlets may need rearranging and so forth. It is therefore critical that customer care is seen as an investment and that accounting procedures value customer care over several years.

Customers' rights and obligations

In law and in marketing, customers have rights and obligations. Customers who buy products have the legal right to receive products of the right quality at prices which are not deceptive and on terms which are clearly explained before the transaction. From a marketing point of view, customers have the right to be valued as customers and treated accordingly. They also have the right to be given the information and support they need in order to be good customers or they will take their business elsewhere. Customers do not have the right to get products, services or customer care at rates which bankrupt the company!

Customers' obligations are to behave as responsible customers. Legally, this means:

(a) taking account of information provided by the supplier
(b) carrying out the transaction within terms publicised by the supplier, subject to these terms not breaking the law, such as the Consumer Credit Act 1974 and the Sale of Goods Act 1979 (eg refusal of refunds for defective goods).

The phrase "buyer beware" was coined long before the emergence of modern capitalism (Latin — *caveat emptor*). However, in the age of marketing, the supplier's job must be seen as that of helping customers fulfil their obligations. These are only obligations in a weak sense in that customers owe it to themselves to fulfil them, otherwise they risk being worse off. These obligations are:

(a) to be conscious of their own needs. A supplier can obviously help a customer explore these needs by offering different products or options

(b) to find out whether the product will meet the need. The supplier's obligation here is to provide the information that will help customers do this

(c) to carry out the relationship with the supplier honestly. Mutuality on the part of the supplier is essential here (untrustworthy suppliers may encourage devious customer behaviour)

(d) to adhere to commitments made beforehand — the mirror image of the supplier's obligation to do the same.

Ignorance and dishonesty

Customer care policy must be set within this framework. Ignorant customers exist and must be educated. This will help them get the best out of the supplier. It may also help customers decide correctly that they should not be doing business with the supplier. Dishonest customers should be identified quickly and discouraged. Every supplier has a long list of bad experiences with customers who lie and cheat their way to get special conditions or terms, damaging merchandise which they claim was already damaged when bought, and so forth. These must be allowed for in all customer care policies.

However, no customer care policies are perfect. A supplier which trusts customers so little that it adopts policies which will guarantee no wrongful return of merchandise and no bad debt will end up with no customers. On the other hand, a supplier which trusts its customers completely, irrespective of warning signs, has a good chance of going bankrupt!

Why so many organisations forget their customers

If customers are so important, why do so many suppliers neglect, or worse, forget their customers? The answer is to be found in the nature of modern management. Most organisations whatever their size use some degree of specialisation. Large tasks and roles are broken down into smaller tasks and roles. These are broken into yet smaller tasks and roles. Policies which were designed with the customer in mind lead to complex management tasks being defined. Once these tasks are broken down again and again, the original customer focus may have been lost. Jobs become a combination of roles and tasks, and customers become part of a task. Internal political pressures then cause staff within the organisation to rank internal issues more highly than customer issues.

Split responsibilities

For example, a product may have been designed with customer needs in mind. The sales policy may have targeted customers with proven need for the product. Yet somehow sales people, in front of the customer, try to sell customers what they do not need. The sales incentive system may be encouraging sales people to sell higher margin products than customers need. Or the needed product may be out of stock, so the sales person tries to sell something else. This has all happened because the responsibility for making profit while satisfying customers has been split between the different groups responsible for:

(a) making products which meet customer needs
(b) overall financial control
(c) sales incentive systems
(d) selling.

In this situation, if sales people are not managed with one of their prime objectives being customer care, then anti-customer selling will occur. Respected customers become "punters" or worse. They may become "debtors" to staff responsible for credit chasing, or "trouble-makers" for those responsible for service.

This demonstrates the importance of integrating customer care with other objectives, down to the very last detail of implementing commercial policy. Otherwise, though customers may not have been forgotten in policy making, they will surely perceive that they have been.

The scope for customer care

Customer care does not just cover sales situations. It covers transactions which are connected with sales (eg reading an electricity meter, receipt of an invoice). It covers service situations which are not directly related to the sale but are in some sense commercial, because the customer may have to pay as a result. Examples of this include emergency call-out of gas service staff to check a central heating boiler emitting fumes (a repair would need to be paid for) or flight cancellation (the customer has paid for a ticket). It also covers uncommercial activities (eg treatment of voters or taxpayers, behaviour of security guards, or even arrest by police).

The perceived transaction period

Customer care is not just a question of face to face transactions. Other opportunities for caring for customers exist in these kinds of situation:

(a) over the telephone
(b) in self-service stores when the customer is confronted by shelves of merchandisc
(c) in self-service petrol stations
(d) at cash machines
(e) when customers receive letters
(f) when customers see advertisements
(g) when customers face computer screens.

In fact, opportunities for customer care exist whenever customers *perceive* that they are engaged in a transaction with an organisation.

This rather "aggressive" view of customer care brings many opportunities and problems. For example, customers who buy new cars may pay two or three visits to the dealer before buying. They may have several telephone conversations with the dealer before and after the sale. They may exchange one or two letters during the transaction. They may visit the dealer after the sale to have a minor problem rectified.

Throughout this period, most customers are likely to consider themselves engaged in a transaction with the dealer. If this period of transaction is well managed, customers are likely to return to the dealer for service and for a replacement car when the time comes. They may also buy a more expensive model, or buy insurance, extended warranty or finance through the dealer. However, the potential for problems is also greater. If this period of transaction is spoiled by failures in customer care and safeguards future revenue opportunities, then customers may not buy additional items. At the worst, they may cancel the deal. So, using "perceived transaction period" in defining customer care opens up opportunities for much better customer care and safeguards future revenue opportunities, but also exposes risks of failure. Figure 1.2 illustrates a typical transaction period and shows how the degree of involvement of the customer may vary over that period.

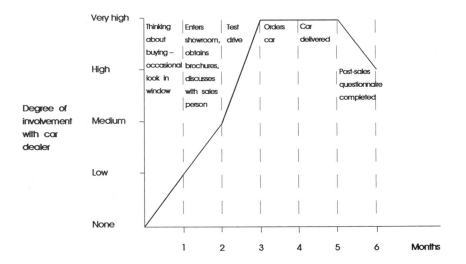

Figure 1.2 Involvement during perceived transaction period for purchase of new car from dealer, period up to and just after purchase

This diagram shows how the customer's involvement increases gradually in the period up to the purchase. It also shows how early in the purchasing cycle opportunities for customer care occur. Many customers feel neglected at the early stages, and this may influence their choice of dealer.

What happens after purchase depends on the state of the delivered car. If it is in a poor state, then involvement may stay high, but negative. If it is in a good state, then a second post-sales questionnaire after 6 months may maintain a reasonably high and positive involvement. This in turn will increase the probability of the customer returning for service.

The service encounter

A perceived transaction period may be composed of a number of service encounters. During each service encounter and over the transaction period as a whole, the customer may go through a range of mental states, such as:

(a) experiencing the need
(b) panic about how to fulfil the need, or whether it will be fulfilled at all
(c) sensitivity — about whether the right choice has been made, or whether to accept the way in which the service is being provided
(d) dependence — a feeling of being as a child to the "adult" provider of service
(e) happiness or unhappiness — according to the degree of success of the encounter or transaction
(f) satisfaction or resentment — after the encounter or transaction is over, according to its result.

Figure 1.3 shows an example of an analysis of service encounters during a perceived transaction period and the resulting emotional states.

Perceptions of care

Perceptions are important not only in defining the period of the transaction. They are even more important in defining the standard of customer care received. Suppliers which aim to achieve high levels of customer care may need to monitor delivery of customer care through internal measures, such as time to answer a query or frequency of a fault recurring. However, the measure that counts is what customers *perceive* they are receiving, and how satisfied they are with it. Measuring service just through internal measures is like behaving as an adult to a child. The organisation is effectively saying: I am an adult and set the standards. The customer [the child] will see the wisdom of this in the long run.

Standards should be set according to customer needs. Because customers have different needs, this implies that standards should be varied according to the type of customer being served.

15

MINUTES

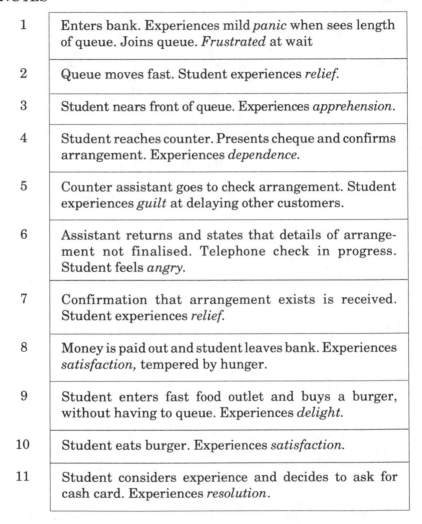

1	Enters bank. Experiences mild *panic* when sees length of queue. Joins queue. *Frustrated* at wait
2	Queue moves fast. Student experiences *relief.*
3	Student nears front of queue. Experiences *apprehension.*
4	Student reaches counter. Presents cheque and confirms arrangement. Experiences *dependence.*
5	Counter assistant goes to check arrangement. Student experiences *guilt* at delaying other customers.
6	Assistant returns and states that details of arrangement not finalised. Telephone check in progress. Student feels *angry.*
7	Confirmation that arrangement exists is received. Student experiences *relief.*
8	Money is paid out and student leaves bank. Experiences *satisfaction,* tempered by hunger.
9	Student enters fast food outlet and buys a burger, without having to queue. Experiences *delight.*
10	Student eats burger. Experiences *satisfaction.*
11	Student considers experience and decides to ask for cash card. Experiences *resolution.*

Figure 1.3 Emotional states during banking transaction

This figure shows the possible emotional states a student might experience when trying to cash a cheque drawn on another branch of the same bank. The student has entered the bank 15 minutes before it closes. An arrangement has been agreed between the two bank branches, but only a few days before, so the student is worried about whether details have been finalised. This figure demonstrates the variety of emotional states that can occur during a very brief period.

The first transaction

The first transaction is important, though not as critical as it might seem. It is true that "you never get a second chance to make a first impression". But a customer approaching a supplier for service has a reason to do so. Some customers may be put off by a poor first impression. Others will persist, particularly if any problems are quickly resolved. The problem is that new customers are those most likely to have difficulties dealing with the supplier. They are less likely to know how to get the best from the supplier. Experienced customers know the "script" that both sides have to follow to ensure a mutually satisfactory transaction. This implies that the first transaction needs to be managed more carefully, paying particular attention to the information flow throughout.

Formal definitions

Customer care

In this book, the level of customer care achieved is defined as:

> How customers perceive that they are treated by the organisation and its people during any period in which those customers perceive that they are in transaction with the organisation.

This is a customer-oriented definition of the level of customer care. It follows the vital marketing rule that all policy should be seen from the viewpoint of the customer.

Customer care policy

The definition of *customer care policy* that follows from this is:

> Everything that the organisation does to ensure it meets its objectives through managing customer transactions throughout the perceived transaction period, so that customers perceive that all their needs are satisfied.

This definition keeps the focus on the perceived period of transaction and perceived levels of satisfaction.

Competitive care

One more definition is needed. This book is about *competitive* customer care. This has a more commercial focus, although it does not exclude organisations which do not have to compete through customer care. In a commercial environment, does it imply just performing better than competitors? Not necessarily. A supplier may want to achieve competitive advantage by providing *much* higher levels of customer service than its competitors. In a mature market, *company differentiation* is important. Here, customer care policies ensure that all a supplier's staff reinforce the desired (differentiated) image.

Even a non-commercial supplier may be subject to comparisons with other suppliers. Most suppliers are in a sense competing with other organisations for the goodwill of customers. Failures in customer care will be unfavourably compared with levels of customer care achieved by other suppliers. This will be true even if they are operating in completely different fields. These different fields are called "parallel markets". Parallel markets have little or no competitive overlap, but still provide a basis for consumers to compare experiences. Once again, it is the customer's perception that counts. If the customer compares the performance of two suppliers, irrespective of the markets they operate in, customer care policy must have a competitive focus. This focus must exist in strategy, planning and operational delivery, as is shown later in this chapter.

The role of the supplier's values

However, this focus must also be consistent with the values of the supplier, or more specifically, with the values customers would like it to have. It often (pleasantly) surprises customers when staff in a store recommend visiting a competitive store to obtain a product which is out of stock in the original store. The staff do this because the value they wish to transmit relates to the primacy of customer needs over the store's need to make a profit. Even competition has its limits!

Customer service and customer care

"Customer service" is now an accepted part of business vocabulary. Many companies now have "customer service" functions which are much more than complaints departments. For example, many computer companies successively named their after-sales activities maintenance, then service, then customer service. In most cases, this renaming was not superficial. It indicated a real transition, through stages which had the following foci:

(a) maintenance — ensuring that failures were dealt with and restoring equipment to its required standard of performance
(b) service — ensuring that the equipment performed to the appropriate standard through the intervention, often on a scheduled basis, of the engineer
(c) customer service — an advanced version of the previous attitude, with more focus on the interaction between the customer and the supplying company at the time of delivery of the service action.

In line with this move, staff who serviced the equipment went through the following (or similar) name cycle:

(a) maintenance engineers or field engineers
(b) (field) service engineers or field service representatives
(c) customer service representatives or officers.

The customer service orientation was an advance on the engineering orientation. It did not deny it. After all, equipment must continue to receive good engineering service or be designed to avoid the need for it. But the customer service orientation moved the focus to the customer. However, the focus was (and in many cases still is) on the supplier's perception. High priority is given to tasks, costs, procedures, management processes and hierarchies, and internally-oriented targets. In the best companies, these targets are based upon customer research.

For example, customers may say that for urgent calls they require service staff to come within two hours — the problem to be resolved within one hour of arrival. But this begs the question that customers know how long the service incident actually takes, and that every two hours has the same value. For example, is two hours over a lunch hour or at the end of a working day worth the same as two hours of prime work time? However, some suppliers insist on asking the question in terms of an absolute number of hours because it is only by hours that they can target their engineers.

The difference between customer service and customer care can best be summarised in this way:

Customer service	*Customer care*
Emphasises tasks	Emphasises customers
Focuses on costs	Focuses on profit and revenue
Procedures restrict responsiveness	Procedures enable responsiveness
Hierarchial management	Supportive management
Technical/administrative environment	Commercial environment

Focusing on customers

The customer care approach focuses on the customer. It considers the customer's perceptions and requirements in the customer's own language and within the customer's own frame of reference. It also focuses unashamedly on profits and revenue or on other objectives that the supplier has. These may include customer care itself. This is because focusing on key objectives normally ensures that customer care is ranked as important as other policies.

Customer care also focuses on the service encounters within the perceived transaction period. In these service encounters there are usually one or more moments of truth in which the customer either becomes convinced that excellent service is being delivered or decides that this is the last transaction because the service is so poor.

Customer care focuses on procedures which allow responsiveness, supportive management and targets which are customer-oriented. This is because much experience and research shows that these contribute to higher levels of customer care.

The role of customer care in policy

If customers are important to a supplier, then the supplier's policy must deliver the right level of customer care. However, customer care is not just a veneer. Failures in customer orientation cannot be dealt with by smiling at customers. If products do not meet customers' needs, if retail outlets are badly located, if advertisements trumpet the virtues of the company and its products without explaining benefits to customers, if staff are treated badly so that they become unco-operative, being pleasant to customers during the service encounter is unlikely to help much.

Inconsistencies in care

Lack of consistency in how customers are dealt with makes the contrast between an apparent desire to care for them and other policies too evident. The consumer who is expertly handled over the transaction period for a major domestic appliance such as a washing machine, and then finds that the machine breaks down on the second wash, is likely to consider that the supplier was working hard not to please but to deceive! The consumer who is consistently faced with polite and smiling refusal when requesting a service which staff have been instructed not to supply will soon feel cheated. Customer care, properly implemented, ensures that the organisation will not fall into this trap, and will deliver the promise implied in advertising or by reputation.

Caring is not easy

The seeds of customer care are sown early on in the business process, by ensuring that customer needs are taken into account. However, taking customer needs into consideration is not easy. Here are some examples of apparently sensible decisions and their adverse customer care consequences:

(a) If a retail outlet is designed with its prime criterion being effective use of space, customers are unlikely to be happy with the resulting arrangement. Aisles will be small and cramped, and displays too high.
(b) If a product is designed primarily for ease and economy of manufacture rather than ease of use and service, customers are unlikely to be satisfied because they will incur higher user costs.
(c) If a self-service machine is designed primarily for security, then customers are likely to find it difficult and time-consuming to operate.
(d) If staff are recruited and trained primarily to do their jobs quickly and accurately, then they are unlikely to handle customers well.

(e) If credit control procedures are designed primarily to reduce credit risk, then many new customers may be alienated by the stringency of procedures.

So for the right level of customer care to be achieved, it must be adopted as an objective at the beginning of any process which affects how customers are treated. This applies to everything, including:

(a) product or service design and manufacturing process
(b) staff and customer training programmes
(c) invoicing and credit control procedures
(d) marketing policies
(e) business planning — strategic and operational.

This approach is of course no guarantee of success but it has the right foundations. Insistence on high standards of customer care and the integration of customer care into policy does much to prevent a gap opening up between customers' requirements and the organisation's delivery.

A general responsibility

Customer care is not something that can be delegated to particular individuals in the organisation. The oft-used slogan "service is everyone's business" captures the essence of the idea. But it needs to be extended to "service of every customer is everyone's business". The TARP figures on the consequences of failure quoted at the beginning of this chapter show that customer care cannot be managed by averages. Five per cent of badly dissatisfied but vociferous customers can destroy a business. So the *general* responsibility must be taken through to dealing with *individual* cases. The responsibility is not an abstract one. Good customer care is experienced by individuals, not market segments, and is enhanced by staff working hard to help those individuals.

The role of planning

Business planning is very important. It is through business planning that all aspects of policy are usually integrated. The customer is normally confronted by the outcome of a mixture of policies which arise from the plan — product, service, staff, invoicing and so forth. The way that these policies affect the customer should be consistent. Otherwise, there is the risk identified above — that one aspect of policy may be badly out of line with others.

"Hi-tech" and "hi-touch"

In planning its approach to customer care, any organisation has a choice between two main approaches, as follows:

(a) *Hi-tech* involves delivery of customer care by the use of auto-mation. It is achieved through information and communication systems, design of the product (eg fault diagnosis), provision of comprehensive documentation and the like.
(b) *Hi-touch* means that customer care is delivered mainly through people, whether face to face or on the telephone.

Of course, the two can be and usually are combined. Hi-tech might be used with experienced users, who prefer to manage things by themselves, and require impersonal support. Hi-touch might be used for inexpert customers, faced with unfamiliar situations. They are likely to need a high level of personal help. Some degree of flexibility needs to be maintained, however. For example, a company whose customers are expert in dealing with routine situations may provide hi-tech customer care solutions for dealing with routine problems. But when a rare problem crops up, customers may require personal help.

The hi-touch approach goes back to personal service as provided in former times by the servant, waiter or corner shopkeeper. This approach, while highly effective, raises problems today. It is expensive. Today, customers expect a high level of service without having to pay a high price for it. It is also difficult to manage and control so that customers are guaranteed a high level of care. So the very largest organisations — giant retailers, banks, computer companies — have tried to produce a compromise between hi-tech and hi-touch that meets the varied needs of customers. The key need is flexibility. This ensures that customers needing more help can switch from hi-tech to hi-touch transactions when they need to.

Hi-tech customer care can be risky. In many service situations, customers are not in control and may therefore be slightly under stress. Their stress level can be reduced if they control the situation themselves, rather than depend on others. For example, self-service petrol stations reduce the customer's need to wait for service and ensure that the customer controls the amount of petrol pumped. Some bank customers prefer to take money from an anonymous but controlled-by-them automatic teller machine (ATM) than receive it from smiling counter staff.

The key need is to use whatever combination of technology and humans that gives the best service, taking into account the customer's required level of control over the service situation and the level of skills which the customer can reasonably attain given the frequency with which the transaction is repeated. Some customers are afraid of ATMs, others take to them very quickly.

The marketing concept — where the customer fits

Above, the importance of customer-orientation and basing definitions of customer care on perceptions of customers was emphasised. These points are fundamental to all marketing. Customer care comes naturally to the market-led company which highlights customer needs to all parts of the organisation. Of course, customer care is not just part of marketing, but an approach which should pervade the whole organisation. Some marketing writers argue the same for the marketing approach. Whether or not this is true, it certainly is difficult for the marketing approach to pervade the whole organisation unless customer-orientation precedes it. Marketing is important because customers are important, not the other way round.

The Seven Ps

Most marketing activities are generally defined as part of "the marketing mix". This consists of policies which are deployed directly in a company's relationship with its customers, to achieve its marketing objectives.

The marketing mix is often defined as the four Ps, which are:

(a) Product type, design and packaging — the specification of the services and how they are presented to the customer.

(b) Prices and user costs — what it costs the customer to obtain and use the service. For more expensive services, finance and payment terms can be very important.

(c) Promotion — marketing communications — how the customer is informed of the service and its benefits, and how the customer is persuaded to buy it. The main disciplines or functions of marketing communication include advertising, direct marketing, sales promotion, merchandising, public relations, exhibitions and other "face to face" events. Packaging is sometimes included here.

(d) Place or distribution — how the service reaches the customer. The main discipline here is choice and management of distribution channels.

There is some overlap between different elements of the marketing mix. For example, direct selling is a mixture of place and promotion. Special discounts are a combination of price and promotion.

Some people include market research and choice of market as elements of the marketing mix, but the former is better defined as marketing support, and the latter as part of marketing strategy.

When marketing policy is being formulated, customer care should be a central focus. It should unite the four traditional elements of the marketing mix — price, product, promotion, place. However, most professional marketers now agree that in marketing a service of any kind there are three further Ps which have a strong effect on customer care:

(a) People — who deliver customer service and should embody the promise of the service by their behaviour.

(b) Processes — in two senses, the process the customer goes through in obtaining service and the process the company goes through to ensure that what is delivered is what customers want. A special element of company processes are programmes which focus marketing resources to achieve specific objectives at specific times. Programmes are very important in marketing, which depends on focus for achieving results.

(c) Presence — how the total company offering — product, price, people, etc is delivered in front of the customer. It is what the customers see and hear when they walk into a store, what they see when they read a letter and what they hear during a telephone call. Corporate design, store layout, letter copy design, telephone call scripting, uniforms — all these have an important effect on presence.

The seven Ps are important because most customers see their relationship with suppliers holistically, and not as a mixture of seven types of policy. This applies whether or not the product being marketed is a service product.

Competitive strategy and customer care

In recent years, competitive strategy has received much attention. Porter's seminal works (eg *Competitive Strategy*, Free Press, 1980) have been adopted as text books in business schools through the world. This competitive emphasis filled a yawning gap. This gap was created because authors in many fields of management tended to assume that the context in which all businesses operated was competitive. They assumed that by pursuing good management norms, businesses would inevitably be competitive.

They reckoned without the strong tendency of managers to divert their gaze from markets and focus on internal procedures, practices and problems. Porter's work was and still is a timely reminder that unless a company focuses on dealing with its main competitors and on achieving a situation where its vulnerability to competition is minimised, it will be much weaker when attacked.

Creating markets

However, the Porter view tends to regard markets as concepts which exist in their own right, determined by customers' needs. Of course, suppliers can gain strong competitive positions by such strategies as dominating markets by sheer economies of scale or quality, or strongly entrench themselves in niches by a high degree of product differentiation. But many markets are in fact consciously or unconsciously shaped by the proponents. The most aggressive competitors deliberately seek to undermine their major opponents. They do this by *redefining* markets or segments and changing the critical success factors. In essence, they change the rules of the game.

Thus, if the prime competitive mode has been by product differentiation to meet the variety of consumer needs, the position of the leader (who may have a number of brands or products to cover the market) may be undermined by:

(a) developing a high quality product which meets all the needs of target customers
(b) a carefully structured marketing communications and sales strategy to hit all segments (a typical Japanese policy, but also the essence of the Marks & Spencer attack on department stores)
(c) a strong customer care position.

Professionalism in marketing

Maintaining high levels of competitive customer care is difficult. It depends on unrelenting efforts to understand customers' needs, and sustained motivation of staff. But being more competitive is no different from being a good manager. The same logical process, from situation analysis (including a very strong emphasis on perception and interpretation), through to setting objectives and strategies, to implementation, monitoring and control can be followed. The difference between strong and weak competitors lies in:

(a) *how* they work this process through
(b) their creativity in perceiving, understanding, defining and managing their markets
(c) their ability to identify where they really add value to customers
(d) their understanding of the actual and potential differentiators between them and their competitors, of where their competitors are trying to drive markets, and of the opportunities opened up by competitors' failure to drive markets in opportunity areas
(e) their ability to follow the more competitive "plan B" or alternative scenario when the opportunity arises
(f) their speed and competence in reacting to competitive challenges
(g) how closely they keep in touch with the market (customers and competition) while implementing their strategies
(h) the attention paid to getting things right at the operational level, including how they manage their people, how they exploit information and other technologies.

This is where customer care comes in. The importance of customer care depends on whether an edge has already been gained by any other players in the market, through care and/or quality. If not, the potential for increased market share and profit is great. But if one or more of the competitors are already leading on quality, then differentiation is the

main option. Customer care is not an option but an essential requirement.

Emulation versus differentiation

However, simple emulation is not a good recipe for success. Differentiation means standing out from the crowd. In most cases, some basic
customer research will show that there are many things that are quite
important to customers but which competitors do badly. Today, most
(though by no means all) suppliers have improved their performance
in areas that matter most to customers. It is in second-order needs that
the key to competitiveness may lie. Being best at things that other
suppliers do badly but which are quite important may be the best route
to success.

However, the professionalism with which customer care is managed
(designed, planned and implemented) does offer scope for differentiation. Positioning is an important part of this too. It supports and is
supported by good customer care. All aspects of customer contact must
be managed and presented to customers so as to reinforce positioning.

Customer care and the product

In competitive markets, a key element in marketing is defining and
bringing to the market products which meet customer needs while
making the right profit for the supplier. However, usually the customer
does not just buy a physical product or a tightly defined service.
Customers buy a product, associated services, and indeed the whole
relationship with the supplier. Customer care is an important component of this relationship. The product can therefore be depicted as
having a number of "skins", the innermost of which is the tightly
defined product, and the outermost of which is the entire relationship
(see Fig 1.4).

Some consumers may be able to differentiate sharply between these
skins, others may not. Whether they are able to do this depends upon
factors such as:

(a) the nature of the product, eg a physical product is easier to
distinguish from other elements of the package than a service
product

(b) consumers' past experience — do they know the product and/or supplier well, have they experienced service from the supplier?

(c) customer needs — do customers want the product and very little service, or do they require more than just the product? If so, what?

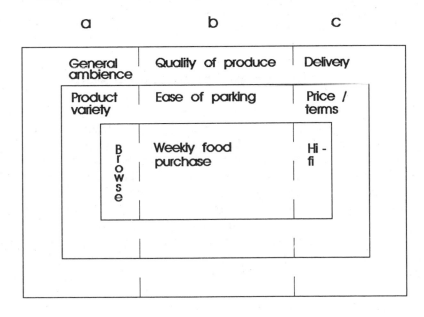

Figure 1.4 Different perceptions of product and service

This diagram shows how a customer might perceive the product/service combination offered by a John Lewis/Waitrose store, on three different occasions. On one Saturday (a) the customer and family may go with no other reason than to browse. It is a *leisure* experience, supported by the product variety and general ambience. A mid-week visit to Waitrose (b) is focused entirely on the weekly food purchase, supported by ease of parking and quality of produce. It is a *routine* experience. Finally, a visit to purchase a hi-fi is focused on the product, which is supported by pricing, terms and delivery. It is an *acquisition* experience.

Most customers' perceptions of the product are affected by their perceptions of other elements of the package, and *vice versa*. Hence the earlier emphasis on consistency of approach.

However, the idea of the product or service coming packaged in a variety of other elements is also a reminder not to ignore what these other elements are. Some may be under control of the supplier (eg sales documentation, packaging, telephone hotline), others less so (eg the retail situation when a manufactured product is bought). So it is important to:

(a) identify all elements of the package which might be perceived by consumers
(b) seek to optimise them, as far as possible.

The customer and the service system

The customer plays an active part in the product/service delivery system of many suppliers. For most services, the customer is present when the service is "delivered" and may take an active part in shaping the service to ensure that needs are met (eg a visit to the hairdresser). The term "servuction" has been coined to describe this combination of a service and production system. In this servuction system, it may make sense to see customers as partial employees of the service system — albeit unpaid. In fact, customers are often sacrificing time while obtaining the product or service. Therefore, they should be handled even more carefully than employees, who are at least paid for their efforts.

The employee analogy is useful. It suggests that while the service is being delivered, the customer is part of the supplier's system. As supplier's own staff are trained to perform the service properly, perhaps customers should be trained in the same way. This perspective corresponds to a good marketing principle. To optimise a marketing situation, policy must take into account the perspective of both sides — the customer and the supplier.

The customer and the brand

The above idea has a strong relationship with branding. A brand is a set of feelings, experiences, perceptions and/or ideas that is associated with a particular product or company. If a brand has strong customer care elements, and if these elements are successfully delivered to customers, then stronger customer loyalty will result. However, establishing such a strong reputation for customer care that it gets deeply embedded in the brand can only be done through a consistent policy of attention to customer care for many years. Once this branding has been achieved, customer care aspects of the brand can be brought out in many ways, from staff practices to advertising. This topic is dealt with more fully in Chapter 12.

Customer care and quality

The roots of the current fashion for quality go back many decades, to just after the war, when (amongst others) the Japanese listened to US experts. They were preaching the gospel of quality control — how to produce products with no defects, first by measuring defects, then by identifying causes of them, and finally by removing the causes.

Since then, the idea of quality has been extended and gradually transformed, from an emphasis on performance to specification, to one of meeting customer needs. The idea of the internal customer arose out of this, as meeting internal customer needs is an important step in meeting external customer needs. Quality programmes brought with them many techniques, all of which are applicable to customer care. In fact, it can be argued that customer care is merely the extension of quality into relationships with the customer. The whole question of customer care and quality is dealt with in Chapter 10.

Customer care in large and small organisations

Earlier, the idea of recreating the benefits of the era of personal service was suggested. This is not identical to the benefits provided by small suppliers. Although the corner shop is often cited as the supreme case of this, the comment applies equally to the waiter in the large hotel, the porter at a railway station, or the door to door collector of unemployment insurance.

Small suppliers may not subdivide tasks between people, but they often have to divide them up over a period of time, as a sequence of activities. This carries just as many risks of failure in customer care. So the need for attention to customer care is as great in small organisations as in large ones.

Avoiding failure in customer care

Customer care is a dangerous phrase. It is compact and alliterative. It rolls off the tongue easily, like competitive advantage, marketing, quality, IT and the other management fashions of the last few decades. The idea of customer care seems logical and obvious. All these are both strengths and weaknesses. They are strengths because explaining the idea of customer care does not take a long time, and it is not too difficult to get large numbers of people committed to it, at least superficially.

The weakness is that most people do not realise that customer care *does* involve reorienting policy, from top to bottom of an organisation. If a supplier has been managed taking into account only its own perspective, then adding the customer's perspective complicates things. The main risk to customer care, therefore, is suppliers taking the idea on board without realising its significance, and then failing to follow it through. Worse, they may hurry it through without working out its full implications. The aim of this book is to encourage readers to apply the ideas of customer care slowly and steadily, experiencing benefits all along the way. Without this level-headed approach and long term commitment, customer care may go badly wrong.

Chapter 2

Customer Care and Service Marketing

Customer care should be seen in two ways:

(a) as a comprehensive approach to working with customers
(b) as one of the service components of any product, whether that product be a physical product or a service.

The first interpretation implies that at every stage of the planning and implementation process, customer care issues should be to the fore. This is demonstrated throughout this book, in the many aspects of the management process viewed from the perspective of customer care.

In its second guise, customer care must be a key focus during service or product design and delivery — the subject of this chapter and Chapter 12. If a supplier aims to succeed with customers, customer care is not a discretionary component of products. It is essential.

The nature of service products

As customer care is a service component of many products, it shares many of the characteristics of service products, as follows:

(a) *People based*

Most service products and customer care policies are people based. With few exceptions, their quality depends on people serving customers. Variations in quality and in the level of customer care achieved may be due to the quality of recruitment, training, motivation and the processes used to manage and control those delivering the service. In many service companies, up to 90 per cent of staff are in direct contact with customers. This compares with around 10 per cent in, say, manufactured product companies.

(b) *Perishability*

Services are perishable. Consumption is simultaneous with production. Capacity unused today is lost forever. Output cannot be stored. An opportunity for caring for a customer, once missed, cannot be recreated on the same terms, although a very similar one can be. The customer's memory of the failure of care is likely to persist.

(c) *Customer involvement*

The customer is involved in delivery. Both service products and customer care cannot exist without the customer. The capacity to deliver service may exist (eg trained staff, an information distribution point). But the service is not being fully provided unless customers are receiving it. As mentioned in Chapter 1, this is the origin of the term "servuction", a system in which production of the service is inseparable from the service itself.

(d) *Importance of perceptions*

Customers' perceptions of the service product are the key to the marketing process. As customers are involved in the creation of the product, their attitudes and feelings strongly influence how they perceive the product. For example, the managers of an airport hotel may believe that they have created an excellent customer care programme. But customers may have very different views if they happen to be in the hotel when three buses full of flight cancellation victims turn up and drown all the hotel's facilities with their demands. This viewpoint is confirmed in a 1987 study by the Leo Burnett advertising agency of customers' attitudes to retail service. In this study, over 90 per cent of customers said that if they felt they had received really bad service, they would not go back. Nearly 90 per cent said they would go out of their way to shop where they believed service was better. 70 per cent would pay a price premium for better service.

(e) *Sensitivity to images*

The customer is likely to be very sensitive to images. The images of the supplier and product are important determinants of whether the customer buys. They affect customers' expectations. For example, people tend to have higher expectations of the customer care levels of big, national brand companies than of smaller ones. Images also affect whether customers are satisfied with their purchase. A good image can create a "halo effect", enhancing the customer's perception of the service or of customer care actions. This brings us to the next point.

(f) *Importance of consumption context*

The customer's perception of a service or of a customer care action is often affected by the context of consumption of the service. The context is determined by several factors. One of the most important is the nature and behaviour of co consumers — those consuming the service in the same location at the same time. Suppose many other customers are visibly complaining at the same time. In this situation, the behaviour of an individual customer will differ from a situation in which the customer is the sole complainer amongst a group of very satisfied customers.

(g) *Delivery over time*

Many (but by no means all) services and customer care actions last for a particular period of time. This time may extend from the moment that the customer perceives the need for the service to the time when the service is delivered satisfactorily. The notion of "perceived interaction period" is helpful when analysing customer behaviour in this area.

Service marketing and customer care

There are many definitions of marketing. The simplest is:

Marketing is the process of attracting and keeping customers — profitably.

Any service supplier must first attract customers, and then provide the service that customers require. Few service providers can live by only satisfying each customer once. However strong the need to

generate return business, the need to give good service is still paramount. "Word of mouth" is one of the most effective builders of
reputations. If service is poor, the customer who does not return or who
hears bad things about a supplier may stop another ten customers
coming.

The day to day contact a supplier has with its customers has an
extremely strong effect on recommendation and consequent reputation.
The power of this contact is often underestimated by managers. Each
contact episode constitutes a "moment of truth", a critical test of the
ability of the organisation to deliver customer care. It also provides an
opportunity to influence the customer's opinion of the organisation.
Focus on "moments of truth" was a central part of the famous turn-
round at Scandinavian Airways. Failure at too many moments of truth
is a very efficient way of losing customers.

Attracting and keeping customers

Whatever a supplier's approach to resource management, marketing
is fundamentally about attracting and keeping customers. They will
only be attracted to a supplier and stay with it as customers if that
organisation offers them a proposition that meets their needs. Customers will only remain customers if they remain satisfied with the
service once they have experienced it. The best marketing businesses
keep a balance between attracting new customers and keeping existing
ones satisfied. Even if a business keeps all its existing customers
satisfied, it would be risky for it to neglect recruiting new ones. "Word
of mouth" recommendation by existing customers is very flattering.
However, it cannot be totally relied upon to bring in new customers.

Some suppliers give the most excellent service (as their customers
perceive it) and have very small capacity relative to their target
market. They may be able to manage without paying any attention to
recruiting new customers. The level of customer care might be such as
to cause their fame to spread by word of mouth. In such cases, rationing
may need to be imposed, by price or waiting lists.

Sometimes, in the life of a business, more emphasis is placed on
recruiting customers. This is most likely when:

(a) the business is new
(b) the company is committed to rapid growth

(c) the company is changing its strategy (new products or new markets).

However, at other times, the supplier may concentrate on improving and deepening its relationship with existing customers. This is most likely when:

(a) the supplier already has a dominant position in its market
(b) the supplier wants to make its position more secure in the face of increasing competition
(c) the supplier wants to make more profit but finds it difficult to attract the resources required for growth
(d) the supplier wants more profit but simply does not want to grow in size
(e) a mature market restricts opportunities for growth.

In the latter case, emphasis on customer care must be greater. Retaining customers and selling more to them is the most attractive option. In terms of marketing costs, this is cheaper than recruiting more customers and selling them small amounts of service. It is much cheaper if, by serving customers well, loss of customers is prevented or slowed down. However, most service businesses need both to attract new customers and to retain existing ones. If the seeds of this are sown early, by adopting the customer care approach, then profitability will grow more quickly, as marketing costs fall in relation to revenue.

What makes a marketing organisation?

There are many views on this. The simple view is that so long as an organisation is providing a product or service, it is engaged in marketing. It may be marketing its services very badly. But once it provides products or services to meet people's needs, it is, perhaps without being aware of it, in the business of marketing.

At the other extreme, it can be argued that unless an organisation adopts a particular attitude, namely that it aims to achieve its objectives by meeting customer needs, it is not really marketing. It is merely supplying the service.

Successful marketing requires a strong focus on customers and their needs and a strong commitment to meeting these needs. If this focus exists, then the customer care approach has a good chance of taking root, together with the marketing approach. The McDonald marketing judgement that customers wanted quality, predictability of product, speed of service, absolute cleanliness and friendliness led to a clear focus in designing the product and associated service. The same can be said for Club Méditerranée and its pursuit of service and quality for a particular type of customer, and Federal Express's pursuit of the ability to give precise tracking of items to be delivered.

Which customers?

If marketing is about satisfying customer needs, it is clearly important to identify which customers one is going to provide services to and care for! Doing this is one of the most important tasks in marketing strategy. One must define which customer groups one wishes to serve and care for. This is called *targeting*. Target groups of customers should be chosen on the following criteria:

(a) the customers are known to have the need for the general kind of services that the organisation supplies (ie the need is there)
(b) their demand is strong enough to be translated into enough buying to sustain the company. In other words, enough customers must be willing to pay for the service. In addition, one should be confident that this situation will continue
(c) they have a particular need which the supplier can supply better and/or faster than other suppliers (ie the competitive advantage is there).

Competitive focus

The competitive point is all too easily forgotten in customer care programmes. These programmes are often unfocused, despite the fact that some customers are clearly more at risk than others. Although it sounds good to proclaim a high standard of care for all customers, it can be very expensive. Worse, the proclaimed standard may be too low for those customers at risk from competition, or for new customers the organisation wishes to attract from the competition and then keep.

Focused customer care depends on focused marketing. Without focused marketing, high levels of customer care are hard to achieve.

The oft-quoted example of the hernia-only Shouldice Hospital in Toronto illustrates this. This hospital is able to deliver exactly the right kind of care for its patients because it chooses them with care. Only fit patients with hernias are admitted. As a result, they are able to administer much of the service themselves, to their great satisfaction.

A key sign of using customer care competitively is the construction of different levels of customer care for different types of customer. For example, when British Telecom was a nationalised monopoly, it offered the same level of service to all its customers, irrespective of their value to the company. When it became one member of a competing duopoly, it improved the level of service to all customers and started to differentiate the care levels it offered. Very large and important business customers were given on-site engineers and special service centres, smaller business customers were given much quicker service response times, and consumers were given improved service times.

Consumers and influencers

As was shown in Chapter 1, behind the customer may lie other groups of people who influence his or her decisions. So selecting a particular group of customers as a target may mean focusing marketing efforts on another group. This applies particularly if a company has to reach the customer through an intermediary (eg a shop). In this case, the intermediary is likely to be a strong focus for marketing efforts.

Some elements of the marketing mix lend themselves more easily to "influencing the influencer" than others. For example, it is easy to advertise to children so that they influence the purchasing patterns of their parents or *vice versa*. It can be more difficult to care for influencers so that they influence purchasers. An example of this would be providing special additional services to the spouse of purchasers of pension policies (eg a specially written guide to the benefits of having a spouse with an enhanced pension).

Ensuring the "right customer" comes

Despite the need for precise targeting, marketers recognise that there is many a slip 'twixt cup and lip. Many customers may end up buying a service that was not targeted at them. So customer care programmes cannot risk being too targeted — they must allow for the need to deal with a variety of kinds of customer.

For example, many services are sold when customers come to a particular site. In this case it is difficult to control exactly who comes. The service (eg an exhibition) may be advertised to one group (eg professionals). However, another group (parents with young children) may come. If the service facilities have been set up to deal with the first group, then problems will result. In such circumstances, flexibility in care policies is important. If this flexibility is simply too expensive, or if providing the additional care would alienate customers in the target market, then policies excluding certain kinds of customer may need to be adopted.

Which needs are to be met?

All suppliers specialise in a particular range of products and services. This means that each supplier aims to satisfy only some of its customers' needs. Customers' needs are complex. Therefore, much of a marketer's work consists of:

(a) identifying what customers need
(b) determining which customer needs can be satisfied profitably or cost-effectively, with which services.

Even the most caring suppliers cannot meet all the needs of all their customers. For this reason, it is important for suppliers to make clear to customers what they can reasonably expect. In other words, customer education is part of customer care.

More complex definition of marketing

Much of the emphasis in service marketing is on direct dealings with customers. But a supplier's ability to deal properly with customers does not depend just on the products it offers and the quality of the service. Behind the scenes many actions take place which determine a supplier's ability to meet customer needs. In a large organisation the quality of information systems affects the ability to process customer information. This in turn may affect the organisation's ability to give good service.

So, a more comprehensive definition of marketing would be:

Everything that a supplier does — whether strategy, policy, structure or management — to ensure that its chosen customers' needs are met while its own resource constraints are satisfied.

A change in service technology (eg new information systems) can improve the quality of a service. It can affect a supplier's ability to meet customer needs. The marketing discipline is to see such a change from the point of view of customers, as well as from the organisation's own perspective (eg saving costs, increasing effectiveness). The marketer would ask the following kinds of question:

(a) Is the improvement to service noticeable?
(b) What is the real benefit to customers?
(c) How could it be drawn to the attention of customers?
(d) What can the customer do as a result of this improvement that could not be done before?
(e) Can a higher price be charged for the service?

Commitment to marketing therefore means that every change that could affect customers is seen from their point of view. Every such change must be "packaged" properly for customers, ideally so as to improve or at least maintain care levels.

The influence of competitive offerings

Marketers are of course very interested in directly competitive products and services — ones that meet the same or closely related needs. In a competitive world, the level of care provided must support the overall market positioning of the supplier. But competing with care is definitely not the same as competing with products. Customers view care as something they have the right to receive from all suppliers, irrespective of the product or service being supplied (hence the notion of parallel market introduced in Chapter 1). So in formulating customer care policies, a much broader set of competitors must be taken into account.

The idea of value

Adding value is a central marketing task. It refers to the tasks that take place in:

(a) transforming the supplier's resources into things customers want
(b) making sure that customers receive them (where necessary paying for them).

Marketing is only one activity which helps add value. Value can be added in a variety of ways. These include service design, site location and making the service available for customers to buy. But marketing is involved from the beginning to end of the process. The main elements of adding value are as follows:

1. Design and development

This involves designing and developing the product or service to meet customers' needs. The marketing function's input here is to:

(a) analyse customer needs, market trends and the competitive situation
(b) recommend or take decisions on the specification of services and on when they should be produced
(c) in some cases to test service concepts and designs.

For customer care, the key need is to focus on the situation in which the customer will be buying, receiving and using the product or service, to identify care requirements and see how the design of the product can make this care easier to deliver.

2. Production

This involves making the product or preparing the service and having it ready for customers. Marketing's role here is to ensure that customer needs in relation to the specification and quality of service are met, by providing information on customer needs and monitoring the performance of the service and customers' perceptions of it. Marketing is often involved in decisions about the provision of facilities or inventory. These decisions depend upon how the service is specified and how demand changes (how orders flow in, whether there are seasonal and other variations in the flow, such as response to promotion).

3. Selling

This means getting the product or service ready for sale and selling it.

This involves packaging (eg in brochures), pricing, promoting (eg through advertising or direct mail) and distributing the product such that it meets the needs of enough customers in the right place, and that (where appropriate) they pay for it.

Adding value through information

If customers are dissatisfied with a service, it may be because they do not know how to choose which of a range of services is right for them. They may need to be given more information or help. Many suppliers do not realise how important information and education are to customer care. This may represent a real competitive opportunity. It can be identified by asking the question: "How much do competitors help customers receive the level of care to which they are entitled, by telling them about it and educating them as to how to obtain it?".

Marketing and other business functions

In a large organisation, the marketing function will be only one of many departments whose actions affect customers. As "custodians" of the customer, at every stage of adding value, the marketing function must state what it believes the supplier must do to meet customer needs and how resources should be deployed to meet these needs effectively. Other functions, for example, finance, operations, personnel, will also state their requirements of marketing.

This insistence on stating customer requirements may seem pedantic, but the reason for this is that suppliers often conceive their services in technical terms rather than as the customer sees them. Some other functions are happy to accept information on the "hard" requirements — typically the technical features of the product or service. But "soft" requirements, the context in which the product or service is bought and used, and what can be done to make it easier for customers, are almost a foreign language to them.

How the functions relate to each other

Marketing is only one of the many functions a supplier needs to carry out to succeed. Most suppliers need to carry out all these functions:

(a) research and design of the service
(b) buy the physical, technical and human resources needed to develop, operate and market the service
(c) raise finance for the above
(d) market the service
(e) deliver the service
(f) collect payment.

A business also requires many support functions to enable it to do these (eg computing services). Figure 2.1 shows how the different functions can contribute to customer care.

Success in meeting customer needs depends upon team-work between all the functions. This team-work is likely to be helped if marketers ensure that:

(a) information about customer needs and about their satisfaction with the company and its products is widely diffused in the organisation
(b) performance measures in all functions have some component relating to customer care and satisfaction.

Similarly, marketers need to know what they can do to make it easier for those actually delivering the service.

Features, advantages and benefits

To help make the transition between the technical aspects of a service and what customers experience, marketers distinguish clearly between the features, advantages and benefits of a service.

Features are technical factors — the specification of the service. Feature language is that used to specify design and service delivery.

Advantages are what these features enable the customer to do.

Benefits relate to the value that customers want, because they enable their objectives to be met. As customers vary, so the benefit of a given feature is likely to be different for different customers. Benefits are harder to generalise than features. This is because the benefits experienced by each customer depend upon the objectives of that customer.

Function	Contribution to customer care
Research and development	Designing products that meet customer needs, that are easy and inexpensive to use, reliable, have variety/options to meet changing needs, etc.
Purchasing	Acquiring inputs (components, materials, sub-assemblies, etc) that support reliability, functionality and cost objectives, and ensuring their availability, so continued supply to customers is guaranteed.
Production/ operations/ distribution	Making/delivering product or service to meet customer requirements (eg cost, reliability, availability).
Finance	Ensuring funding is available to continue supply to customers. Fixing payment terms that are "fair" to customers. Ensuring that debtors are managed carefully.
Personnel	Ensuring that staff are recruited, motivated and trained to perform all the tasks required to satisfy customers, and, if appropriate, remunerated to do so. Ensuring that performance management takes into account customer needs (eg through appraisal process).
Marketing/ sales	Ensuring that information on customer needs is provided to all in the organisation who need it. Specifying products and services that will meet customer needs and organising their delivery to customers. Ensuring that customers have all the information they need to get the best out of the supplier. Ensuring that control mechanisms incorporate measures of success with customers. Monitoring competitive delivery.
General management	Creating and managing organisational processes so that they deliver customer care. Ensuring that performance measures relate to customer care. Exercising customer care leadership.

Figure 2.1 Contribution of different business functions to customer care

The variety of potential benefits applies to customer care too. The objective of competitive customer care is to find the combination of actions which provides the required variety of benefits, cost effectively.

Communicating benefits

Benefits can be communicated through many different media — advertising, direct marketing, sales promotion, selling, customer education and so on. The fact that the same features create different benefits for different customers is important when it comes to communicating the benefits. It is important not to assume that all consumers derive the same benefit from a particular product or service or from the care associated with it. Research may be needed to identify groups of customers deriving similar benefits, before that benefit can be communicated. Also, because benefits are more personal, communication of them tends to be more powerful when expressed in the way that customers would express it themselves (ie in their own language).

Benefits and value

Adding value means creating the right set of benefits, which customers want and (where appropriate) are prepared to pay for, expressing those benefits to customers, and then delivering what is promised.

Controlling the costs and benefits to the customer

Marketers often want to control the exchange of value, in terms of what benefits customers receive or what price is paid for the product or service. But if the service is being sold through a third party, such as a dealer or retail outlet, control may be limited. In these situations the marketer works by influence. What is required is a set of policies which will result in final customers getting the value marketers think they should. It is not too difficult to control the physical features of the offering — the product, its packaging and the like. It is harder to control the level of care offered to customers. This usually requires a significant investment in communicating with and training customer-facing staff, as well as in the development and installation of processes for dealing with customers (see Chapter 11).

The other area of value which the marketer must focus on is what is called the "user cost". This is defined as what the customer has to sacrifice (including money) to use the service. The marketer can influence some of these costs, but others are less amenable to influence.

Who is the supplier?

It sometimes surprises marketers how little some customers know about the supplier. This applies even in cases where knowledge about the supplier is an important component of value (eg because it provides reassurance about quality). For many services, therefore, much marketing effort is devoted to marketing the supplier as well as the product or service. This is particularly so for products where the customer may suffer badly if the product is not delivered properly.

Sometimes there can be outright confusion about who is the supplier. In such cases the branding presented to the customer is usually that of the company taking responsibility for the quality of the product or service or of the customer care delivered with it. For example, if the customer buys a piece of complex technical equipment from an authorised dealer, who is trained by the equipment manufacturer to deliver high levels of customer care, which one does the customer perceive to be responsible for the care — the dealer or the manufacturer?

The role of information

Once upon a time, models of economic behaviour were developed which assumed that on both sides of the market, supplier and customer, perfect information existed, about what was for sale, at what price and so on. This situation is rare. There are some good examples of it, such as commodity markets, town markets and financial markets. But much of a marketer's work involves identifying potential customers and making sure that they know what the company is, what it does, what services it supplies, what benefits they provide and how to buy them.

It is not easy to distinguish between the provision of information and advertising. However, the fact that many customers are prepared to pay good money for market information of this kind should be proof that information itself has a value and is an important benefit provided by marketing activity. If customer care considerations dictate the provision of high volumes of information to customers choosing or using products or services, but this information is expensive to provide, then it may be sensible to consider charging for it. This does not violate the principles of customer care, provided that customers understand the arrangement from the beginning. Indeed, there is a view that what comes free is not valued.

Customer orientation

The dominant principle of good marketing and of customer care is "customer orientation". This does *not* mean giving the customer everything! It *does* mean striving to identify customer needs and meeting them profitably. Customer orientation is not just an attitude of mind, it is a complete way of working.

To achieve this, an organisation must subscribe to the following principles:

(a) Customers are the greatest asset. Without them, a supplier cannot survive. Building and conserving this asset is the central task of marketing.

(b) To do this, the supplier must understand its customers' needs better than its competitors. It must use this understanding to meet these needs better than its competitors do.

(c) The supplier will only be able to understand and meet its customers' needs if it puts its customers first. This means managing its day-to-day work to deliver the best results to customers. Customers do not belong to the supplier by right, but by the hard, customer-oriented work of the suppliers' staff.

Lack of customer-orientation is common. Many suppliers are inward-looking, more concerned with solving their own problems of product design, production or sales, or internal politics, rather than the needs of their customers. A customer-oriented supplier starts with customer needs as the foundation of its policy. It identifies customer needs before designing services. It determines administrative procedures according to customers' requirements, rather than administrative convenience. It listens to customers before promoting services to them. It promotes in terms of benefits to customers, not features. It determines success by customer satisfaction indices, responses to marketing campaigns and customer loyalty, as well as sales.

As a supplier becomes more customer-oriented, it starts to use a variety of measures of its success in meeting customer needs. These measures are transformed into targets for managers responsible for different groups of customers. These measures are needed because increased customer orientation cannot be achieved without increasing *accountability* for customer orientation.

These are the main things that indicate the strength of an organisation's customer orientation:

(a) when the supplier's services meet customer needs, or even when they are slightly ahead of customers' immediate requirements, the customers rapidly "latch on" to them because the services open up new areas of possible satisfaction

(b) when services required by customers are available when the customer wants

(c) when customers' requests for information are answered accurately and promptly

(d) when customers' problems are solved promptly

(e) when communications from the supplier seem appropriate, relevant and intelligible to customers

(f) when contact with the organisation leaves the customer feeling more satisfied than before the contact

(g) when customers recommend the supplier to others with similar needs

(h) when the customer base continues to grow almost without loss of customers, with new customers being attracted partly by the supplier's reputation for handling existing customers.

Following the principles and practices described in this book will help to achieve this state.

Marketing as a professional discipline

Marketing and selling

Where marketing starts with customers' needs for benefits, selling starts with the supplier's need to sell. But selling is a vital part of marketing. Once products or services are ready to be sold, customers will not necessarily come in droves to buy, even if they would benefit greatly by so doing. Selling means getting customers to buy, by identifying customers, getting into a sales relationship with them, persuading them to buy, taking the order and ensuring that money is received.

Selling is a vital part of what is called the marketing mix. Forgetting that the product needs to be sold is a recipe for weak marketing, as many an experienced sales person will claim. Forgetting the needs of the person doing the selling is just as serious a crime!

The marketer's job

Customer care thrives in a professional marketing atmosphere, one in which it is recognised that the job of marketing is to:

(a) set feasible objectives
(b) determine strategies to meet these objectives
(c) put detailed plans together to make these strategies happen
(d) implement these plans
(e) monitor and control achievement against these plans
(f) do all this with energy, creativity and flair.

In more detail, the steps involved in marketing are:

1. Defining the business that the supplier is in. "Business definition" is critical. Unless a supplier does this, it will not know which markets to target in step 2, or which customers to care for.
2. Defining and understanding target markets, competition and the supplier's own capabilities. This is often called "environmental analysis", because it deals with the state of affairs in and around a supplier.
3. Setting marketing objectives which are realistic in the light of steps 1 and 2, taking into account the resources at the supplier's disposal.
4. Determing overall marketing strategies before fine tuning details of policy. The strategies should be based solidly on the analysis under step 2 and aim to achieve what was stated under step 3.
5. Setting out detailed action plans to achieve strategies, remaining faithful to the analysis under step 2. In other words, it is important not to lose sight of the conclusions of the environmental analysis once the stage of detailed action planning is reached.

6. Implementing these action plans professionally, using all the right techniques of general management, in particular communicating with and managing people, managing projects and keeping tight financial control.
7. Measuring results of actions and forming conclusions about what worked.
8. Making sure that these conclusions are taken into account in the next marketing plan.

However, there are many factors at work to destroy this logical view. These factors are very powerful. Many suppliers carry out their marketing planning very professionally. But the end result, in terms of what the customer sees and experiences, is not what the supplier thought it had agreed to deliver. Many failures in customer care are caused by the same policy flaws.

The factors responsible for this include:

(a) An unrealistic business definition. This may be too wide, so that it implies taking on too many competitors with too few resources. Or it may be too narrow, so that it does not take account of developments in closely associated businesses which may end up absorbing or destroying the target market.
(b) A poor information base. The information on which the plan is based does not reflect realities. For example, information on customers may have come from market research rather than from staff who deal daily with customers, or directly from the customers themselves.
(c) Time — the time taken to plan is too long, so that by the time the plan is to be implemented, it is out of date and so ignored.
(d) Communication — the plan is not communicated properly to the staff supposed to be implementing it. They do not understand what the plan is, and why they are being asked to do things differently.
(e) Motivation — staff involved in implementing the plan were not involved in producing it, so they do not feel accountability or ownership.
(f) Control — there is no proper mechanism for measuring whether the plan is being put into practice properly. Typically, all that is being measured is final results, by which time it is too late to do anything.

(g) Other priorities — staff in the field are given too many priorities. Marketing is particularly at risk here if it is perceived to be a luxury, not essential for the immediate survival of the organisation.

(h) Organisation — related to the above point. If no one's job depends upon making marketing work, then other priorities are likely to dominate.

(i) Lack of acceptance of the concepts of marketing and caring for customers. If staff refuse to believe that their jobs hang on the organisation's ability to attract and keep customers, they will never achieve the customer-orientation that is so critical for any supplier.

(j) Short-term emphasis, which produces a focus on short-term profit opportunities and not on real customer needs.

(k) Power conflicts — an unwillingness to give control to or share it with another function or department, despite the fact that this is likely to produce better results for customers.

The catalogue is almost endless. The consequences of these for customer care are shown in Figure 2.2.

This is not a book about the failures of customer care, but the reader is now warned about some of the problems that are encountered. It is now possible to see what must be done to ensure that marketing and customer care do work. Answering the above points, a supplier must:

(a) define the business, taking into account economic and social trends and what its customers say about what choices they make

(b) make sure that the information it bases its marketing on is as fresh as possible, and comes as directly as possible from the ultimate source. Information on customers should come directly from them or from staff who service them. Information on competitors should come from recent reports. Information on the supplier's own capabilities should come directly form staff "at the coal face", and not be filtered up through layers of management

(c) ensure that information about customer needs, overall and specifically for care, form a prime part of the planning process

(d) not take too long to plan

(e) write the plan so that it works as a communication and as motivation. Follow production of the plan with actions to communicate it, get feedback on it and motivate its staff

Cause	Effect on customer care
Unrealistic business definition	Over-optimistic promises to customers, wrong level of care, turning customers away.
Poor information base	Ignorance of customer needs, and consequent mismatch of care to needs. Business priorities out of line with customer priorities.
Poor timing	Services and care levels targeted at past needs of customers, not present and future needs.
Poor staff communication	Staff do not understand how supplier wants them to handle customers. Local improvisation causes inconsistencies and quality problems. Some staff react by defective "system maintenance" behaviour, at expense of customers.
Poor staff motivation	Staff not committed to improving customer care. Attitude may become obvious to customers.
Poor control	Variations in quality of customer care. Some actions positively anti-customer because priorities not being followed through.
Confused priorities	Staff not knowing which priorities to follow. Customers suffer because customer care priorities lost in confusion.
Organisational focus confused	No-one sees it as their job to look after customers. Customers find it hard to obtain satisfaction.
No acceptance of marketing and customer care	Staff believe that customers are less important, and focus on own tasks. Customers' needs are not taken into account in policy-making. Customer care absent or poorly matched to customer needs.
Short term emphasis	Lack of acceptance of benefits of investing over long term in meeting customer needs. Customers suffer because their needs are met only if their behaviour brings quick rewards to supplier.
Power conflict	Inconsistency of policies of different functions. Level of care experienced by customers varies according to function they are in contact with. If customer needs an outcome which involves crossing functional boundaries, customer is unlikely to gain satisfaction.

Figure 2.2. Examples of effect of poor marketing planning and implementation on customer care

(f) make sure that it gets regular progress reports on implementation of the plan, not just on final results, and then check the
validity of the reports

(g) measure everything (within reason) that the supplier wants to
change as a result of marketing and learn from what it succeeded
or failed to change

(h) make marketing part of everyone's job, but also make sure that
some people are *totally* accountable for it.

The importance of process in marketing

Many of the marketing problems identified above occur because of the
absence of a marketing process developed with a view to achieving high
levels of customer care. The following chapter describes what a good
marketing process looks like, while Chapters 7 and 8 show how to
integrate customer care into such a process.

Chapter 3

The Marketing Process in Detail

In Chapter 1, it was shown that:

(a) customer care can be seen as a special aspect of service marketing
(b) marketing works through applying a more or less structured process to information about customer needs to work out ways that a supplier can achieve its objectives.

In Chapter 2, the marketing process was broken down into a number of simple steps. These were:

(a) business definition, corporate objectives and strategies
(b) environmental analysis
(c) setting marketing objectives
(d) determining marketing strategies
(e) drawing up action plans
(f) implementing action plans
(g) measuring results
(h) learning from results for next time.

In this chapter, each of these steps is described in more detail.

1. Business definition, corporate objectives and strategies

This describes which market(s) the supplier serves and, very broadly, how. It provides the answer to the question "What business is the supplier in?". Some people prefer to use the term "corporate mission". This is an enduring idea, the thing the supplier wants to achieve above all, irrespective of other objectives it might want to follow year by year.

Business definitions are meant to be very simple. A simple business definition is needed to ensure that the organisation stays on its chosen path. It provides an immediate test of all proposed variations. Managers try to achieve good results by focusing the application of resources to achieve the direction contained within the business definition. So any change in business definition usually implies diversion of resources and management time. There must be very good reasons for any deviation.

Market definition

Market definition is more precise than business definition. It defines more precisely which kinds of customer the organisation sees itself as serving, and which of their needs it will try to fulfil. There may be several stages of iteration between setting objectives and market definition. For example, an exploration of marketing strategy may reveal that there is no way that particular kinds of customer can be satisfied by what the supplier has to offer. This will lead to redefinition of the market. Questions that need to be resolved in market definition include:

(a) How large and profitable is the market?
(b) How mature is the market, in terms of sophistication of buyers and clarity of purchasing standards?
(c) What are the relative strengths of buyers and sellers?
(d) How strong is the competition and what policies are they following?
(e) What competitive advantages does the supplier have in serving customers in this market?
(f) How profitable are the suppliers serving this market?
(g) Are there any long term technical, social or economic threats to the market?

Setting objectives

The business definition "sets the scene" for determining the supplier's objectives. It also suggests what should be analysed under "environmental analysis" — eg which groups of customers are to be served and, of course, cared for. The business definition or mission should lead directly to the overall objectives and strategy of the organisation. Overall objectives cover areas like profit, revenue, employment, market leadership and development of assets. Strategies cover areas like commitment to producing particular kinds of products and services and involvement in particular geographical markets.

Corporate strategies are very "high level" policies, involving every activity in an organisation. Examples of corporate strategy might include:

(a) getting out of one line of business into another
(b) taking over major competitors
(c) investing in complete renewal of production facilities
(d) joint ventures with other suppliers and so on.

In a large organisation, corporate mission, objectives and strategy constitute a key part of the policy framework "handed down" to the marketer. Marketing will (or should) have made a big contribution to them. But by the time they are fully worked out and stated, they will be, so to speak, set in stone. They will then be applied to every business function, eg operations, personnel, finance. This will lead to each function being asked to produce and deliver a plan which embodies the vision, helps meet objectives and supports achievement of strategies. Small organisations, which rarely separate these functions, simply have to check that each policy they adopt squares with these objectives.

In private sector companies, the main overall objectives are likely to be financial, eg return on capital, net profit before tax. Sometimes, the mission may be set up as an objective which holds true for many years, irrespective of financial objectives for each year. The type of financial objective adopted will be based on the company's financial profile.

For example, a company which needs a lot of investment is likely to have a return on capital objective. This target return is likely to be used in all investment appraisal. An organisation which does not need much investment, but relies for success on skilled staff, might set a target of revenue or profit per member of staff. Companies whose principal activity is buying products and selling them on (eg retailers) are likely to use margin on sales as their key measure of success. It reflects their success in marking up what they buy. Companies for which a key competitive dimension is the fight to acquire and retain customers may measure success in terms of profit per customer.

"Market presence" objectives are ones which relate to the size and scope of an organisation's activities in the market. For private sector companies, without success in the market, financial objectives will be hard to achieve. In very competitive markets, market share is likely to be top of the list. Service levels are usually important to service companies, as they indicate likely repurchase rates (whether consumers are likely to buy again).

Resources and skills are important to all service organisations. If staff require a high level of training investment or a long induction period, an organisation may have as a key objective to keep staff turnover below a certain figure.

Overall objectives and strategy should not be confused with marketing objectives and strategy. The latter identify the contribution that marketing will make to achievement of overall objectives. Of course, overall objectives cannot be set independently of the situation in the market. A particular objective simply might not be feasible in the markets the organisation operates in. It can be argued that the most critical test of whether the supplier's objectives are sensible is in the market.

2. Environmental analysis

Before a supplier can set marketing objectives, it must understand its business environment. It would be rash simply to translate corporate objectives and strategies into marketing objectives with no regard for:

(a) what the market allows (customer needs, competitive policies, etc) or
(b) what the organisation is capable of (the internal environment — resources, skills).

Environmental analysis is not a once-off affair. It goes on all the time. In a large organisation new policies are likely to be tested in the light of formal conclusions resulting from this analysis. The length of time it takes to progress a change in policy from conception to delivery gives plenty of opportunity for this testing. In a small supplier, contact between customers and those making marketing decisions may be very close. Changes in marketing policy may be implemented from one day to the next, or even the same day. In this situation, the likely test against the market is usually based on the owners' or managers' sense of what their customers would like. They may be in the position of being able to ask customers directly. If the owners' or managers' decide that they need to improve the way customers are being cared for, they may be able to make some changes straight away.

As a marketing proposal takes shape, checking market needs becomes more precise. A large organisation may want to test a new service only in part of its operation. A small supplier may decide to make the change across the board, but on a trial basis.

Environmental analysis involves looking at markets, economies, technology, society, legislation, competitors, parallel markets and, of course, customer needs. At this stage, market definition is likely to be considerably refined. The aim of this analysis is to identify how the supplier's objectives might be achieved by serving particular markets. In practice not every aspect of the market can be analysed. Even in a large organisation, market research budgets are usually limited. In a small organisation there may simply be no money available. So the analysis must be very focused.

SW/OT analysis

The idea of SW/OT analysis (strengths, weaknesses, opportunities and threats) is often used to structure environmental analysis. Without a methodology, environmental analysis could lead to the production of many facts and no conclusions. Marketers need to know:

(a) what their organisation's strengths and weaknesses are
(b) where the organisation is exposed to risks
(c) what possibilities are open to it.

Note that this means marketing must get involved in analysing the "internal environment". This is a clumsy but convenient way of referring to the organisation's own resources and capabilities. The internal environment determines what the supplier can do to meet market needs.

Environmental analysis involves obtaining and analysing information about all the factors which affect the organisation's ability to achieve its direction. These include:

(a) Customers — who they are, what their characteristics are, what their needs are and what they buy. They may be direct customers. They may be distributors who take the organisation's products and sell it on. They may be people who strongly influence customers.

(b) Competitors — these may be direct competitors, which supply the same or similar products. However, indirect competitors, which sell products which are close substitutes for the supplier's own products, must also be included.

(c) Economy and society — insofar as they affect the market (customers and competitors) or the ability of the supplier to function (eg cost of finance, labour availability and costs).

(d) Legislation and regulation — whether there are "official" limitations on what the supplier can do.

(e) Technology — what is technically feasible. In service industries, the biggest changes have been in information systems. These now allow information to be made available more quickly and sales to take place almost instantaneously.

(f) Internal factors — what resources and capabilities the supplier itself has, what process it has for meeting customer requirements. This provides the basis for understanding the implications of external factors.

Most of the data for the external factors listed above comes from either market research or from information flowing directly from customers (transactions, complaints, etc). Data for analysis of the internal environment is likely to come from managers' knowledge of their organisation, operating reports and special analyses.

SW/OT analysis smoothes the policy transition to setting marketing objectives and strategies. This analysis should generate strategic options by matching different strengths (eg market and technological). Strategy should capitalise on opportunities, be based on the organisation's strengths and, if possible, aim to reduce weaknesses. Policies may also be required to neutralise or avoid threats.

3. Setting marketing objectives

Setting objectives is one of the most important tasks any marketer does. Set the objectives too low and the result may be performance that is below potential. This could in turn lead to opening up the market to competition. Set the objectives too high and the result may be that in trying to achieve the impossible, the organisation fails completely. For this reason, objectives should be set only after a thorough analysis has been undertaken of what the organisation is capable of (its resources, skills, etc) and what the market (customers, competition) will allow it to achieve. Examining what competitors have achieved is also a very useful exercise.

4. Determining strategies

This involves putting together overall organisation objectives and strategy with analysis of the environment, to come up with the main lines of marketing policy. These are what the marketer believes will allow objectives to be met in current circumstances. Strategies are "big picture" policies. Examples include:

(a) to enter a new market
(b) develop a new range of services
(c) withdraw a range of services
(d) greatly change the scale of operations
(e) make very significant changes to the way the marketing mix is deployed
(f) radically improve standards of customer care.

Strategies normally involve significant changes in deployment of resources. In some cases, marketing resources may be the only resources involved. However, other resources (eg production) may also be involved.

At this stage, it is particularly important to identify several strategic possibilities. Too many strategic decisions are chosen from a list of one! Having more than one option forces the organisation to develop criteria to evaluate them and then to choose the best.

5. Drawing up action plans

This is more detailed. It is often described as "what makes strategy work". Suppose, for example, that an organisation decides to develop a new range of services for a particular market. It will need to develop a number of services and market them through the right channels, at the right price and with the right promotion and packaging, with the right people, process, and presence. For the supplier to know whether it achieves its targets, action plans should contain measurement processes.

6. Implementing action plans

This is achieved through *marketing operations*. To make policies stick, a supplier must have a way of making things happen. These include issuing instructions and making sure they are implemented by recruiting, training and motivating people and giving them processes within which to work, money to spend on marketing services, information systems to support them and so on. In a small organisation one or two people may do everything, from setting objectives, strategising, devising and then implementing action plans. All this may happen within a space of days. In a larger organisation, responsibilities for these actions are likely to be divided between different groups of people.

7. Measuring results

Once plans have been put into effect, the results of actions must be measured and analysed, and remedial action taken if things are not on track. The essence of good marketing is that measurement takes place routinely, not as a special exercise. Sales data should be produced routinely and in a form which can be readily analysed. Computerisation has made a big difference here.

8. Learning from results for next time

Results are measured not just to provide details to accountants. They are measured to provide information on what worked and what did not. Armed with this information, the marketer can then improve marketing policy next time.

The skill of the marketer is to use this (or a similar process), adapting it to the needs of their particular organisation and the markets it serves. The process is summarised conceptually in Figure 3.1.

Does this process work in practice?

The points covered above are expressed as a hierarchy. In the real world, decisions are not made in a hierarchical way. There may be a plan which marketers are managing by, but decisions are not made in such a logical way in most organisations. However, the value of the framework is based upon much experience. This shows that if the logical hierachy of ideas is not thought through well and then communicated to everyone who makes or implements policy in the organisation, then many problems arise. For example, if a supplier is not following a consistent strategy, then different parts of the marketing mix may not "fit" with each other.

Keeping it simple

Although it is important to keep policy simple, it is also important to recognise that much work has to be done to produce and implement simple, coherent marketing. Consider, therefore, the process described above in more detail, from the point of view of the marketing manager.

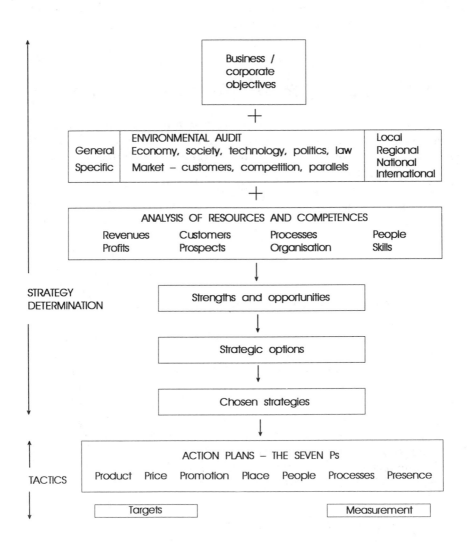

Figure 3.1. A view of the marketing process

In moving from objectives and strategies to action plans, even in a small organisation, the manager may have gone through quite a complex process of identifying options, researching and evaluating them. Just being small does not necessarily make the process simpler — there is just less time to manage it. This can make getting marketing right more difficult for the small business, as shortage of time is the common problem of small businesses. This is because most of managers' time has to be spent doing things.

A larger organisation can spend more time on determining marketing policy. The marketing director might spend a long time on strategy, reviewing policy options prepared by marketing staff, checking implementation and reviewing performance reports. Some time will be spent planning. Some time will be spent making sure that the plans have been implemented and are working. Some time will be spent checking the consistency of policy with organisation requirements. Finally, time will also be spent communicating marketing policy to the whole organisation.

Perhaps because of this, marketing management may find that it has little time to spend with customers. This is one reason why senior marketing staff can get out of touch with customers and make mistakes. Therefore, in some companies marketing staff take part in programmes designed to keep them in touch with customers. Reviewing market research and sales reports is not enough!

In a big organisation, the marketing director is likely to see the above hierarchy of topics as stages of a cycle of planning and implementation. This is likely to be in the form of an annual planning process. At the start of this process, corporate objectives and strategies are set (ideally not changing too much year to year and the mission being constant for even longer). Towards the end of the planning process, the detailed actions for marketing and sales people will have been planned. In a small organisation, planning might be confined to a day or a week each year!

This process is summarised in the following diagrams. The items in the earlier diagrams tend to determine those towards the bottom. Financial objectives affect nearly everything. But they affect in particular the marketing performance ratios, pricing in the marketing mix, targets, incentives and controls. They also affect market choice (costs of entry, likely profitability of different markets), service range policy, new service development costs, rates of return and so on. The function of these diagrams is to show interdependencies. They also give an idea of the logical sequencing of marketing decisions. The diagrams towards the end show what is required to make marketing happen and what the outcomes are.

Marketing process diagrams

Financial	*Market presence*	*Resources / skills*
Margin on sales	Share	Operations facilities
Return on assets	Service quality	Operations technology
(RoA)	Customer loyalty	Marketing
Asset turn	Image	General management
Cash flow	Service levels	
Total assets		
Revenue		

Figure 3.2 Corporate objectives and strategy

This diagram identifies three main kinds of corporate objective.

Financial objectives clearly relate to the main financial flows in the business — how much money is made, how much of that is profit and what value of assets is used in making that profit. The key ratios are critical, as they determine the health of the business. Return on assets is simply profit divided by assets. It indicates the efficiency of use of assets in making profit. Asset turn is revenue divided by assets. It indicates how much in the way of assets is required to generate income. There are many ways of reducing the use of assets. If an organisation already has assets, they can be sold and leased back. Or they can be leased in the first place. This merely converts assets into costs, as leasing charges must be paid for.

Market presence refers to the impact the supplier has on the market place. The most obvious indicator is market share. But strength of image is also important. If an organisation's image is strong in its target market, it has a better chance of achieving its target market share. Customer loyalty is closely related to this. The other indicators are quality indicators — the fundamental quality of the service and how customers are handled. All these represent significant overall objectives for the business. They cannot be achieved by marketing efforts alone.

Resources and skills refers to objectives a supplier might have in terms of the development of the main resources by which it achieves its results.

Resources and skills	General external	Immediate market Customers / prospects	Competition
Financial	Technology	Needs	Numbers
Operating/technology	Economy	Buying power	Resources
Marketing skills	Legal	Behaviour	Skills
Customer loyalty	Political	Numbers	Behaviour
Channel presence		Types	
Channel loyalty			

Figure 3.3 Internal and external environment

This summarises the points that need to be covered in the environmental analysis. Channel presence refers to strength of representation in distribution channel outlets. Channel loyalty refers to the loyalty of agencies to the supplier.

Sales / profit	Stance	Services	Markets	Customers	Channels
Value/volume	Aggressive	Range	Number	Number	Suitability
Share	Reactive	Leadership	Spread	Loyalty	Penetration
Asset turn	Leader	Quality	Variety	Type/size	Loyalty
RoA/profit	Follower	Number	Penetration	Distribution	Stability
Margin	Specialist	Technical	Export	Buying power	Cost
Cash	Efficient	strength	Growth rate		Added value

Figure 3.4 Marketing objectives and strategy

This summarises the main areas for formulation of objectives and strategies. *Stance* summarises the main competitive thrust of marketing strategy. For example, some suppliers always lead the market in developing new services. This may involve specialising in meeting the needs of a particular group of customers — innovative ones. Others prefer to be what is called *fast followers*. This involves picking up on ideas which other suppliers have marketed. Other companies prefer to lead on low cost and efficiency.

Under *service strategy*, market leadership might be achievable by a combination of customer-oriented service targets, intense advertising, high quality customer care, and features designed to appeal to a large number of customers. However, it might also be achieved through a very specialist stance.

Customers, markets	Services, brands	Prices, user costs	Customer communication	Distribution representation
Number	Types and range	Margin	Target customers	Channel choice
Value	Leadership	Flexibility	Objectives	Trade margins
Spread	Quality	Negotiation	Budget	Terms
Variety	Number	Discounts	Means/media	Motivation
Penetration	Technology	Lead pricing	Message	Support
Export	Customer care	Promotions		Training
	Financing			Promotions

Figure 3.5 Action plans — marketing mix

This gives more detail on the particular marketing policies that an organisation might pursue. The largest service companies need to cover all these areas to deliver their marketing strategies. Smaller companies tend to concentrate on defining their service offering, getting the general price level right, and a little market targeting and customer communication.

Information, analysis & assessment	Decision making	Planning	Organisation	Targets, incentives	Control productivity
Obtain & analyse data on internal & external environment for use in decisions & planning	Create & evaluate choices Decide marketing mix	Review/ audit situation Co-ordinate decisions Provide for targets & control	Structure to achieve all aspects of plan	Fix group & individual targets Provide incentives to achieve	Control performance & expenditure

Figure 3.6 Action plans — marketing operations

This diagram covers all the management actions that need to take place to ensure that marketing policy is made and implemented.

1. PERFORMANCE

Revenue / profit	*Market share*	*Customer attitudes*
Total	Revenue & physical	Loyalty
By customer, area	By services, customer	Participation
service, market	area, market,	in buying decisions
division	division	Positive opinion
Growth	Number of customers	
RoA & asset turn	Type of customers	
Margin (gross/net)	Representation in	
cash flow	outlets/agencies	
	Depth of distribution	
	Market coverage	

2. PRODUCTIVITY

Financial	*Semi-financial*	*Physical*
Marketing cost/	Revenue per unit	Unit sales per unit
revenue	input	input
Gross or net	(sales representatives,	(items sold
contribution of	brochure, hotel room)	per sales
marketing spend	Unit sold per £ spent	person)
	on marketing	Inter-output ratios
		(service X vs. service Y)
		Inter-input ratios
		(advertising per sales-
		person or per outlet/
		/establishment

Figure 3.7 Results

This diagram summarises the two main kinds of result. Performance describes results in the market place. Productivity describes the relationship of that performance to resource inputs. "Semi-financial" productivity is a way of describing ratios that combine money and physical performance. Physical productivity measures do not refer to money. Each supplier develops its own performance measures through experience.

How the marketing process helps customer care

How does following this process help achieve better customer care? Perhaps the best way of showing this is to demonstrate what happens if a supplier does not follow such a process. Some examples of this are shown in Figure 3.8.

Corporate objectives and strategy	Omission of objectives for customer loyalty and customer care. No strategy for caring for customers.
External environment analysis	No analysis of what makes customers loyal and how well they respond to different policies aimed at encouraging them to do so.
Internal environment analysis	No analysis of supplier's capabilities in relation to keeping customers.
Marketing objectives and strategy	Marketing objectives and strategy focus on profit, sales and market share, not on long term impact on customer loyalty.
Action plans — marketing mix	Action plans focus on short term sales and margin increases, not on winning and keeping customers.
Action plans — marketing operations	Focus on efficiencies of procedures, not effect on customers.
Results	Track sales and profit, not customer inventory movements.

Figure 3.8. Example of effect of not following marketing process properly

The test of marketing — the market

This framework provides a good discipline for an organisation to marshal resources to achieve the required effect on customers. If this discipline is observed, customer care policies will be much easier to design and implement. It will be quite clear what the organisation is trying to do with different sets of customers. However, reaching this position is contingent on developing a clear picture of customer needs, the subject of the next chapter.

Chapter 4

The Customer's Perspective

In a competitive environment, customer care is not a luxury but a necessity. Without it, a supplier will not achieve success with customers. Customer care can be a source of competitive advantage. But it is not something that a supplier needs a certain amount of, so that when it has this amount, it will succeed. Customer care opens up many new opportunities for a supplier to achieve success with customers while meeting its other objectives. This, however raises two questions:

(a) What types of customer care policy are required?
(b) How far should each policy go?

Customer requirements

The answers to both these questions lie partly in customer needs and perceptions. Customers are reasonable. Many are quite realistic about the level of care suppliers can provide, given resource constraints. Those whose expectations are unrealistic can be educated as to what is realistic.

However, customers also have a sense of what they have a right to expect, irrespective of resource constraints. These rights include:

    (a) a basic minimum level of customer care
    (b) common courtesy on the part of staff
    (c) complaints handling procedures that work.

and the like. In a consumerist age, customers tend to have such views about every organisation from the most famous private sector company to a tax collector or an office of a local public administration.

Different kinds of service

In analysing customers' views about customer care, it is important to remember that the period during which customers perceive themselves to be in transaction with the supplier may be quite long. Customer care opportunities occur throughout this period and indeed before and after it. These opportunities are particularly great from the time the customer specifically requests a service, until immediately after that service is delivered. For as soon as customers request attention, they become much more alert to what the supplier is saying and doing. They are on the look out for positive customer care and much more sensitive to poor customer care.

The kinds of service customers may request include:

    (a) having problems resolved or complaints handled
    (b) receiving routine maintenance, service or information
    (c) receiving exceptional maintenance, service or information service and so forth.

Many customers distinguish between major contact episodes and less important ones. For example, a car being booked in for its annual service may start with a minor contact episode — calling to book the service. The next step may be more significant — telling the service manager what problems the car has got, or putting it in writing. Then comes the day of the service, when the customer leaves the car at the garage. The customer may be worried all day. Uncertainty may be felt about whether the car will be ready in time, whether all faults will be rectified and what the cost will be. Then comes what is arguably the most important contact of all — when the customer collects the car and pays the bill. Care at this point is critical. If the car is going to take longer to service, the customer should be telephoned if possible. This will prevent the awful situation of waiting for the car, which adds to the customer's doubt — will the service staff start to hurry and not do the job properly?

So, customers' requirements for care are likely to vary according to the significance, as they perceive it, of each transaction with the supplier. When booking in the car, the customer may require brisk and efficient service. When confronted with the bill, the customer may require careful explanation of why the service cost so much!

Attributes of service

Many products and services are bought as a package, with customer service being a greater or lesser part of that package. As has already been noted, suppliers often see the attributes of service in terms of its technical features. Customers tend to see service from a very different point of view. They are likely to view service as it impinges upon them in terms of factors such as:

(a) The amount of time it takes for the service to be delivered or performed.

(b) The importance of the service element of the package relative to other elements, at different times in the relationship. The balance between customer service and other elements of the package may vary over time. In the case of the relationship between a car dealer and a customer, the service element of the package is particularly important before, during and immediately after the purchase, around the time of regular service and at any time of breakdown. For the rest of the time, the physical product and its performance are the dominant elements of the package.

(c) The extent to which the customer wants to or perceives the need to be in control and the kinds of control that are exercised. Customers may be in control by doing, knowing or deciding.

(d) How much effort is required on the part of the customer in order to receive the service (eg give instructions, make telephone calls, check quality).

(e) How dependent the customer is on the supplier for the period during which the service is being delivered.

(f) How important the service is to the customer (ranging from critical to peripheral).

(g) How efficient or reliable the supplier of the service is perceived to be and therefore the extent of the risk felt by the customer.

(h) How dependent the service is on staff or equipment.

(i) How much direct contact with staff or equipment is required during the performance of the service.

(j) How much the supplier's staff are perceived to need to control the situation.

(k) How much and what kinds of contact with other customers is expected/wanted during the course of service delivery. For example, overcrowding in a supermarket leads to more difficulty in examining the shelves and thus reduced purchases.

(l) How much skill and/or professional expertise is expected and/or required of service staff.

(m) The degree of routineness of the different encounters that take place. Some encounters are totally routine, with known and certain inputs by customer and supplier and known and certain outputs (eg filling the car with petrol). Others may require a more intense dialogue between customer and supplier, and the outcome of the service episode may not be known until the end of the episode.

(n) The number and complexity of stages and/or service encounters involved in the customer obtaining the service.

(o) The emotions anticipated and experienced by customers as they go through the different stages (eg anger, dissatisfaction, irritation, surprise, pleasure, satisfaction) and how these vary according to how well each stage is performed.

For example, many self-service services take a short time, are controlled by the customer, require some but not too much effort on the part of the customer to obtain the service and have little human contact. Usually, customers are not too dependent on the supplier (except in the case where the self-service machinery fails, eg an ATM). For such services, the customer's requirement of customer care is usually very different from that for services which, say, are performed by personal service over a long time with a high degree of dependence by the customer on the supplier (eg personal financial services). Of course, both kinds of service require high levels of customer care, but of a different kind. For example, financial services may require a more attentive and informative approach on each contact than when the customer is filling a car with petrol! This is partly due to the routineness of the latter.

Some examples of how a particular customer might perceive how different service products might vary along these different dimensions of customer need are given in Figure 4.1.

Of course, different individuals will view the same service in different ways. For example, some customers have a high propensity to participate in transactions, while others prefer infrequent and distant contact. More experienced or veteran users may see a given service as much more routine and less risky than novices. The former may prefer to obtain instructions through machinery, but the latter may prefer a helping human hand. If this is true, it implies that the role of the customer in the service-production or "servuction" system can be expanded as the customer's experience grows.

Levels of customer care

The idea of the level of customer care expected by the customer has already been introduced. However, this notion must be expressed more concisely if policy is to be built upon it. In most cases, customers have an idea about the *minimum acceptable* level of customer care which should be provided, and the *desired* level. If they already have experience of dealing with the organisation there may also be a *perceived* level — the level they perceive they receive. Perceptions are perhaps the strongest influence on satisfaction levels. Perceived levels contrast with *actual* levels, which is a statement from the supplier's point of view as to what customer care actions were definitely carried out.

The above definitions of care levels are well-established in analysis of technical dimensions of service. For example, in maintenance of technical equipment which requires calling out an engineer, the *response* time is defined as the time between the request for maintenance being communicated to the supplier and the engineer arriving. Customers who are regular users of this service usually have a clear idea of desired and minimum acceptable response times. They may also perceive that a particular response time is achieved, on average or at the last call. It is worth noting that perceived response times often vary significantly from actual response times, and are often subject to a *halo effect*. The better the relationship with the supplier, the more optimistic the perceived response time. Figure 4.2 shows how these different levels might be related for an individual customer and Figure 4.3 shows how the different levels might be distributed over a group of customers.

Delivery time	Engineer called on weekly area rota. Inflexible.
Importance of service element in total package	Critical. Service is the total product.
Need for control	Wants to control timing of service and be consulted about cost.
Effort required by customer	Minimal — phone call and sign cheque.
Dependence on supplier	High — no other trusted service supplier.
Importance of service to customer	Critical. If service not performed, family will have no clean clothes.
Efficiency / reliability of supplier	Excellent, except for rigidity of area calling rota.
Dependence of service on staff	Total. If engineer is not good, service will be poor.
Dependence of service on equipment	None. Tools are basic.
Supplier's staff's need to control	Engineer prefers to work alone, except when needs co-operation.
Kind of contact with other customers	None.
Skill / expertise required	Basic technical expertise.
Routineness of encounters	Very routine, unless repair requires unavailable part or machine requires replacing.
Number / complexity of stages	Only two main stages (telephone, visit). Within visit, three stages (greeting/ briefing, servicing, payment/farewell).
Emotions anticipated / experienced	Fear if service late or fails, or if cost too high. Relief if service on time, quick, cheap.

Figure 4.1. How a customer might perceive a visit from a washing machine service engineer

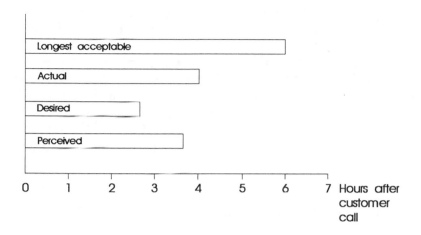

Figure 4.2 Response time relationships — individual customer

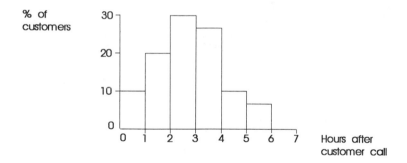

Figure 4.3 Distribution of desired response times

It is also possible to provide too high a level of customer care. The simplest example of this is *over-attentive* service. A customer may go into a store which is laid out to enable browsing. The customer may expect to do it at leisure, without interference from a store assistant. In this case, if the store assistant approaches the customer with the standard question "How can I help you?", the customer may react with the standard answer "I'm just looking". Shortly afterwards, the customer is likely to leave the store! The "hovering waiter" is another well-established popular image of over-attentive care. In response to this the customer may not be able to leave immediately, but is less likely to return. In telemarketing, if a customer calls the response-handling centre and the call is answered immediately after the first ring, customers have no time to collect their thoughts after dialling. This "thought collection" time is particularly important in countries which are switching from other methods of call connection to electronic methods, where the ring follows the dialling much more quickly. This kind of service is defined here as *excessive*.

Some customers may have threshold levels of satisfaction and dissatisfaction. There may be a band of service levels within which they are more or less indifferent. The possible relationship between these levels of care is shown in Figure 4.4.

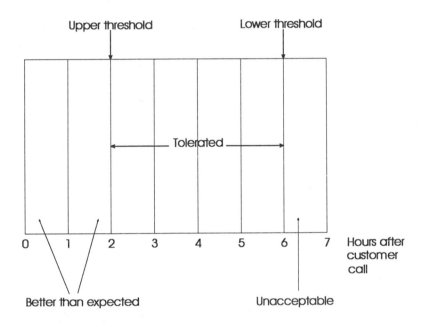

Figure 4.4 Thresholds of tolerance of response times

The effect of experience

Customers form their requirements and perceptions as a result of several influences. The most important of these is experience, whether with the supplier, a competitor or some other "benchmark" company.

As has already been stressed, all suppliers of products and services are in some sense in competition with each other when it comes to customer care. In a consumerist age, it is not unusual to hear customers making explicit comparisons, say, between a retail store and British Rail.

The extent to which customers make such "parallel comparisons" has been increased by the consumerist values of the age. Thus, issues of consequential liability following late arrivals of trains have been paralleled with the liability implied by product defects. As leading commercial organisations improve their standards of customer care, so public service organisations are under pressure to do the same. This is because customers *do* compare and form expectations which are transferred across different suppliers of products and services.

Where customers have a well-established relationship with a particular supplier, their expectations and requirements are likely to be conditioned mainly by their experience with that supplier. For example, suppose customers have no choice but to travel by bus to a particular destination. The actual level of service is that buses always arrive late and in groups. This is the popular myth but sustained by probability theory. This states that if buses leave at regular intervals and are subject to random delays, their arrival will bunch. This bunching will be exacerbated if they are unable to overtake each other which is often the case in busy traffic conditions.

The intelligent customer may understand all this and not expect any better. Customers uneducated in statistics may be highly frustrated by matters, but still expect no better, because things have always been the same. The gap between perceived and desired levels of service may be so great that customers resign themselves to it. They may transfer their requirements for improvement to other aspects of the service, eg polite treatment by bus crews, improved waiting facilities and warmer or more comfortable vehicles.

But this resignation on the part of customers should not console the supplier. For as soon as customers have the choice, they may move to alternative ways of travelling (eg cars). This has been the experience of many commuter rail networks as people's income grew, enabling them to buy first or second cars. This lesson is particularly important, therefore, for companies with strong market positions. Low standards of customer care may be tolerated, but only if there is no competition or no way of influencing standards of care.

In a directly competitive environment, customers who stay in relationships with particular suppliers do so because the total package they receive from the supplier (product, service, price, credit, customer care and so forth) is right for them. But there is no room for complacency. Suppose that a retailer maintains a high market share through its wide, low cost product range, but provides low standards of customer care. Check-out queues are long. Stock is poorly displayed. Staff are surly. Payment terms are cash only. Tills are not automated and charging errors are frequent. Parking is difficult, and there is always a shortage of shopping trolleys and baskets. Customers of this store will have low expectations of customer care and may also believe that they have low requirements. They may have "talked themselves into" accepting the idea that low standards of customer care are worth tolerating because of the very low price charged. However, if competition emerges based on low prices but high standards of customer care, customer requirements may change.

Behaviour often lags behind experience. A supplier with a good record of customer care may occasionally lapse. Customers do not immediately switch suppliers. They have learnt that their supplier has provided good experiences in the past. This learning takes time to undo. This customer behaviour gives suppliers the opportunity to recover from episodes of bad care.

Word of mouth

As Chapter 1 showed, the power of word of mouth is often quoted in terms of how satisfied or dissatisfied customers communicate their experience to others. More specifically, customers who are totally satisfied or who are dissatisfied and then have their problems resolved by the supplier, can become powerful *advocates* for the supplier. They tend to recommend that supplier to their friends. If the latter are dissatisfied with *their* supplier, then the recommendations can be particularly effective. The power of this recommendation is so strong that it is often portrayed in television advertisements (usually housewives recommending detergents to friends).

The force of recommendation is as powerful in organisational markets as in customer markets. Information about perceived levels of customer care may be communicated within the buying centre and between other buying centres. In buying centres which are making important, high risk decisions, it is particularly important for members of the buying centre to be *and to appear* knowledgeable. Any piece of information about the experience of others is often seized upon and given great status.

The above analysis indicates how important it is for suppliers to understand how their customers make their decisions — whether to buy for the first time, to stay with the supplier or leave it. A number of concepts which have been found useful in explaining customer behaviour are described below.

The time problem

In most service situations, customers have some consciousness of the passing of time. Delivering customer care takes time. If the customer is in a hurry, the care needs to be tailored to the requirements. The problem for suppliers is that despite shorter working hours and longer holidays, many customers are *less* tolerant of the time it takes to receive a service. Perceived scarcity of free time can make customers want to achieve more in a short time. This can also make customers worry about the differences between what they want to achieve and what they actually achieve, and of course what others achieve.

If customers perceive that they are short of time, saving time will paradoxically be an important proposition even in customer care. However, the time problem varies by age group. The older and richer the customer, the less the perception of the time problem. Marketers focusing on older customers may well promote the length of time it takes to get the full pleasure out of a service! This applies particularly for more up-market products.

How customers choose

There is a view that customers always act rationally — they test services (as they perceive them) against purchasing criteria, which are based on their needs, to come up with a choice. In fact, people buy in many different ways. Their perceptions of products can change quickly. The speed with which they choose can vary tremendously. This does not imply irrationality, merely that it is hard to model customer choice using simple models based on assumptions about customer needs, awareness of products and perceived product attributes.

But to choose between different services, customers must first be aware of those services. Consideration is probably given to a limited set of services before the choice is finally made. If customers do behave in this way, then the following definitions can be used in analysing customer choice:

(a) total set: all services capable of satisfying a given need
(b) awareness set: services the customer is aware of
(c) unawareness set: services the customer is unaware of
(d) consideration set: services in the awareness set which the customer considers buying
(e) infeasible set: considered services which are unavailable, unaffordable, etc
(f) choice set: services between which the final choice is made
(g) excluded set: considered services which are not in the choice set
(h) actual decision: the service finally chosen.

This (rather exhaustive) enumeration of all the possibilities helps identify what marketing policies are needed in order to get customers

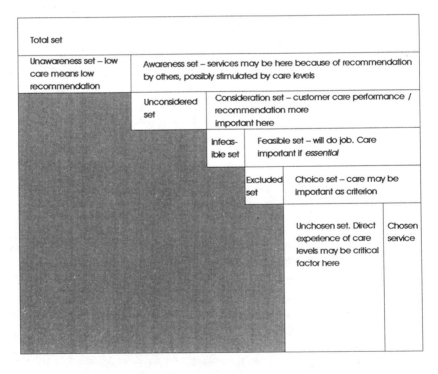

Figure 4.5 Customer care and the choice process

to buy or experience the service. Figure 4.5 shows how levels of customer care can affect this choice process.

The ladder of loyalty

The above discussion assumes that the purchase is what is called "one-off", ie not to be repeated for some time. However, many services are not like this. Provided that the customer is satisfied, a repeat purchase may take place. The term "ladder of loyalty" is used to describe the ascending stages of loyalty to the concept and the supplier. The type of "steps" that are in the ladder depend on the nature of the service, its potential frequency of use, and the severity of competition. This is how the ladder of loyalty might look for a car manufacture:

Step 1   Does not drive
Step 2   Drives parents' car
Step 3   Buys used car of manufacturer's make from friend
Step 4   Brings car in for service at authorised dealer
Step 5   Buys new car from dealer
Step 6   Buys extended warranty from dealer
Step 7   Trades up to larger new car from dealer.

A key objective of customer care is to move customers further up the ladder or, at a minimum, to maintain them at their current position.

The steps in the ladder of loyalty correspond with attitudes, ranging from "neutral" through "positive" to "enthusiasm". "Advocates" are so firmly established on the higher rungs that they try to persuade others to mount or move up the ladder. Conversely, disenchanted customers may try to persuade others to move down or get off the ladder. Market research may be used to classify customers in this way, allowing differentiated service strategies to be adopted.

Why do customers buy?

The use of customer care as a way of retaining loyalty requires a good understanding of the general forces which influence customers' buying behaviour. A full listing of all the factors which determine why customers buy a particular service would be as follows.

(a) *Social, economic, psychological and cultural*
  (i)   Purchasing power — which in turn depends on income, assets (liquid and others).
  (ii)   Cost and availability of finance.
  (iii) Reference groups — including peer groups (neighbours, friends, colleagues), aspirational groups (eg royalty, film stars, superiors at work). Neighbours, friends and work-mates are particularly important. Word of mouth is one of the most powerful influences on buying behaviour.
  (iv)   Demographic — life cycle stage, size and composition of family, age, occupation, ethnic origin. This includes the influence of the family decision-making unit, as discussed in Chapter 1.
  (v)   Family influences — position of the individual customer in the family, degree of influence he or she has on the type of decision in question.
  (vi)   Geographic — rural/urban, neighbourhood type, location relative to the point of service provision.
  (vii) Media behaviour — frequency/intensity of exposure to different media, propensity to respond to different media (eg does a customer respond better to television, direct mail, or telephone?). This is particularly important in helping suppliers determine how to reach potential customers.
  (viii) Life-style — the general patterns of behaviour the customer follows, and psychographic — how people think and interpret the influences of the world around them.

(b) *Product / supplier experience*
  Previous experience in relation to the service or the supplier — whether repeat or first time buyer, degree of satisfaction with product, how problems were handled, expectations, etc. This can be summarised as the customers' position on the ladder of loyalty. Of course, if the customers' experiences are negative, it would be more appropriate to talk about a pot-hole of disloyalty. Given the importance of word of mouth recommendation, complaint handling procedures are particularly important for service providers.

(c) *Channel experience*
  (i)   Pattern of channel use (eg loyalty to particular retailer, dealer or agent). This is related to responsiveness to different promotional media.

(ii)   Awareness, experience of and satisfaction with different channels. This is the ladder of loyalty to the channel rather than to the supplier.

(iii)   Location in relation to outlets.

(d) *Marketing mix*

These factors all relate to the effect on the customer of different elements of the marketing mix. When a company is trying to analyse the effect of changes in the marketing mix on customers, it is not wise to assume that all changes are perceived accurately by customers. In researching the effect of any of the variables below, it is important also to research perceptions of them (eg whether advertising was seen, what a service was perceived to cost). The key variables include:

(i)   which services are available to the customer (not all customers are in the served market)

(ii)   the price of the service

(iii)   the packaging of the service

(iv)   effectiveness of customer care

(v)   quality of staff dealing directly with customers

(vi)   how the service is promoted (advertising, PR, direct marketing, etc)

(vii)   prices of the service in question and of substitutes and complementary goods

(viii) other aspects of the marketing mix of competitive services

(ix)   competing service products

(x)   user costs other than price.

(e) *Natural factors*

(i)   Time — of day, week, month, season and year.

(ii)   Weather — not controllable, but of great influence.

Figure 4.6 shows how some of these factors can be affected or affect customer care.

The buying decision

The nature of the buying decision can be classified using the "buygrid", a concept borrowed from industrial marketing. It defines certain "buyclasses", as follows:

Factor	Relationship with customer care
Purchasing power:	Ability to afford higher levels of care.
Reference groups:	Types of group affect recommendation patterns.
Family:	Determines care needs of total group, according to age, gender, number in family, etc.
Geographic:	Rural/urban split may affect deliverability of care levels.
Media behaviour:	Determines ability of supplier to influence care expectations.
Supplier experience:	Good experience of past care levels enhances receptiveness to supplier's offers.
Pattern of channel use:	Habit of using particular channels mean care policies need to be focused on those channels.
Price of service:	May create care expectations.
Packaging of service:	Care may be part of packaging. Packaging may bring promise of care.
Competing products:	Customer experience of competitive products may condition expectations.
User costs:	These may determine customer attitudes to involvement in service, control, etc.
Timing:	If customer demand peaks at particular times, delivery of care must be attuned to them.

Figure 4.6 Buying factors and customer care — examples

(a) *New task* — the customer has no experience of the product type. In this case, the customer will need much information about the service, and may ask friends for information about it.

(b) *Straight rebuy* — a routine re-order without any modification, often handled routinely.

(c) *Modified rebuy* — where the buyer seeks to change supplier or some other aspect of the purchase, but wants the same general kind of service.

Figure 4.7 shows how the importance of customer care varies between these types of purchasing decision.

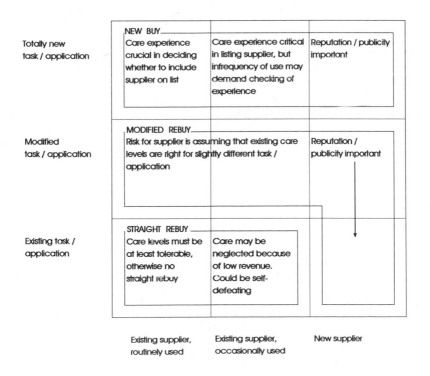

	Existing supplier, routinely used	Existing supplier, occasionally used	New supplier
Totally new task / application	**NEW BUY** — Care experience crucial in deciding whether to include supplier on list	Care experience critical in listing supplier, but infrequency of use may demand checking of experience	Reputation / publicity important
Modified task / application	**MODIFIED REBUY** — Risk for supplier is assuming that existing care levels are right for slightly different task / application		Reputation / publicity important
Existing task / application	**STRAIGHT REBUY** — Care levels must be at least tolerable, otherwise no straight rebuy	Care may be neglected because of low revenue. Could be self-defeating	

Figure 4.7 Relationship between buy classes and customer care

High involvement and low involvement decisions

Many purchases require little or no explanation. Often, purchase motivation is already understood. In others there is little that *needs* to be understood.

This is particularly true of routine purchases, eg a bus trip by a customer who makes the same trip every day. Basic products and services are *commodities*. They are purchased for functional reasons and carry little or no symbolic meaning. Their unit price is low, whichever brand is selected. They are routinely purchased. The risk a customer takes by making the wrong choice of supplier or product is low because economic, psychological and social commitment to the product is low. These are *low involvement* products. However, not all low price, frequently purchased products or services are low involvement products. Commuting journeys by train are certainly not!

In some cases, the customer may feel a high degree of psychological and social risk in making the wrong choice. It is a choice that is in a sense "worn" by the customer. Many products are "worn", not just clothes, but also cigarettes, alcohol, cars, books, home furnishings and the like. These are *high involvement* products and services. They are particularly important for customer care. Appropriate levels of customer care supplied in high involvement situations greatly reinforce customer loyalty. Poor customer care provision in such situations leads to customer disloyalty and strong word of mouth condemnation.

Branding

When it comes to the purchase, corporate and product/service branding are very important. But they also have a strong effect on the customer's expectations and perceptions of customer care. "Presence", the branding of the relationship between the supplier and customers, is one of the most important of the seven Ps of marketing. A strong brand, developed over a long period, gives customer care a strong platform. Without it, customer care almost has to start from scratch with every customer transaction.

Customer loyalty

Customer loyalty and branding are closely connected. Highly visible and positive branding cannot exist without customer loyalty, and customer loyalty depends on good customer care, in the long run. If customers are treated well, they will tend to be loyal and this will provide the opportunity for branding to get to work. Branding requires the strong imprinting of ideas about the product in customers' minds. These ideas will be positive if customers have frequent good experience in buying and using the product or service. The more positive each experience, the further up the "ladder of loyalty" the customer climbs, from first transaction with the supplier, through frequent and regular transactions, to where the customer becomes a firm advocate for the supplier.

Disloyalty occurs when customers switch suppliers or brands. Sometimes this occurs when customers decide they need a change, not because of any problem with the previous product or supplier, but simply in search of variety. These random changes cannot be avoided, although high levels of customer care can do much to ensure that customers return. Switches which are due to significant price differences are also difficult to prevent through customer care, always assuming that the cheaper product is not lower quality.

Switches that are due to problems with the product or service, or poor levels of customer care, can and should be avoided. In service situations, the unresolved problem which the supplier does not know about is the most dangerous. It festers, and eventually the customer switches away. Customer care which encourages complaints and ensures that they are dealt with well is the best defence against this cause of switching.

The high involvement decision process

If a decision is important to the customer, then considerable thought may be devoted to the purchase. If the product is bought frequently, more thinking is likely to take place when the customer is considering switching between suppliers or products. Once the new purchasing pattern is established as a habit, purchases are likely to take place routinely, without much thought.

Usually, the purchasing process goes through the following stages, sometimes sequentially, sometimes with different stages combined.

Existence of the need — the need comes into existence. The customer may not be aware of it, but it is there.

Identification or realisation of need — the need comes to the "front of mind".

Problem recognition — the need exists for a reason, typically a problem that needs to be solved (eg meeting a want). The customer recognises that the problem exists.

91

Search for information — information is sought about products and services which will solve the problem. This is triggered by the need for problem resolution — the dissonance (disharmony) that is felt when a problem is recognised triggers a drive or motivating force that leads the customer to resolve the problem and restore the state of psychological balance or consonance.

Evaluation — when all the relevant accessible information required to make the choice which will resolve the problem is gathered and analysed. The customer may or may not have established choice criteria. Even if they are already established, during evaluation they may change. Patterns of deliberation are also important. Some customers rely more on personal advice than on information provided by suppliers. So the outcome of the evaluation will depend on various factors, varying from personality and past experience to the way different suppliers provide information.

Where customer care is concerned, it is particularly important to understand the criteria customers use to evaluate different suppliers, products and services. For it is the answer to this that provides the link between customer care and financial success. If levels of customer care are used to choose between suppliers, products and services, then the commercial justification for investing in customer care is not difficult to produce.

If information on evaluation criteria can be obtained by research, then segmentation by customer care criteria provides the key to determining the level of care that should be provided to different groups.

Choice — some choices are impulsive, or at least seem so to others. But many are deliberate and rational, based upon systematic processing of information. Such processing leads first to the formation of an intention to purchase, which is determined by the formulation of beliefs about the product and its likely performance.

Post-purchase review — after the decision, the customer re-evaluates it in the light of any new information (eg information about product performance). In some post-purchase situations, customers experience cognitive dissonance. They feel unhappy about what they now know. They may experience doubt, even anxiety, if the product does not come up to expectations. This may be resolved in various ways. Customers look for information which supports their decision (eg others who made the same decision). They may focus on the "good deal" they got in an attempt to convince themselves that they made the right decision. They may even ignore, avoid or distort incoming information which is inconsistent with what they want to believe. High levels of customer care after the sale make it easy for customers to justify the decision they made, even if there are problems after the sale.

How needs trigger behaviour

Needs only trigger behaviour when the customer *perceives* the need. At this point it makes sense to examine the process of perception. This is defined as "the process of organising sensory stimuli in a meaningful way". Seeing is a purely neurological process and does not imply giving *meaning* to what is seen. Some of these stimuli are purely biological, of course, and produce automatic, reflex reactions. Hunger is a good example of this. But marketers focus particularly on the mental processing of external information, notably advertising messages.

However, *intrinsic* forces are more important in determining what is perceived and how it is perceived. These are listed below.

Needs

Needs may be functional (eg the need to replace a faulty dishwasher or a superannuated car). Such needs cause the customer to pay more attention to the technical specifications of the product or service, and to customer care that facilitates the achievement of functional requirements, eg delivery on time, quick rectification of faults. Needs may be emotional, eg to reward oneself. In such cases, customers pay more attention to the emotional side of customer care, such as whether they are well looked after during the purchasing or service process.

Perceptual vigilance and defence

Customers tend to recognise aspects of customer care that relate to their particular values and needs more quickly than those which do not. For example, if in work life a customer is a highly effective manager, customer care which is delivered in an efficient, professional way will be singled out for attention, irrespective of the emotional values conveyed by supplier staff. On the other hand, if the customer is a very affectionate type, with time for anyone with a problem, he or she may single out for attention examples of customer care in this personal style, and may look very negatively at customer care delivered in the "efficient" style. Put more technically, customer care which is delivered in a style which is not consonant with the customer's needs and values may not be recognised at all or may be misconstrued.

Cognitive consistency

Perceptual processes are important in maintaining customers' values and beliefs, even in the face of conflicting evidence. Customers try to maintain a consistent view of their world. They accept messages that support their beliefs, rejecting ones that threaten them. When threatened, they experience cognitive dissonance and the need to reduce it. Much of this dissonance or dissatisfaction occurs *after* purchase. Therefore, a key role for customer care is to reassure purchasers that they have made the right decision.

Personality

Personality types and characteristics are likely to be linked to perception. For instance, deeply prejudiced personality types are likely to perceive selectively and distort the meaning of what they see. This can work positively or negatively. The "efficient business type" described above may see efficiency in customer care where it does not exist and exaggerate perceived inefficiencies.

Motivation

Once customers perceive a need they are in a motivated condition. They are energised to seek to satisfy the need. In other words, motives link needs and their satisfaction. Motivation is therefore a *process* or a *state*. Some types of motivator are more common than others. The more common ones are of particular interest to marketers and include:

(a) making money
(b) helping the family
(c) pleasure
(d) saving money
(e) saving time/effort
(f) impressing others
(g) self-improvement
(h) feeling secure
(i) belonging.

Customer care policies can affect the way in which most of these motives are put to work. Customer care can save much time, effort and money for customers. The shop assistant who takes the trouble to ask a few simple questions to find out customers' needs is more able to provide them with the right service than the assistant who asks nothing and assumes everything. In providing customer care, one should try to establish what customers' motivations are in buying or using a product or service. This will have important implications for the type of customer care that should be provided.

Many so-called motivators are necessary to maintain behaviour rather than increase it. Their absence will demotivate but their presence will not motivate. These are "hygiene" factors. The presence of soap and clean towels will not motivate people to work harder. But their absence causes people to grumble and become dissatisfied. Thus, offering customers different ways to pay for a product may not increase satisfaction but limiting the number of ways to pay may reduce satisfaction.

In some situations, customer care will be a hygiene factor. This will tend to be where the core product or service characteristics do not involve a close or extensive relationship between the customer and supplier, eg buying a chocolate bar on an impulse. But as the relationship with the supplier gets deeper and the involvement with the product higher, customer care factors are likely to become more important. They will cease to be hygiene factors and become *prime motivators* for purchase, eg choosing a make of car and a garage to supply and service it.

Learning

Motivational states lead to rewards (or "punishments"). These experiences, of motivation leading to behaviour followed by reward or punishment, form the basis for learning. Customers learn to associate the benefits of buying at a store with the smiling faces of the shop assistants that they see when they enter the store. Customer learning may be unconscious or rational, as expressed in "I got good service from them, so I'll buy from them again".

Personality

Personality plays a key role in motivation and learning. Unfortunately, personality is easier to recognise than explain or even understand. Much work has been done on personality *traits* (sociability, gregariousness and aggression are examples of traits). Personality types are clearly identifiable in much customer market segmentation and should form the basis for analysis of customers for customer care purposes. In many cases, training should be given to staff on how to recognise and react to different personality types.

Attitudes

Attitudes are the outcome of learning and reasonably good predictors of behaviour. The attitudes that are relevant to a particular service situation can usually be divided into attitudes towards the service that is being bought or used and attitudes towards the way in which that service is being delivered. Thus, a customer may have a very positive attitude towards a car insurance company, perhaps because it handled the last claim very well. But the attitude to renewal of a policy may be negative because the company has a rather complex renewal process.

The social environment

Man is a social animal and functions much of the time as a member of a group. The group can be the *family*; it can also be at *work*, at *school* or at *play* (social groups).

In any purchasing or use decision which involves a group of customers, the kind of roles that they play will be affected by how the group has been set up, the processes by which they work and the pressures at work. For example, a married couple may be served a low quality meal in a high quality restaurant. The wife may want to complain, while the husband just wants to get the meal over with, pay and leave. The husband sees the situation as yet another example of spending time on unimportant things, an issue which has arisen many times in the family. The wife may see the meal as having been a great disappointment. She requires compensation for this. This particular group, the wife and husband buying centre, has a history which is being played out in the restaurant. The customer care solution, if the restaurant wants the couple to return, is to make the husband feel that complaining can be done quickly and painlessly, while ensuring that the wife is compensated. An observant waiter would see the drama being played out and intervene with a discrete question and the offer of an immediate refund.

Control and automation

The psychological needs described above indicate that customers are motivated by the need for security. This need for security leads to a requirement by some customers to be in control of their relationship with their supplier. However, many service situations create a perception among customers that they are totally without control over the situation. The classic example of this is the airport, where customers are processed by display screens, rows of anonymous counters, conveyor belts, crowded departure lounges with limited facilities and rooms without enough seating in which customers are assembled before embarking. In such a situation the customer feels totally at the mercy of the system. Those who fly first class, however, are given more control of the situation. Their time in queues is reduced, they are escorted to lounges with enough seating and attentive but not over-attentive service, embark directly and sit in a more spacious cabin. This is a good illustration of the benefits and costs of customer care.

Even in the worst situation, every attempt should be made to explore how to give customers who wish to be in control the feeling of control. In some cases, a slight price premium enables suppliers to provide this. For example frequent business travellers tend to want more control, so they are usually provided with some benefits similar to those of first class travellers but less expensive. These facilities are funded either by a club membership fee, or the additional profit generated by the loyalty of this group of customers.

The idea of *locus of control* is useful for analysing this kind of situation. In most service situations other than self-service, the locus of control is with the supplier. It is the supplier who determines at what rate and when the service will be delivered. But as with all marketing, it is the perceived locus of control that it more important than the actual locus of control. Customers can be persuaded to think that they control the service.

If customers' control over a situation is less than they want or indeed if they feel they are being asked to control a situation when they are incapable of doing so (eg unqualified, without the right information), levels of stress can rise. This can result in anxious behaviour, which might show as rudeness or lack of co-operation. The answer here is to give the customer the degree of control required (ie give real control or take over control). If a new product requires, for its success, for customers to be in control (eg because of a high self-service element), customer education must form an important part of the product launch package. The nature of this customer education package will of course vary with the ability of the target market to absorb such instructions.

Perhaps the best example of this is efforts made by microcomputer manufacturers to educate their customers. These efforts take the form of rather long but (in most instances) well-indexed and cross-referenced manuals. The target market consists mostly of well-educated customers. If this customer education is successful, the number of calls to the helpline by new customers is significantly reduced. A more-down-to-earth example is the clarity of labelling of supermarket aisles. The more complex the product or service, the higher the level of customer education required for the locus of control to be successfully transferred to the customer. Figure 4.8 demonstrates this point.

Some customers do not want to be in control. Their need for security may be best fulfilled by cocooning them, so that they do not have to take any initiative. Wherever possible, suppliers should offer the two main options for service — control or be managed.

Some customers prefer to be in complete control. A close approximation to it can be achieved by self-service. Bank automatic teller machines, self-service petrol pumps and the like all suit this need. There is some evidence that customers who prefer this kind of option tend to prefer to be in control, however complex the service they are receiving. However, the same customer who prefers self-service for a routine transaction may prefer closely attended service for a more complicated transaction. Groups of customer may be segmented according to their need for control and given different degrees of control. But this is not always possible. For this reason, flexibility and personal attentiveness to customer needs must be retained.

As hinted above, there is likely to be a difference between *equipment-based* and *people-based* services, from the customers' point of view. Customers have very strong attitudes to people. Some customers like being with other people and receiving service from them. Others do not like being with other people and dislike being dependent for service on them. The latter are often happier to receive service from a machine or to administer the service themselves following clear instructions provided by the supplier. Where this is not available, the telephone may be preferred to face to face situations.

The last point is a reminder that customer care can be delivered through a variety of media, depending on the nature of the care action. Information can be provided face to face, on the telephone, on a video screen, through a loudspeaker and in print. Problems can be solved in front of customers or in the "back room". Equipment can be maintained on the customer's site or (for smaller items) at a service centre.

PRODUCT /
SERVICE
COMPLEXITY

	Low	Medium	High
High	High / very high	High	High / medium
Medium	High / medium	Medium	Low / medium
Low	Medium	Low / medium	Low

EXTENT OF CUSTOMER
EXPERIENCE WITH PRODUCT /
SERVICE

Figure 4.8 Level of customer education required to transfer locus of control to customer

Replacement of people-based services by automated services

This provides a challenge to the delivery of customer care. The best examples of this are in simple transactions. These include:

(a) withdrawal of cash from a bank or payment of credits through a bank
(b) telephone directory enquiries or provision of other information through an automated helpline
(c) self-service petrol and car-wash
(d) video hire through a machine.

These transactions are handled best if the supplier carefully investigates the full range of customer requirements that will need to be satisfied by the automated approach. Often, while carrying out a simple transaction, customers take the opportunity to check facts or receive information. When petrol is bought with personal service, checking oil and water levels and perhaps tyre pressures is also undertaken. When withdrawing or crediting money, information is often sought about account balances or about the clearance of recent transactions. Video cassette renters might seek information about the popularity of certain videos. Sometimes, such information can be provided automatically as part of the transaction. In other cases, additional self-service facilities must be added (eg tyre pressure check).

Following the script

The customer forms part of the service system. In many service situations supplier staff are trained to follow a script. Customers can also be trained or educated to expect a script and then to follow it. If customers agree to follow the script, their chance of being satisfied increases because the script is designed to identify their needs and then guide them through receiving the right level of customer care. This is at its most explicit in the telemarketing script, when a customer calls in to request a repair service for equipment or a quote for insurance. If customers can be conditioned to expect questions to identify their needs, and then to co-operate in subsequent actions to ensure that the right level of service is delivered, then both the supplier's and the customer's objective will be reached.

Customers who prefer to be in control of the service process need to be handled more carefully. Typically, supplier staff must have higher levels of training, so that customers believe they are scripting the situation, even though the supplier is in control of the logic and the coverage of the script.

Customers still have a tendency to ignore the script. Perhaps the best example of this is failure to read instructions, the part of the script that precedes human intervention. This may be because this early script is badly written or presented. It is more likely to be that once customers need service, they prefer human media to printed media.

Some companies are using expert computer systems to help them manage the dialogue with different kinds of customer in different service situations. Obviously, this is easiest in telephone-contact situations, but the approach is also being used to provide instant simulations of the consequences of different financial arrangements (life insurance, pensions) or the costs and benefits of different major computer configurations.

How customers perceive the supplier

The idea that the customer's attitude to the core product or service may differ from that towards the context in which the product or service is bought or used has already been introduced. One of the most important "context attitudes" is that towards the supplier. A positive attitude towards the supplier can produce a halo effect, causing a beneficial perception of customer care. However, if the level of customer care deviates too much from the expected level, the positive attitude can change.

In situations of high stress, often caused by the locus of control being in the wrong place (from the customer's point of view), the attitude towards the supplier is key. If the supplier is perceived to be receptive to customer feedback and flexible enough to change, the customer may have no hesitation about giving the feedback that the supplier needs in order to be able to meet customer needs. In this case, the feedback will concern the customer's need to have more control, or for the supplier to control the situation better. If, on the other hand, the supplier is regarded as inflexible and unreceptive to customer feedback, a vicious circle will develop. Customers will not give feedback, the supplier will believe that things are all right and eventually customers will just leave the supplier. Suppliers who are aware of this risk take the trouble to educate their customers to deal with different types of control and to have realistic expectations (ie ones which accord with the supplier's real capabilities to respond to needs).

The visibility of service

Much of the service delivery process may be visible to customers. Their perceptions influence their attitudes towards the supplier. Some suppliers have used this to their advantage. The Disney idea that all service staff are on the stage in front of customers has been approximated by fast food restaurants such as McDonalds. However, suppliers that avoid this issue by trying to conceal the service delivery process may find that this policy backfires.

If customers want to believe that they are in control of the service process, what better approach to use than to play out the service "performance" in front of them, not behind closed doors. Companies offering technical service have found that exposing their service processes and facilities to customers has brought immense benefits to their relationship with suppliers, not just in terms of creating trust, but also in terms of educating the customer as to how to obtain the best service from the supplier.

Organising customer analysis

This chapter has shown the variety of attitudes that customers may have in relation to customer care and how these attitudes are affected by the nature of the buying process. The next chapter shows how to make sense of all this information.

Chapter 5

Identifying and Analysing Customer Requirements

In the previous chapter, the variety of customer behaviours, needs and perceptions has been covered. The key questions for the supplier trying to decide what levels of customer care to provide are:

(a) Who are the customers whose needs are to be met?
(b) What are customers' behaviours, needs and perceptions? What is their relative importance (eg do they constitute a hierarchy)?
(c) How far do the supplier's policies meet customer needs today?
(d) What are relevant competitive offerings against which the supplier should position its offerings?
(e) What are its customers' experiences of its services?
(f) What do the supplier's staff believe about the level of service they are providing?
(g) What do commercial indicators of success show (eg brand loyalty, market share)?
(h) Can customers be grouped into coherent segments to enable customer care policy to be structured to meet their needs?

Making sense of customer data

Except in the smallest organisation, customer care policies cannot be completely tailored to the needs of individual customers. Therefore, customers should be grouped. The most relevant way to group them is according to their attitudes and likely responses to customer care policies. Customers can be grouped in many ways. Each type of grouping may have different care needs. Examples of ways of grouping include:

(a) Demographic (eg age, marital status, number of children) — for example, hotels often offer a customer care package tailored to families with children (eg arrangement of room, baby listening service, rooms or areas for changing babies' nappies).

(b) Socio-economic — social class, occupation, income, assets. In many service markets, more "up-market" customers may be offered higher standards of care (according to their ability to pay). However, the challenge is to make good basic standards of care available to customers with less ability to pay.

(c) Geographical — where the customer is (absolutely and relative to where the service is offered). For example, the telephone is often the key to offering higher standards of care to customers who are remote from the supplier. Some distributors of industrial equipment use dealers or agents to handle customers in certain areas. Here, the challenge is to make the right level of care available through the third party. This is usually achieved by a combination of process design, contractual obligations and motivational programmes.

(d) Behavioural — how customers act. A more popular term for this is "life-style". General life-style based segmentation is quite useful. In particular, it provides a common denominator for analysis of customer behaviour in respect of widely different products and services. Customers might, for example, be segmented into those who readily complain and those who do not. The latter group's needs may be hard to establish, so specific research programmes may be mounted to discover them.

(e) Psychographic (eg extrovert–introvert, optimist–pessimist, planner–improviser). This refers to the underlying determinants of behaviour, or what people think, perceive and feel. Perhaps the best example of this is the customer's need for control in service situations.

Segmentation has become popularised through the use of acronymic versions of segment names. The best known examples include "yuppies" for young, upwardly mobile people and dinkies — dual income, no kids. Thus, a retailer would be interested in whether dinkies tend to be clustered in certain geographical areas and visit certain kinds of store. A public utility might be interested in whether dinkies differed from other customers in their attitudes to delayed service visits because one of the couple needed to stay at home specially to receive the service visit.

Market segmentation has moved way beyond these rather simplistic segment definitions. They are still useful in providing a focus for marketing, but it may be more useful to segment by behaviour in relation to the particular kind of product or service in question, and in particular towards customer care. For example, it would be interesting to see whether customers could be grouped into acceptors and complainers.

The importance of segmentation

Segmentation is just another word for putting customers into groups which share similar characteristics which affect their behaviour in the market (buying, media, etc). Segmentation is used because:

(a) It gives a better basis for understanding the whole market. Even if a company markets the same service to segments which behave differently, it will understand the whole market better if it knows how different segments behave. However, if customer care is an important part of a complex product/service offering, then it is possible to adjust customer care levels to different types of customer, while making the same core offer.

(b) If different segments respond differently to marketing policy, and if policies can be attuned to different segments, companies can achieve their objectives more easily than if they followed an undifferentiated policy (ie applied to the whole market). If the care needs of different kinds of customer differ quite radically, then the total product/service offering may be differentiated purely or mainly in terms of the level of care offered. Examples of this include first class air travel.

(c) Segmentation can bring benefits of focus, concentration and specialisation and hence differentiation. These benefits include increased profit or sales, lower costs, prevention of competitive entry. This is because a focused marketing policy makes a company very good at meeting the needs of its chosen segment. If the customer care needs of each segment are analysed in depth, an organisation is in a strong position to fine tune its care offering so as to meet the needs of its chosen segment.

Customer care policies can be anything from very general — applicable to the whole market or highly differentiated, with different procedures being followed for different kinds of customer and care situation. Suppliers aiming to meet the needs of many different types of customer may opt for a core care offering with "add-ons" which are targeted at specific segments.

Taking the customer into account

The foregoing analysis shows that customers cannot be treated as just one-dimensional objects. They are a complex mix of personality, motivations, attitudes and needs. They prefer particular kinds of experiences and learn from them. Customer care policy must take this into account. Obviously, it is not possible for every member of staff, whether working with customers face to face, on the telephone or by letter, to understand every one in such depth. But it is important to understand the customer's perspective in order to be able to meet customer needs.

The demand for attention

Customers have some idea of the kind and level of care they want, and what level of care they do not want. Between neglect and excessive care lies a wide range of possibilities. How can a supplier possibly allow for the wide range of requirements that customers might have? Of course, no supplier can provide every possible level of customer care. Remember, too, that customer care is composed of a number of separate elements. These include:

(a) giving information about products and services
(b) providing reassurance

(c) providing information on the status of the relationship
(d) providing a relaxed atmosphere
(e) helping the customer buy or use, to obtain maximum benefit
(f) minimising waste of time
and so on.

Customers will have requirements of different levels in all of these. So there is clearly no way a supplier can meet all these needs. The solution to this problem lies in early planning of customer care. In particular, four stages must be gone through:

(a) deciding which customers are to be cared for
(b) researching and modelling needs
(c) determining the levels of care that should be provided, to meet customer needs and supplier objectives
(d) building flexibility into the customer care delivery system so that individual variations within the general requirements can be met.

(a) Choosing customers

Not every supplier has the luxury of being able to choose customers. For example, public utilities and retailers must normally do business with any customer, no matter how problematic or litigious. But the issue is not simply one of what customers can do in principle. Rather, it is a question of which of these customers are most encouraged to buy. By branding, marketing communications, store layout, pricing, product range and all the other items of the marketing mix, particular kinds of customer can be attracted while others can be deterred. For example, customers requiring a high degree of personal service understand from the layout and staffing of a self-service store that they are unlikely to get their required level of service. In a department store, the layout and numbers of assistants gives a different message.

A key principle of customer care is that it is hard to meet all customers' needs all of the time. It is therefore essential to prioritise customers and needs. Competitive survival requires meeting the most important needs of the most important customers. Competitive advantage is obtained by doing this and meeting the needs of customers which are not being met by competitive providers.

For this reason, suppliers must have a good understanding of the needs of the different groups of customers being served and prioritise customers and needs. But there is a prior decision — which groups of customer should be served. Customer care must be part of mainstream business strategy. However, the decision as to which customers' needs are to be met must take into account the likely care needs of customers. The issues involved in ensuring this are dealt with in Chapters 7 to 9.

(b) *Researching and modelling needs*

If the supplier is marketing oriented, it is likely that some research into customer needs will be carried out. Research may already have been carried out as part of the customer targeting exercise described above. If so, information on customer care requirements may have been included in the calculation as to which customers should be targeted. If not, now is the stage at which customers or types of customer with care requirements which the company cannot meet cost-effectively are filtered out (either by excluding them or by not attracting them).

Many suppliers make the mistake of amassing large amounts of data on customer needs. This data, not surprisingly, usually shows that:

(a) customers have a great variety of needs
(b) these needs influence customers' buying behaviour in all sorts of ways.

It is therefore essential to try to develop a model of customer behaviour and how it affects customers' attitudes towards the supplier. Although such a model will require (often heroic) simplifications, it is essential if customer care needs are to influence policy. Management rightly finds it hard to integrate very complex statements of need into policy.

Such models are simply statements of the main requirements of customers and of how these requirements influence customer behaviour and the consequences for the company of this process. Figure 5.1 gives some examples of models for different situations.

Modelling of customer needs should take into account the idea that there are different levels of service need. In particular, customers' needs differ according to whether a problem has been encountered. On a normal day to day basis, a customer might have quite tolerant attitudes towards the supplier. When a problem occurs, a different attitude of mind is demonstrated and different images of the service

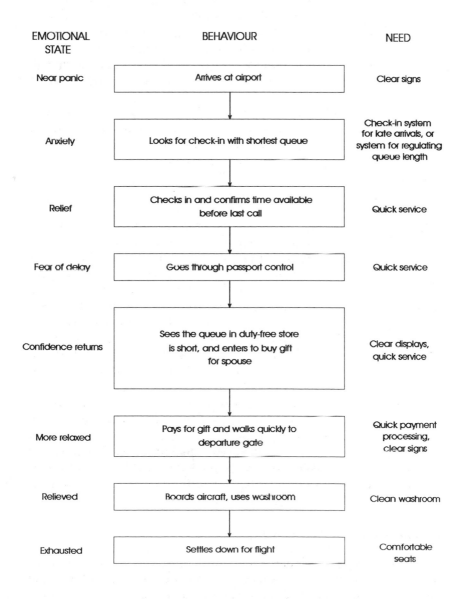

Figure 5.1 Modelling customer needs and behaviour. Example — airline traveller arriving close to departure time

and the supplier are called up. Customers' prejudices about the supplier start to be articulated and they might be quite negative. This is why problem-handling techniques have to differ in their speed and professionalism from normal care delivery techniques.

Similar differences in attitude occur when customers need to change the type of service they are receiving or are approached by the supplier to change.

This is the service version of the "modified rebuy" or the "new buy". Figure 5.2 gives an example of how needs and attitudes change in these different types of situation. It is a model of a hierarchy of service needs which can be used in planning different aspects of a company's service.

(c) Determining care levels

If it is assumed that the broad customer care requirements of customers still in the target group have been identified through research, the next step is to determine target levels of care. If must be decided where on the spectrum of customer care the customer wishes to be, between neglect and excessive care. Given that care requirements are dependent on customer types and the needs of the moment, exact positioning of customers will not be possible. The supplier must therefore determine the base level of care that should be provided. Variations around this level must be achieved either by contractual variations or by flexibility of care delivery. The base level of care should be determined on strategic, competitive grounds, as an important component of marketing strategy. Likely variations in requirements should be analysed and grouped, so that meeting them can be done without too complex a process. There should also be frequent feedback from customers about the level of service they are receiving and their attitudes to it. This will ensure that broad policies are correct and that, at the front-line, the right attunement to individual needs is taking place.

(d) Building flexibility in

The larger the organisation, the more difficult it seems to be to remain flexible to customer needs. So it is important to allow staff some flexibility, without causing confusion to the supplier's organisation. For example, if a customer asks for a particular delivery date, the person receiving the call can give a precise response if scheduling

Situation	Needs
Normal service (straight re-buy)	Quick receipt of dial tone Fault-free, clear line Fault-free telephone No congestion Low call failure rate No wrong numbers No cut-offs Quick call set-up Clear invoicing
When fault occurs (modified rebuy, may be translated into new buy if supplier consistently fails to meet needs)	Quick access to right person Quick diagnosis Immediate action Quick communication of action Successful outcome Permanent rectification Appointment choice Appointment kept Clear, accurate invoicing Clear complaints procedure Polite, friendly staff Only need to give details once Reassurance of supplier competence Quick reimbursement of any credits

Figure 5.2 How needs change with situations. Example — telephone service

information has been provided on-line. If information systems are not capable of delivering this kind of information, then some leeway may be given to the person receiving the call to reduce the customer's uncertainty about delivery dates, with provision for a later call back to confirm date and time.

Market research

Market research can be defined formally as:

> The objective gathering, recording and analysing of all facts about problems relating to the transfer and sales of goods and services from producer to customer.

The aim of market research is at the very least to reduce the risk in decision making, and at the most to guide the details of a marketing programme from concept/product development through to sale and later evaluation of the programme. Market research is an essential component of customer care policy. Without it, no supplier can be sure that it has understood customer needs.

Main techniques used in research

Desk research includes analysis of reports on previous studies of customer needs and how they are met. These show the variety of customer needs, but also indicate how these needs can be grouped and what sorts of policy have been used to meet them. Of particular value is the work done by behavioural scientists of various kinds in exploring different basic needs. For example, the literature on the customer's need to control the service situation has been particularly valuable in developing care concepts.

Group discussions are used for:

(a) concept testing
(b) basic need studies for new product or service idea creation
(c) new product idea or concept exploration
(d) product positioning studies
(e) advertising and communication studies
(f) background studies on consumers' frames of reference

(g) establishment of the vocabulary consumers use, as a preliminary stage in questionnaire development
(h) determination of attitudes and behaviour.

Group discussions are particularly useful for exploring customer needs when:

(a) customers normally experience service in close contact with other customers
(b) the level of control by the customer is relatively low (eg airline or train travel, mass market retailing, theme parks).

Customers may be more likely to give voice to their needs when talking about the situation with other customers who have undergone the same experience.

Depth interviews are usually used to find out:

(a) why customers buy various products
(b) what buying, owning and using means to them
(c) what improvements in service and care customers want.

This method can uncover basic predispositions. People's attitudes can be probed and their cause, intensity and implications can be uncovered. If the subject is sensitive or personal, depth interviews can be better than group discussions. Depth interviews are therefore more likely to be useful in very personal situations of customer care. This is because in such situations, customers might not like to reveal their innermost concerns to other customers (as they have to in group discussions). An example of this would be personal financial services.

Mail questionnaires are used when a company wants a large enough sample to derive a statistically valid result. If qualitative information is required, this can be elicited through asking consumers more detailed questions about why they respond in particular ways to particular questions. Mail questionnaires have these advantages:

(a) they are more economical and convenient than personal interviews
(b) they avoid interviewer bias
(c) they give people time to consider their answers
(d) they can be anonymous

and these disadvantages:

(a) the questions need to be very straightforward if the response is to be valid
(b) answers must be taken as final
(c) respondents see the whole questionnaire before answering it
(d) it is impossible to be sure that the right person answers it
(e) many recipients may not respond
(f) non-response may lead to bias in results, because those not responding are different in some way from those responding (eg they may be less interested in the service, less loyal as customers).

The higher the response rate, the more valid the result. But the only way to check this is by chasing up a sample of non-responders.

Response can be increased by:

(a) using a covering letter explaining what the survey is doing, how the respondent's name was selected, and why the recipient should reply
(b) telling the respondent the benefits of replying
(c) explaining why the survey is important
(d) enclosing a stamped, addressed or business reply envelope
(e) giving a premium for responding
(f) follow up.

An example of a postal customer questionnaire is given in Figure 5.3.

Telephone questionnaires are used in very similar contexts to mail questionnaires, with the notable addition of questionnaires administered when customers call in to respond to a promotion. Telephone surveys are normally more accurate than mail surveys and combine many of the advantages of mail questionnaires and in-depth interviews, in that:

(a) they are private
(b) they are one to one
(c) the consumer cannot see the whole questionnaire
(d) any problems of understanding can be dealt with
(e) careful scripting helps avoid interview bias
(f) computerised routing of questionnaires allows for complex patterns of behaviour to be captured

Most questions are answered simply by circling the appropriate number.

1. Name_____ _____Company_____

2. Which Star equipment is
   currently installed in any
   location in your company?

		Year installed
1	Hartley	_____
2	Auditor	_____
3	Convergent Technology	_____

3. How often are you in contact with Star personnel, by phone, letter or personal visit? (Note: A call made by yourself and returned by Star counts as one contact)

	Salesman	Client support	Technical support	Engineer	Accounts	Senior managers
Once a week or more	1	1	1	1	1	1
Once every 2 weeks	2	2	2	2	2	2
Once every 3 weeks	3	3	3	3	3	3
Once a month	4	4	4	4	4	4
Once a year	5	5	5	5	5	5
Less often	6	6	6	6	6	6

4. How easy is it to obtain the person you wish to contact:

	Salesman	Client support	Technical support	Engineer	Accounts	Senior managers
Very easy	1	1	1	1	1	1
Easy	2	2	2	2	2	2
Alright	3	3	3	3	3	3
Difficult	4	4	4	4	4	4
Very difficult	5	5	5	5	5	5

5. If you reported a computer printer failure to Star at 10am on Monday, what response time from an engineer do you receive and what do you need?

	SAME DAY			NEXT DAY		LATER
	Before 12	12–2pm	2–7pm	am	pm	
Average achieved	1	2	3	4	5	6
Desirable if failure during critical run (e.g. payroll)	1	2	3	4	5	6
Acceptable if failure during non-critical run	1	2	3	4	5	6

6. How long does it take to repair a printer on site after the engineer's arrival? What time is acceptable?

	Up to 1 hr	1–2 hrs	2–4 hrs	More than 4 hrs
Average time achieved	1	2	3	4
Acceptable time	1	2	3	4

7. If a software problem stops you carrying out an operation, and you contact Client or Technical support for help at 10am on a weekday, what percentage of problems are solved immediately (ie via the coupler)?_____

8. If a software problem is not resolved immediately, when does Star generally have the problem solved? What desirable and acceptable times would you specify:

	SAME DAY		NEXT DAY		WORKING DAYS			LATER
	Before 12	After 12	am	pm	Up to 5	5–10	10–20	More than 20
Average time achieved	1	2	3	4	5	6	7	8
Desirable if problem critical	1	2	3	4	5	6	7	8
Acceptable if problem not critical	1	2	3	4	5	6	7	8

Figure 5.3 Star client survey

9. Please rate your Star hardware and software for the following characteristics:

HARDWARE	Very Good	Good	Average	Poor	Very Poor
Reliability	1	2	3	4	5
Overall performance	1	2	3	4	5
Value for money	1	2	3	4	5
Ease of upgrade	1	2	3	4	5

SOFTWARE	Very Good	Good	Average	Poor	Very Good
Reliability	1	2	3	4	5
Overall performance	1	2	3	4	5
Value for money	1	2	3	4	5
Ease of upgrade	1	2	3	4	5

10. How would you rate Star's maintenance in terms of value for money?

Very Good	Good	Average	Poor	Very Poor
1	2	3	4	5

11. Is the £75 'no call' bonus attractive?
Yes 1   No 2   Don't know about it 3

12. What are the implications for your business if your Star equipment fails totally?

No adverse effect	1	Staff idle	2	Revenue loss	3	Cash flow delay	4
Clients lost	5	Goodwill loss	6	Data loss	7	Other (specify)	8

---

13. What is your opinion of the professionalism of Star personnel?

	Very Good	Good	Average	Poor	Very Poor
Salesmen	1	2	3	4	5
Sales managers	1	2	3	4	5
Client support	1	2	3	4	5
Technical support	1	2	3	4	5
Engineers	1	2	3	4	5
Accounts	1	2	3	4	5
Senior Managers	1	2	3	4	5

14. How good is the service and support you receive from Star compared with the past?

	Much better	Better	Same	Worse	Much worse
Compared with 6 months ago	1	2	3	4	5
Compared with 1 year ago	1	2	3	4	5

15. Would you recommend a Star system to others?

Yes: 2   No: 2   Maybe: 3

16. If you wish to amplify any of your answers, or comment on other aspects of Star service and support, please do so here, or use an additional sheet of paper.

_____

_____

_____

_____

_____

Figure 5.3 Star client survey contd.

(g) response rates are higher — customers can be called until they reply

(h) costs are lower than personal interviews

(i) the telephone is a way of life to business

(j) speed — telephones get higher priority than post and the results are immediately available.

Their disadvantages are that:

(a) some consumers object to the approach

(b) the costs of setting up a telephone questionnaire can be high

(c) calling costs are higher than postal costs

(d) it is a voice medium only, so customers' reactions cannot be seen.

In telephone, postal or face to face interviewing, there is now much accumulated expertise about how to design questionnaires to elicit customer care needs and attitudes. The recommendations arising from this experience can be summarised as follows:

1. Do not rely on satisfaction ratings alone. This may give a useful idea of the extent to which customers are satisfied, but it does not give a good indication of specific requirements. So questions should be oriented to identifying specific needs.

2. Customers have many needs, so it is important not to try to condense them into a few simple questions. It is usually a good idea to carry out a few depth interviews or group discussions to identify the variety of needs, particularly those that customers find hard to articulate, then to design the questionnaire with as many questions as are needed to cover the variety of needs.

3. Questions should be as specific as possible. General questions bring imprecise answers which cannot be acted upon.

4. The reliability of answers should be cross-checked, by asking the same question in different ways and possibly by combining postal, telephone and face to face interviewing to check consistency across the different techniques.

5. If comments are asked for (often at the end of the questionnaire), they should be requests for specific recommendations, eg improvements to particular aspects of particular services. General comments have little value.

This gives examples of a number of types of question which can be incorporated into features research, in this case for a technical equipment product. Statistical techniques (eg factor analysis, cluster analysis, regression analysis) are then used to identify:

- Which types and levels of feature tend to be required together
- Which features contribute most strongly to overall customer satisfaction.

1. Please rank the factors below in order of their relative importance to you in your decision to buy product X.

    —— Advertising   —— Speed of supply of product
    —— Price   —— Experience with the supplier
    —— Product availability   —— Past experience with the product
    etc.

2. Which of the following should be standard with product X?

a	Yes/no	One year's free service
b	Yes/no	One day's free training
c	Yes/no	Phone number for priority service
d	Yes/no	Guaranteed replacement in case of complete failure
e	Yes/no	Five year parts guarantee
f	Yes/no	Regular information about product changes
g	Yes/no	Customised invoicing arrangements
h	Yes/no	Guaranteed service response time
i	Yes/no	Guaranteed availability of equipment for use
j	Yes/no	Guaranteed maximum repair time

    etc.

3. Which of the following are provided by your supplier of product X?

a	Yes/no	One year's free service
b	Yes/no	One day's free training
c	Yes/no	Phone number for priority service
d	Yes/no	Guaranteed replacement in case of complete failure
e	Yes/no	Five year parts guarantee
f	Yes/no	Regular information about product changes
g	Yes/no	Customised invoicing arrangements
h	Yes/no	Guaranteed service response time
i	Yes/no	Guaranteed availability of equipment for use
j	Yes/no	Guaranteed maximum repair time

    etc.

4. Please write in the space below the letters corresponding to three vital features, the absence of which would cause you to look for an alternative supplier, and three features whose absence would not be too important.
    Vital features   —— —— ——
    Less important features   —— —— ——

5. We are now going to ask you to tell us what levels of service you would like for certain features. Please use the units stated.

a) SERVICE RESPONSE TIME (HOURS)
    Longest tolerated ——   Shortest needed ——   Reasonable level ——

b) TIME BETWEEN EQUIPMENT FAILURE AND RESUMPTION OF WORKING
    Longest tolerated ——   Shortest needed ——   Reasonable level ——

    Longest tolerated ——   Shortest needed ——   Reasonable level ——

Figure 5.4 Features research

Figure 5.4 gives an example of a questionnaire designed to elicit specific information about service feature requirements.

Competitive research is vital. Using customer care competitively requires knowledge of how competitors are treating their customers and also what they are doing to achieve their standards of care. Some information on this can be gathered from customers using the techniques mentioned above. But experiencing competitive service is vital. This is parallel to the manufacturing practice of buying competitive products and stripping them down, to find out how they are made, how reliable they are and what they can do. To experience the service, competitive locations should be visited, helplines should be called, and so on. Finally, it is important to try to envisage what competitors' own customer care strategy is likely to be.

All the above information sources should be integrated with the results of other kinds of feedback from customers. Staff feedback should also be used, as it is critical to get staff views on what is happening to the relationship between the organisation and its customers, and what the organisation is doing to help staff improve it.

Customer feedback

This used to be the most neglected form of research. It was treated by many suppliers as "complaints". The information arising from complaints was used to rectify the situation the customer was complaining about. Perhaps letters with compliments were passed to the appropriate staff. But the rest of the information was lost. This led to a vicious circle. Customers viewed giving feedback as pointless, since they received no acknowledgement and saw no results in company policy. Staff failed to pass feedback on. This was because:

(a) they saw no actions resulting from their efforts
(b) the "shoot the messenger" syndrome was present.

An additional point to bear in mind is that customer behaviour lags behind changes in levels of satisfaction/emotion. For example, a customer who has for many years been satisfied with the level of care of a particular supplier will go on buying from that supplier for a time after the care level starts to fall, and may not complain for some time. Conversely, when matters improve, it may take time for customers to hear about it, realise it, and so on. So they may not return or increase their purchasing/loyalty for some time. This can lead staff to become indifferent about customer feedback, as they do not see the immediate effect of it in company performance.

However, today, many large companies realise that improving care levels provides good long term benefits. They are deploying a variety of techniques to channel customer feedback into points where it can be dealt with quickly and effectively *and* used to produce information to steer policy. Some examples of this include:

(a) Goodyear Tyre's integration of information from toll-free telephone numbers, comments cards, point-of-purchase surveys and focus groups
(b) the use of structured programmes of management visits to the field to produce information (common to many service companies)
(c) making the giving of comments easier, eg British Airways Videopoint booths for customers to record comments, Marriott Hotels' 24 hour hotline, the Maine Savings Bank's $1 per suggestion.

Perhaps one of the most comprehensive programmes in this area is Nippon Telephone and Telegraph's Orange Line Customer Service Network, which was launched in 1982. It was set up as a response to the company's failure to provide a route for customers into the company and the absence of a mechanism for processing feedback.

The colour orange was chosen because it signifies freshness, warmth and kind consideration in Japan. The Orange Line consisted of:

(a) Orange Counters — desks in offices and showrooms where customers could hand in their opinions and requests
(b) Orange Numbers — telephone hotlines
(c) Orange Customer Panels — customer discussion groups
(d) Orange Monitors — housewives and young people who monitor aspects of service
(e) Orange Surveys — customer surveys
(f) Orange Committees — committees in every office to evaluate feedback
(g) Orange Reports — to announce the changes NTT makes as a result of feedback.

Segmenting for research

It is clearly important to ensure that the respondents chosen for research represent the target market properly. Where relevant, respondents should include users, recommenders and others who influence the buying process, as well as the buyers themselves.

The research process

The research process should be integrated closely with the policy process. Information is not being gathered for its own sake but to influence policy. This means that the content, coverage and timing of research should be integrated within the planning process. Figure 5.4 shows how a customer care research programme was designed to be integrated into a service marketing programme. It demonstrates the following principles:

(a) each piece of research should have specific objectives
(b) each piece of research should improve the quality of the next piece
(c) each piece of research should have clear policy outcomes.

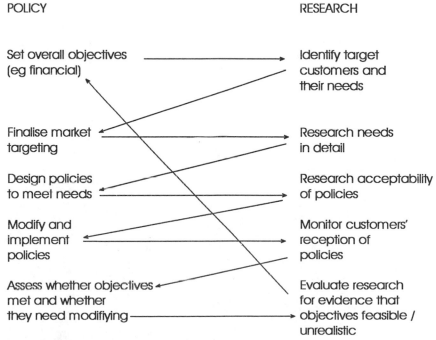

POLICY

Set overall objectives
(eg financial)

Finalise market
targeting

Design policies
to meet needs

Modify and
implement
policies

Assess whether objectives
met and whether
they need modifiying

RESEARCH

Identify target
customers and
their needs

Research needs
in detail

Research acceptability
of policies

Monitor customers'
reception of
policies

Evaluate research
for evidence that
objectives feasible /
unrealistic

Figure 5.4 Integrating research into planning

Chapter 6

The Supplier's Perspective

Until this point in the book, customer care issues have been viewed largely through customers' eyes. This chapter sees them through the eyes of the supplier.

The classic conflict

Many customer care problems are caused by the difference between these viewpoints. However, it is not just a question of perception. A real conflict can exist between caring for customers and achieving objectives. Take the example of a store selling electrical appliances, such as washing machines. Suppose a customer's washing machine breaks down irreparably. The customer has seen model X advertised by the manufacturer. The store is visited and the customer finds that model X is not in stock. The sales assistant, unwilling to lose the opportunity of a sale and the consequent bonus, tries to persuade the customer to buy model Y. It is made by the same manufacturer, but has more features and is slightly higher priced. The customer feels uncomfortable, senses the pressure that is being applied, but is too weak to resist. Model Y is bought, but the customer is dissatisfied. Any problems arising later are likely to be blamed on the sales assistant and the store. The sales person too may have felt uncomfortable. But behind the sales person lay a whole apparatus of sales targeting, bonuses and inventory policies which caused the situation.

This situation has arisen because the store's objective of making profit has over-ridden the customer's objective of buying model X. Although it is clear that too many customers treated in this way will do long term damage to the store's profits, in the short term, profits rise. Of course, the sales assistant could have recommended another branch of the store or even a competitive company. But the commercial pressures and incentives under which store staff work militated against it.

This example demonstrates the most common area of conflict between customer and supplier objectives. Everyone agrees that, in the long run, satisfied customers are the best safeguard of success for a supplier. But in the short run, organisational structures, control processes, procedures and operational necessities often bring supplier and customer into conflict. The secret of competitive customer care does not, therefore, lie in customer care programmes which only deal with the immediate interface between customer and supplier. Customer care which works in both short and long runs usually requires the supplier to reconsider every aspect of policy.

Planning for customer care

A supplier's ability to meet customer needs depends upon:

  (a) its *objectives* — what it aims to achieve and whether these objectives require customer satisfaction
  (b) its *strategies* — the translation of objectives into the main lines of policy
  (c) its *policies and action plans* — the translation of strategies into practical work
  (d) its *procedures* — the norms and rules by which its staff work
  (e) its *resources* — which are allocated to achieving different policies
  (f) its *people* — perhaps the most important resource because they can contribute so much to customer care. If they are wrongly allocated, managed or trained, their effect on customer care can be devastating
  (g) its *planning processes*, which match resources to objectives and harness resources through particular policies, working to particular procedures.

The effect of each of the above on customer care depends on whether a focus on customer needs is maintained. Much of the emphasis of customer care programmes is often placed upon people and procedures. But, as the above list indicates, these are largely *outcomes* of a comprehensive policy process. Even in the smallest organisation, a one-man business, this can be seen. Consider the following example.

The smallest company

Scott Williams is a manager with a large company. The company suffers a financial set-back and decides to offer early retirement to all its managers above 50. Scott has just turned 50 and decides to accept, believing that his management training skills could be deployed in the market for management consultancy. The redundancy payment, combined with the possibility of an early start to pension, means that he would be financially secure, but not at the high standard he had anticipated. His daughter is about to get married and is likely to require considerable financial help. His son is just about to start university and will also require help. Fortunately, his work over the years has brought him into contact with many other companies, so he has a long list of contacts who might be able to provide business. He decides to set up his business. He realises that he will be in competition with other independent consultants, as well as medium and large training and management consultancies.

He considers three options for setting up. The low cost option is:

(a) call a few of his closest contacts to see if they have any work going
(b) buy a combined telephone answering and facsimile machine
(c) print a business card.

The medium cost option is:

(a) mount a direct mail campaign to all his contacts
(b) install an additional telephone line for a facsimile machine and put an answering machine on his original line
(c) acquire a mobile telephone
(d) produce a small brochure indicating his skills and the benefits that might accrue to companies using them.

The high cost option is:

(a) take three months off, in which to undergo additional training
(b) also during this three months, write some articles for the training press, to establish his positioning in the training market and to provide interesting material to send to potential clients
(c) then rent space in a managed office which provides all business services
(d) mount a direct mail campaign with an expensive brochure to all his contacts and to prime prospects (companies he knows have large training budgets)
(e) be prepared to take on a junior partner if required.

The low cost option might bring the earliest additional revenues but is also likely to lead to early occurrence of customer care problems. He is unlikely to be able to get through to his contacts first time. If his contacts call him back they may well find his line engaged. He may not be able to contact them again, particularly if he has to make initial visits to a number of contacts. Also, the long term consequence of pitching straight into the market may mean that he attracts a high volume of low-cost "commodity" work, where he is being used not for any specific expertise but as a general trainer. He might become overworked and the quality of his training work might start to suffer. Unless he has very good contacts who are prepared to tolerate this low level of customer service compared with that provided by larger consultancies, he is almost certain to be confined to commodity work.

The medium cost option would minimise customer care problems in relation to contactability. But there might still be problems caused by the high workload. The high cost option, while the most risky, is most likely to provide high-quality, premium-rate work, in which Scott will be able to concentrate on delivering quality. It is most likely to enable him to compete on nearly equal terms with larger consultancies and thus attain high rates.

The choice between each of these options depends upon Scott's attitude towards risk, the quality of his contacts, his ability to develop a special competitive edge, and also on home factors (eg the attitude of his family to him working at home). Each option is viable and each has different customer care consequences. This demonstrates how, even in the smallest business, customer care is determined by overall business policy.

The largest company

Now consider an example from the other end of the spectrum. Megaleisure is a large hotel chain in the UK. It is facing increasing competition from overseas competitors. The latter are using a more structured approach to the UK market than any domestic competitors. They are acquiring existing hotels, identifying well-defined target markets for each (eg luxury, high quality business, family, basic stop-over), branding them accordingly and promoting them heavily. Megaleisure's own market research makes it clear that its own undifferentiated approach is causing many problems, ranging from lack of profitability to customer alienation. The latter is caused by trying to be all things to all men. For example, business travellers are not happy about fighting for dining room space with families with young children and coach parties.

Megaleisure therefore decides to follow the same carefully segmented policy as its overseas competitors. It carries out market research to identify how to segment its market — by customer type and geographically. This gives it the ability to adapt its facilities to the main types of customer. It then groups different types of hotel under a sub-brand, which clearly conveys the type of hotel to the target market segment. In some cases, where it is not financially sensible to allocate a hotel to one brand, dual branding is used for different times of the week or year. Thus a hotel which is a business hotel during the week might become a family or conference hotel at the weekend, or over the summer. To achieve this, "conversion packages" are developed, covering everything from room lay-out, through menus, to staff behaviour. Within each type of hotel, it provides the features and staffing appropriate to the segment. Of course, it also trains its staff to deal with customers typical to the segment. For example, families need a different kind of care from business travellers or wealthy tourists.

This approach leads to a much higher level of customer care than had been achieved under the old approach. It also demonstrates that the customer care is achieved not just by staff training but by marshalling all the resources of the company to meet customer needs.

The customer care life cycle

In many companies it impossible to identify a customer care life cycle. This is a final stage of development of the cycle of production–sales–product–marketing orientation so often described in marketing text books. Although the cycle is a great over-simplification, it is still instructive, because it allows suppliers to position themselves, historically and against competition. It also facilitates identification of the implications for planning and management approaches.

Production orientation

This often arises when a supplier has plenty of customers clamouring for its product and services. The whole focus of the organisation is on "getting the goods out of the door", irrespective of quality or features. This approach was common in the period immediately after the second world war, when world-wide shortages of goods had developed. Top management focused on production volumes. Anything that got in the way of increased output was disregarded, including customer complaints. The attitude to customers was "take it or leave it — we've got plenty of other customers".

Although this attitude is often dismissed as a historical aberration, it is surprising how easy it is for suppliers to slip back into this frame of mind. Companies with strong competitive positions and some state monopolies and public administrations often demonstrate this attitude. For example, tax office management might focus on the number of cases processed, hospitals on the number of cases treated, educational establishments on the number of students educated. This approach is also common in times of financial pressure. Managers may be told to maintain the workload while the budget is reduced. The focus is on the numbers processed, not the quality of the processing.

Many service suppliers are production-oriented. They focus on achieving the throughput demanded by high fixed investment or large amounts of pre-booked capacity. Where fixed capacity is high and the product is perishable, the sales force is usually *extremely* short-term driven. Their targets may be weekly or even daily sales. Targets tend to be fixed in volumes. In such circumstances, marketing as a concept finds it hard to survive.

Sales orientation

At some stage, finding customers gets more difficult. Customers are no longer knocking on the door. So the supplier starts knocking on theirs! Sales forces are recruited and trained to prospect intensively and close aggressively. Customer needs are taken into account only to the extent of identifying which customers might need the supplier's product. Once there is evidence that a customer might need it, the strong arm of persuasion is used. In consumer markets aggressive sales promotion and high advertising spend may be used. Advertising focuses not on branding but on persuading customers to try the product.

Product orientation

As the situation becomes more competitive or as customers start to become more discriminating, focus switches to the nature of the product or service itself. But the focus is rather a technical one, ie on the features rather than the benefits. Engineers focus on designing the "better mousetrap". Service industry product planners try to define service products which will meet the needs of ever smaller market segments. Engineers and product planners are king. The better product is seen as the key to competitiveness. The rate of new product launch, and failure, increases. Customers' needs are taken into account primarily in terms of their demands for product features, rather than their need to be treated well by the supplier.

Marketing orientation

At some stage management wakes up to the fact that just having a better product and selling it hard is not the recipe for long term success. A more integrated approach is taken. Customers' needs are analysed not just in terms of their requirements for products, but also in terms of their deeper needs (as discussed in Chapter 3). An integrated marketing approach is taken, whereby the whole marketing mix is deployed to act upon customers, so that they feel that the product or service fully meets their needs. Strong product branding is achieved, creating extremely well-defended competitive positions.

Customer orientation

The well-researched and strongly-branded position works very well for individual products. But it leaves one chink in the armour — the customer's overall relationship with the supplier. The best marketed product may suffer from a poor relationship between its supplier and its customer. This might be visible in a number of ways:

(a) inconsistent products being promoted or sold to the customer
(b) customers not understanding which product or service would best meet their needs
(c) customers having difficulty contacting the supplier or resolving problems
(d) products in high demand being out of stock too frequently or requiring a long waiting period
(e) sales staff having a poor understanding of products
(f) sales staff treating customers badly
(g) inadequate documentation of products and services
(h) customers being poorly trained to use the product
(i) conflict between users, decision makers, buyers, etc within buying decision making units,

and so on.

The role of customer information

The cause of these and similar problems may be that information about customers and their needs is not available or taken into account during the planning process. This in turn can often be due to management not being open-minded enough about the variety of customer needs.

Consider the case of a local government department whose objective is to provide support for people who are caring for relatives and friends who are mentally ill. The afflicted people are not necessarily resident with the carers — they may be in their own accommodation or in some kind of institution. But they are still in a situation where having someone caring for them can make a big difference to the quality of their life.

The department has worked hard to identify those carers with financial difficulties, eg who need to travel some way to the cared-for person. Financial support has also been given for the acquisition of special facilities. The carers are very happy about all the support services that have been provided. But a survey shows that although the department has provided a high level of material support for carers, the real need is for a different type of relationship. In fact, many carers do not need the financial support. Caring for mentally-ill relatives and friends is a lonely business, and can limit the carer's other opportunities of friendship. Carers need mutual support and counselling.

Meanwhile, the department focuses on efficient processing of requests for help and indeed prides itself on the quick turn-round of requests, rather than providing a warm, caring approach. The overall effect is to make carers feel more isolated, as the very department which can provide the help they really need is seen by them as an efficient but rather cold bureaucracy. Both product and customer care are at fault. The answer lies in a refocusing of policies and staff to provide different kinds of support (a different product policy) with a different type of care (with the emphasis not on efficient processing, but on friendly helping).

In general, where mis-orientation is due to a drive for production volume, sales levels or getting new services accepted, moving to targeting based on longer term measures of success, such as medium term profitability, and introducing the ideas of marketing and customer care through cautious, well-planned pilot projects can work. It shifts the emphasis to acquiring customers, retaining them, selling-up, selling across and selling extras, all of which require a proper marketing approach to succeed.

Characterising the servuction system

Much conceptual development has taken place in the area of production or operations management. The servuction system, in which customers play a key part in the delivery of service, has its own concepts, as this book demonstrates. From the supplier's point of view, the key characteristics of a servuction system are:

(a) The relative degree of dependence on equipment or staff.
(b) The complexity of the service delivered. A complex service requires complex procedures and scripting.
(c) The depth of contact with customers. If the customer is closely involved in delivery of the service, more careful scripting will be required, while staff will require more skill in handling people.
(d) The frequency of contact with customers. Infrequent contact, particularly if it is also shallow, makes the service manageable like a manufacturing situation. Frequent, deep contact must be managed more according to service industry norms.
(e) The degree of repeat business — a service which is delivered to large numbers of customers who return only infrequently must be managed very differently from one which has a few, frequently returning customers.

(f) The time-criticality of the service delivered. For example, if the customer has to wait while the service is being delivered, more attention must be focused on speed of service and on what is done with the customer while service is being delivered. On the other hand, if the customer can be involved more in the delivery process, time criticality may fall.

(g) The skill levels of staff required to deliver the service.

(h) The degree of variety in the service provided to individual customers, and the relative degree of involvement of the supplier and customer in customising the service.

The role of staff

The reasons why so much customer care work focuses on people are:

(a) People dominate the way that customer care is presented. Using the definitions of the seven Ps in Chapter 1, people work through procedures to deliver products, achieving a particular presence. The other three Ps of the marketing mix — price, promotion and place — are also affected by how people work.

(b) People are not automatons — they are individuals with their own roles, personalities, perspectives, skills and moods. Even the best-designed, most customer-oriented processes will fail if they are not implemented properly.

(c) People working with customers need to provide input into the supplier's work on customer care. Processes for looking after customers which do not take into account the insights of people who actually look after customers are likely to be unrealistic or inappropriate.

This subject is covered in detail in Chapter 14. For the time being, note that customer care depends not only on customer-facing staff (those who deal directly with customers). Back office and management staff are also important. The way they approach their work has a significant influence on the level of customer care delivered. This is for four reasons:

(a) In many service situations, so-called back office staff are actually visible to customers. Their behaviour can influence customers' perceptions.

(b) Back office staff handle cases passed to them by front office staff. If they see cases as technical issues to be resolved rather than as people needing help, their ability to provide the right customer-oriented solution will be hampered.

(c) Back office staff's input is also used in determining procedures for handling customers.

(d) Management staff determine procedures for handling customers. The degree to which they can identify with customers and understand their viewpoint affects their ability to create a customer-oriented organisation.

People and care — an example

Here is an example. In consumer and small business banking, the lunch-time rush hour poses a problem. This is the time when consumers take a lunch break and rush to the bank to complete their transactions. It is also the time when many small businesses (except of course retailers, who are busy with lunch-time consumers) are less busy. So the work load peaks dramatically. Many bank branches are now designed so that back office staff are clearly visible to consumers. From the consumers' point of view, what they see when they walk into a bank branch during the lunch hour is a long queue, a large number of back office staff processing transactions (and sometimes on the telephone), and the occasional member of staff leaving the back office or counter position to go to lunch. Managers may also be seen at this time leaving for lunch.

Consumers and small businesses want quick service so they can get back to work. What they see when they arrive is not pleasing. Front office staff are working fast to process the queue. If a customer produces a difficult query, they may have to leave their position to resolve it. Meanwhile the queue grows. But the back office staff have their jobs to do. They have not been given procedures to empower them to deal with overload. Nor are they trained that queue reduction is one of their most critical tasks. They may feel slightly oppressed by the sight of so many pairs of anxious eyes peering through the glass and wondering what they, the back office staff, are doing!

Contrast the situation in some fast food chains. Here, staff are trained that at peak periods, they must all rally round to maximise the speed of service. Any tasks which do not lead immediately to customers being served must be deferred. Long queues are seen as a challenge to be quickly reduced, with everyone benefiting by the increased success of the outlet. Role definition deliberately allows for this requirement to switch roles, even if it means leaving other jobs unfinished until the pressure dies down.

Of course, maintaining an approach which is so flexible to customer needs is not easy. If efficient back office processing of cases is hampered by constant rushing to the front office to serve customers, then transactions may start to take longer to complete or, worse, may be improperly processed with error rates rising.

The back office staff are, in a sense, the production staff who serve those distributing the service. The normal tension between manufacturing and marketing is visible. Manufacturing usually thrives on high volumes of standard products produced with minimum interruption. Marketing thrives on attuning products to customer needs. However, manufacturers are moving increasingly to flexible manufacturing systems, which allow them to undertake cost-effective short production runs and even to manufacture several items on the same production line at the same time.

The analogy with services is clear — systems and procedures must be designed to empower back office staff to work flexibly without risking quality. If a member of the bank back office staff is in the middle of processing a complex transaction on the computer, then the system must be designed to allow the transaction to be frozen while that member of staff goes to the front office. The system must also allow for switching of work between different members of staff to maximise flexibility.

Systems, procedures, scripts and boundaries

The idea that the relationship between supplier and customer follows a script was introduced in Chapter 1. What the supplier sees as a set of procedures should be thought of as a customer script, for situations in which the customer is interacting with supplier staff (or equipment). If the script is followed, there is a reasonable assurance that the quality of the outcome of the service episode will be as required. The script therefore needs to be worked out carefully, communicated to customers and, where necessary, form the basis of customer training (for complex scripts).

The script is also a way of giving customers a perceived level of control. For if the customer learns the script properly, the service episode is effectively managed by the customer. A good script makes the customer feel that the outcome of the episode is more predictable too, reducing stress levels. Of course, not all customers require a high degree of control, so a script may not be necessary if each service episode is managed with close personal service.

A good example of detailed scripting is the Goodyear Tyre customer script, telling customers how to get good service. It runs as follows:

(a) If you aren't happy, tell the store manager, who wants to know if you've got a problem.
(b) If the store manager can't resolve your problem, call our Customer Assistance Line, giving this (specified) information.
(c) If you still can't resolve your problem, call your local Better Business Bureau, letting us know that you have done so via our Customer Assistance Line.

The script should also make clear where the boundary lies between the server and the served. This boundary is both a physical one (where one stands, for example, to receive service) and a mental one (what are the expectations of the customer as to the extent of action required to achieve the desired service). In situations of stress and uncertainty (eg major problems), it is natural for supplier staff to feel insecure and to reassert boundaries. A good example of this is:

Just wait there while I get the manager.

The message here could be:

Don't follow me, because I want to warn the manager about you.

The importance of the boundary depends upon a number of factors, such as:

(a) The degree of direct contact between customers and staff. Boundaries are more important when there is more direct contact.
(b) The relative status of customers and staff. For example, in restaurants most staff are usually "lower status" than customers, except for the manager. In a professional services environment (eg accounting, law, medicine) the opposite is often the case. Too much deference to boundaries (eg between queuing and

service areas) can make customers feel oppressed and highly dissatisfied.

(c) The newness of the relationship. For example, a first time visitor to a very upmarket restaurant might be more hesitant about calling a waiter over than would a frequent visitor.

The role of experience

Uncertainties about script and boundary can be very damaging to the relationship between customer and supplier. This is where having experienced customer-facing staff helps. Paradoxically, however, suppliers often put the most experienced staff in charge of the most experienced customers, leaving the novices to deal with each other. Examples of this include:

(a) A new business sales force for finding new customers, composed of inexperienced recent trainees, contrasting with senior account managers for dealing with long-standing accounts.

(b) Putting the most experienced air stewards on flights with experienced business travellers, leaving tourist flights to newly graduated stewards.

Of course, this is done to give higher levels of care to the most important customers. In some circumstances, experienced staff are much better at dealing with disputes between customers (not infrequent in air travel). Also, experienced staff can become hardened, so they are less capable of dealing with new customers. The solution lies in the team mix. There should always be some experienced staff in teams dealing with inexperienced customers.

Experienced staff are seen by suppliers as having another important advantage. They know when and where they can break rules to give customers better service, without affecting the overall efficiency of the operation. Novices have not accumulated experience in this area. However, if customer care depends on experienced staff breaking the rules, this is a poor recommendation for management. The aim should be to empower customer-facing staff to meet customers' needs, by giving them the right to make concessions, within a controlled framework. This should also ensure that concessions are recorded, so that the fundamental processes of the organisation can be re-examined in the light of the type and frequency of concession.

Acting and over-acting

An interesting question facing management today is how far to go in the direction of encouraging staff to "act it up" while serving customers, following the Disney theme park model. One reason why staff like to do this is that over-acting can help them deal with conflicts which are inherent in the role. By acting, they put on a new personality, and shed their original concerns. Acting can also make customers feel happier about the service they are getting. In some restaurants, staff recruitment advertisements now specify the need for acting skills and the desire to perform in front of customers.

This is a logical extension of the idea that, from the customers' point of view, customer-facing staff are already actors. They are under observation by customers, particularly if the customer has to wait. So why not make the most of it? The answer to the question whether this represents a good move depends, of course, on the customer. If the customer likes it, and views it as an enhancement rather than a distraction, then there is no reason not to do it.

Learning from experience

The example of local government carer support given earlier demonstrates a critical point — that knowledge is the key to customer care. This knowledge is of two kinds:

(a) knowledge of customers — what they currently perceive, need and expect and how this situation may change in the future
(b) knowledge of one's own organisation — its capabilities, what it actually delivers to customers, and how these will be affected by future policies.

Knowledge of customers

Knowledge of customers comes in many ways. These include:

(a) formal market research and observation
(b) transaction information — responses and enquiries, sales, etc
(c) competitive information — what customers are buying from other suppliers

(d) complaints and compliments

(e) feedback from customer-facing staff.

Techniques for gathering and co-ordinating this information were described in Chapter 5. The issue for this chapter is whether the organisation is sufficiently customer-oriented. Does it demand and thrive upon feedback from customers? Or does it regard customer information as an intrusion into its work? Customer care cannot thrive without a thirst for customer feedback and without a proper process for taking this feedback, digesting it and identifying from it any opportunities for improving customer care.

Consider two examples — one of a company that uses customer information only where necessary, the other of a company which uses it to provide structured input into policies for improving customer care.

The companies concerned are both in the automotive business, selling luxury cars through a small, select group of dealers. Company A is less concerned with customer care than Company B.

Use of formal market research and observation

Company A carries out market research mainly for these reasons:

(a) to test new product concepts

(b) to see whether its advertising is hitting the right targets

(c) to see whether its dealers are achieving the required levels of visibility in their catchment areas.

Company B also researches for these reasons, but in addition researches:

(a) whether customers are happy with the frequency of communication from the company and from dealers

(b) what type of communication they require

(c) how satisfied they are with sales and after sales service by dealer staff

(d) reasons why customers switch to different makes

(e) reasons why customers switch to its make.

Observation research is also carried out to see how customers behave in showrooms and what draws them towards different models.

Transaction information

Company A only analyses sales and enquiry information to see:

(a) which models sell best through which dealers and in which areas
(b) which media yield the most productive responses to promotional campaigns.

Company B does the above but also analyses sales and enquiry information to find out which kinds of customer order and why. It matches this information with other sources to correlate satisfaction with pre- and post-sales service to identify the impact of customer care on buying decisions. The speed with which enquiries are handled is also analysed and the results correlated with subsequent purchasing behaviour.

Competitive information

Both companies obtain market share information from the industry trade association and other sources. This suffices for Company A.

Company B researches a sample of acquirers of its own and competitive models, to see whether (amongst other variables) customer care has an important effect on buying decisions. It focuses particularly on customers who have switched makes. This information is matched with information on competitive dealer policies and the subsequent performance of those dealers. A programme of incognito visiting and telephoning of competitive dealers has been initiated, to test pre-sales customer care. This information is matched with the market research to identify the impact of different levels of customer care.

Complaints and compliments

Company A passes compliments and complaints onto the relevant staff. If too many complaints are received, disciplinary procedures may be initiated. This may lead to a dealer losing the franchise.

Company B logs all complaints and compliments by type of customer, model of car and type of complaint. Clear follow-up procedures have been installed, and time to resolve the complaint and nature of the solution are also logged and analysed. This is one of the key sources of data for quality improvement programmes. Compliments are used as one basis for a staff incentive programme. This data is also used to provide training material for dealers.

Feedback from customer-facing staff

Company A never surveys these staff. Company B has a regular survey aimed at finding out:

(a) how staff perceive their jobs and whether they are happy in them
(b) what are the main barriers they perceive to serving customers better
(c) what are the main opportunities for improving customer care.

This information is then analysed to provide a structured programme for improving the interface between staff and customers.

Finally, all the information Company B derives from these programmes forms part of the market environment analysis for corporate and marketing planning. At Company A, the information is edited down to basic market share and trends.

Not surprisingly, Company B has no problem in identifying how to improve its customer care. Company A has no real picture of what customer care it delivers, let alone where its deficiencies lie.

Knowledge of own organisation

The two key questions that need to be answered here are:

(a) How is the organisation *structured* to deliver customer care?
(b) How is the organisation *managed* to deliver customer care?

In a large organisation, with many tiers of management or with many branches or subsidiaries, these questions must be asked at each level.

Structuring to deliver customer care is a question of putting authority to deal with individual customers as close to the customer as possible, while maintaining the controls required to ensure that the organisation meets its financial or other objectives. "Closeness" does not necessarily imply geographical proximity. Many national suppliers have found that for handling individual queries, central telephone helpline offices which deal full time with queries are a much better solution than having many offices around the country which deal with queries part time. Many suppliers, large and small, have also found that a pre-requisite for customer care is making it easy for customers to contact them. Until customers find this easy, it is almost impossible to judge what levels of customer care are being delivered. This is because customers may be largely cut off from the organisation, except when the latter wants to contact them.

Managing to deliver customer care is a question of having management procedures and control processes that allow staff to meet customer needs (the subject of Chapter 11) and recruiting, training and keeping staff informed so that they have the skills and capability to meet customer needs (the subject of Chapter 14).

Neither structuring nor organising is a theoretical affair. It is easy to draw up organisation charts or show system or process designs which appear to demonstrate that the organisation is able to deliver customer care. But the only evidence that counts is that of customers themselves, closely followed by that of customer-facing staff. The customer evidence outlined above should be combined with evidence of staff surveys and internal management statistics (eg numbers of complaints received, speed of problem resolution, to diagnose whether structure and management are correct). In a large organisation, it may be possible to compare branches or stores to identify whether issues relate to the nature of policies themselves or to how these policies are implemented. For example, many automotive companies audit their dealers using complaint statistics and customer survey data. Similarly, management can be audited using feedback from staff surveys.

Warning signs to look for include:

(a) needing to refer too many decisions to senior managers
(b) long lead times for decisions
(c) systems not allowing staff the flexibility to deal with customer needs
(d) work pressures not allowing staff to complete tasks (customers often go to the end of the queue in such circumstances)
(e) poor quality information being given to staff, so that they do not know what to tell customers
(f) motivation, appraisal and other people-management systems giving inadequate attention to success in dealing with customers.

Learning in practice — the role of leadership

It is one thing to have a great deal of data and ideas about how well an organisation cares for a customer. It is another to do something about it. This is where customer care leadership comes in. Ideally, in every organisation which depends on dealing successfully with customers, all staff should be customer care-oriented. However, getting to such a situation is not easy. Change normally requires leadership. In a large organisation, this leadership is required at every level. Leaders function as coach, communicator and monitor. They identify problems, propose solutions and motivate people to change. They initiate programmes to implement changes to systems and procedures. Without a good sprinkling of customer care champions around the organisation, even the best customer care drives are likely to grind to a halt.

The customer care leader

The first role of the customer care leader is to make sure that the learning is properly absorbed by the organisation. This means taking the conclusions to the right people and showing the evidence that customer care pays (or satisfies some other basic objective). This may means demonstrating the severity of the problem or the competitive opportunity.

At this stage things can go badly wrong. For once an organisation, however large or small, has accepted the need for improvements to customer care, the next step is definitely *not* a customer care programme. As Chapters 7 and 8 show, the next step is to take the idea and benefits of customer care into the core policy-making process and ensure it does its work there. Once the idea and methods of customer care are absorbed into this process, then customer care leadership works within the procedures and systems of every department, not as a challenge to them. At every stage, the focus should be on learning from what customers and customer-facing staff say about their past experiences with each other, and working out cost-effective ways of achieving improvements.

The importance of a clear corporate strategy

It is easy for an organisation to become confused about customer care.

The "headless chicken" analogy, running around in every direction without a clear goal, is a perfect fit. Today, customer care consultants are two a penny. Articles extolling the virtues of customer care are part of the daily diet of managers. In this situation, a manager might rush into an ill-considered customer care programme. This would be exactly the wrong thing to do.

Customer care is one approach to looking at how an organisation works. Whether the customer care perspective is the correct one depends upon what the organisation's objectives are, how it aims to achieve them, and with which customers. The wandering street trader, who sets up stall, sells merchandise cheap and then disappears to another town, only needs a little bit of customer care — watching and listening to the customers gathered in front of the stall to identify those most likely to buy and gently easing them into the purchase. No after sales care is required! At the other extreme, a company selling complex industrial equipment and services and involved in long term business relationships with a small number of customers needs to care for its customers intensively. Such a company could measure the value of customer care in terms of increased loyalty. Between these two extremes lie most suppliers. Any supplier can only determine whether it should be investing more time and money in customer care through a proper analysis which is part of its normal planning process — the subject of Chapters 7 and 8.

Chapter 7

Building Customer Service into Business Plans

Customer care is not a veneer, to be applied to an organisation to make it look good for customers. Of course, a customer care veneer can be applied, but it cannot change a supplier's basic character. Failure to focus on customer needs will show through.

The only way to ensure the right level of customer care is to build it in from the beginning. Where, however, is "the beginning"? The answer to this question depends on how a supplier organisation makes policy. In particular, it depends on whether an organisation has a *formal* process for making policy, or whether it evolves its policies in a less structured way.

Formal processes

Larger organisations tend to have more formal policy processes. This is because they need to co-ordinate a variety of resources in order to implement policies. These resources — human, financial, material, property, systems and so on — are acquired, assigned and then managed and controlled so as to implement the required policy.

Many large organisations have not only formalised their planning processes, but also their customer care processes. For example, Citibank has a permanent customer care programme. Its programme aims are defined by its customers. The programme aims to deliver differentiated service to its customers, with the core idea being that Citibank should make the right promises to its customers and then keep them. The principles of programme management are as follows:

(a) the programme is led by senior management
(b) staff are given the tools to do the job
(c) staff are service professionals, through motivation, understanding and training
(d) standards and measurement are used (200 indicators in all, of which 15 are priority indicators). In addition, techniques such as "mystery shopping" are used to check
(e) performance is communicated.

Marks & Spencer and British Airways use similar combinations of process, training, communication, commitment, measurement and other techniques to achieve high levels of service. Without formal process, the risk is of too many customer care initiatives proliferating and even conflicting with each other.

Smaller organisations are able to change their policies without formal policy processes for making and implementing policies. The extreme (and most common) case of the small organisation is the one man business. Here, the owner can change policies from hour to hour. However, this does not imply that small business policy-making should be any less well thought through. But the small business has fewer resources to marshal. The trap that many small businesses fall into is to avoid thinking through policy in a rational way — one of the benefits of a formal planning approach. The consequence of this is that many small businesses are extremely poor at marketing, a discipline which really does require "perspective". If a business fails to anticipate customer needs, it will face problems.

Failure to anticipate customer needs make it very difficult to care for customers. So the need to build customer care into policy is no less important for the smaller business. Many smaller organisations would benefit considerably from adopting a more formal approach to policy making, tempered of course by the speed and cost-effectiveness with which they need to work.

Given all this, it seems sensible to outline a formal process for building in customer care, and then leave it to the judgement of the person running a small organisation as to how to adapt the formal process to the decision processes of that organisation.

However formal or informal the process by which a supplier decides what it should do, customer care must be an integral part of that process. It should be taken as an objective, right from the beginning.

The business development cycle

In most organisations, a business development cycle can be discerned. Again, this may be of varying degrees of formality. It starts with information gathering (research and review of progress) and objective setting, and proceeds through implementation, monitoring and control. During each cycle and whenever a cycle is completed, review of experience provides the basis for improvement. This is the philosophy underlying the customer care process model described below.

The customer care process model

The model presented here is based on these ideas:

(a) The conventional policy process works for customer care just as well as for any other area of decision making. It is vital not just to throw resources at customer care. Customer care does cost money, so resources should be invested in it with care, and results should be measured every year.

(b) This process consists of:

(i) Research and analysis to identify what is possible and what customers need. This should cover the product and service portfolio, service standards and customer behaviour.

(ii) Determination of objectives, policies and main projects to ensure that the policies required to meet customer needs are adopted.

(iii) Agreement on the details of policies and implementation of projects to ensure delivery of the policies.

    (iv)   Measurement and control to ensure that the policies are properly implemented and the need for any modifications picked up.

(c) This policy process must encompass four areas:

    (i)   What products and service customers need and how they should be provided. This provides the answer to these questions:
- What features do customers require in products?
- How can these features be delivered to customers in practice, using different combinations of technology, human, financial and other resources?

This part of the process is defined as *core product and technical development.*

    (ii)   How the supplier's customer care will cause it to stand out from that offered by other suppliers — whether directly or indirectly competitive, or just suppliers whose standards of customer care are likely to provided a basis for comparison. This answers the question "How well should the supplier be perceived to be performing, when compared to other suppliers?". This is defined as *competitiveness.*

    (iii)   What should be done with these resources to ensure that customer needs are met, ie the answer to the questions "What does the customer want to happen in the relationship with the supplier?" and "What does the supplier want to happen so that these customer needs are met?". These are defined as *service performance requirements.*

    (iv)   How staff must behave to ensure that customer needs are met, ie the answer to the question "What do staff need to do to ensure that what the customer wants to happen actually does happen?". This is defined as *behavioural requirement.*

Putting (b) and (c) together gives a four by four matrix of issues, shown in Figure 7.1. The first two steps in the process — research and analysis and defining objectives, plans and projects — are dealt with as separate stages in this and the following chapter. Once the main lines of policy are determined, then implementation relies upon a combination of top management leadership, procedures, marketing techniques, people and performance control, the subjects of the following chapters.

	Research and analysis	Objectives, policies and projects	Action details	Measurement and control
Core product and technical development	Customer views on products Customer require-ments Staff views on product and how far they are given tools to support delivery Portfolio, margin, sales and market performance analysis	Formulation	Portfolio and process changes	Product performance tracking, eg warranty Post-launch research Product / service monitoring
Competitiveness	Customer and staff views of competitors' products and capabilities		Competitive marketing programmes	Loyalty / share measurements
Service performance requirement	Feedback on current performance from staff and customers Staff views on targets Analysis of performance against targets		Quality improvement projects Operational target setting and performance monitoring	Performance measurement Testing / sampling
Behavioural requirement	Customer views of staff behaviour Staff views on customers' desired behaviour		Motivation, reward and internal marketing programmes	Customer feedback after service Complaints monitoring

Figure 7.1 Matrix of planning issues

(Examples are given in cells of matrix — there are many more areas.)

Research and analysis

Core product and technical development

This starts with identifying customers' needs for particular benefits. For example, customers may require the ability to get to work cheaply and reliably each day in a situation where there is no public transport. The features required to achieve this might be embodied in a particular design of a town car.

Customers' views on current products are an important guide to needs. For new products, market research, concept testing and similar techniques may be required to tease out needs, as described in Chapter 5. As the ability to care for customers depends partly on the quality of the core product or service provided, customers' needs for quality must also be determined.

At some stage in this analysis the need to segment the market will emerge. The decision to segment offerings, ie provide different products or services to different types of customer, may be a later decision. One role of research is to find market segments which require different core products or services. This is likely if the supplier has determined that the best way to achieve its objectives is by finding well-defined niches which are less subject to competitive attack.

In a public service or a monopoly, the task is to find groups of customers whose needs are not well catered for. The aim here is either to minimise public dissatisfaction or to identify additional revenue opportunities. Different groups of customers with different sets of needs must be identified if the rest of the process is to deliver results. It is not enough to segment by simple variables (eg consumer income, type of industry). Segmentation must be based, at least, on needs and behaviour.

The core product or service will often be delivered to customers through people — typically at the point of transaction (eg point of retail sale, reception in a doctor's surgery). But it may be elsewhere. With an automatic vending machine, the closest point of contact between the customer and supplier's staff is usually with the person who comes to stock up the machine and perhaps service it. The attitude and behaviour of this person towards the machine (and the consequent level of care devoted to the process of restocking, servicing and checking it), will be no less important to caring for customers than the attitude and behaviour of the doctor's receptionist towards patients. If the product is a true service (eg maintenance of customer equipment, receiving guests in a hotel) then staff's feelings about their work will affect their performance. For these reasons, an important component of research and analysis is finding out how staff relate to the work that they are doing in providing the core service.

The above information relates to what customers need and what staff see themselves as providing. To this must be added information on what core products and services are actually supplied. The final result of this part of the analysis should be a comparison between:

(a) what core product or service customers want
(b) what core products and services the supplier is supplying (or currently planning to supply).

This comparison should take into account the attitudes of staff to supplying those products or services. This will lead, in the next stage of policy making, to conclusions about what sort of core products and services should be supplied. It is, in effect, a product audit followed by product planning.

Competitive position

Who are the competitors?

This involves identifying key competitors and assessing their quality of customer care. This immediately raises the question as to who should be regarded as competition. The answer to this lies mainly with customers, at least as far as the present is concerned (the future is more difficult, see below). Customers have their own basis for comparison, so it is enough to ask them. For example, retail grocery customers are normally quick to voice opinions about the relative customer care performances of Marks & Spencer, Tesco, Sainsbury, Asda, Gateway, the Co-op and perhaps their corner shop.

However, as has already been shown, where direct competitors are absent or are not very large or effective, consumers may choose "parallel" organisations — those they see as involved in similar activities or as similarly large. Thus, telecommunications may be compared with other utilities such as gas, water and electricity. However, utilities may be compared to retailers, as the latter provide most consumers with their commonest experience of interaction with large commercial organisations.

In other markets the situation may be more complicated. A computer supplier's performance may be compared with other computer suppliers but the actual users of computers may also compare the supplier's performance with that of their in-house computer department. Comparisons may also be made with other suppliers of industrial equipment. Purchasing managers are particularly likely to have standards which they apply across a wide range of suppliers.

Customers of public sector organisations may compare the performance of, say, school teachers with that of doctors or even shop assistants. Bases for comparison may be affected by the politics of the day. In the UK, consumers have been overtly encouraged to compare the level of service provided by public sector organisations with that of major private sector suppliers.

What are competitors delivering?

There are two aspects to this, as follows:

(a) the levels of customer care competitors *are* delivering.
(b) what customers *perceive* them to be delivering.

The latter is dealt with in the next section. Customers' perceptions about what is being delivered are of course determined partly by what is actually being delivered. This is turn is determined by the policies competitors have in place to deliver it. Obviously, it is not always possible to get detailed information on competitive policies. Strategies for doing this include:

(a) Direct (formal or informal) exchange of information with competitors. This is most feasible when
(i)   competition is indirect
(ii)   customer care is not seen by top management as a major factor in overall competitive success
(iii)   competitors have to work together on specific customer projects (eg as industrial equipment suppliers often have to).
In acutely competitive situations, information is sometimes obtained by hiring competitive staff.
(b) Briefing market research agencies to collect data. This can be done through:

(i)   agencies interviewing competitive staff
(ii) using agencies to set up "multi-client studies", in which competitors pool information on an anonymous basis.
An example of a questionnaire of this kind is given in Figure 7.2.
(c) Experiencing customer care by becoming a customer of the company concerned.

Competitive issues needing research

Particular issues to examine are:

(a) How reliable is the delivery of customer care; is it variable in quality, timing, etc?
(b) What does the delivery depend upon? Is it staff conviction, clearly identified and properly followed procedures, financial incentives or some other factor, or some combination of these?
(c) How much does it cost to deliver it? This may need to be based on informed guesses about the kinds of policy, procedure and resource that are being used to deliver customer care.
(d) What benefits does the organisation derive from it? Information on this may be derived from market research on customer loyalty.
(e) The competitive future — researching the current competitive position is not enough. Relying solely on today's information would lead to customer care policies designed to meet past requirements and situations.

Service performance requirements

This starts with defining customers' wants for particular levels of service. If the core product is a service, it still makes sense to talk about service performance requirements. For example, one of the core services provided by a hotel receptionist is to check guests in. This might include the following actions:

(a) validate booking
(b) give key to guest
(c) arrange for luggage to be handled
(d) check meal arrangements
(e) check optional requirements (eg video).

This questionnaire was used in a quick study in the machine tool industry.

PLEASE TICK THE BOXES WHICH APPLY

1. Does your company offer a range of clearly defined maintenance options?

   Yes ☐   No ☐   If no, go to question 3

2. How are they differentiated from each other? (Tick all boxes which apply)

Response time	☐	Hotline/helpline	☐
Uptime	☐	Dedication of engineer to particular customers	☐
Repair time	☐	Equipment performance reports	☐
Service visit reports	☐	Audits of customer maintenance needs	☐
On-site parts provision	☐	Exchange parts/equipment	☐

   Other (specify) ——————————————————————————

3. What methods do you use to market contracts? (Please rank in order of importance. Equal rankings are allowed.)

   Engineers at time of installation of equipment ☐
   Engineers during maintenance ☐
   Engineers during special calls for this purpose ☐
   Engineers at other times ☐
   Sales staff at time of sale of equipment ☐
   Sales during special calls for this purpose ☐
   Sales staff during sales calls for other puroses ☐
   Reminders at time of contract expiry ☐
   Account reviews ☐
   Telemarketing ☐
   Direct mail ☐
   Catalogue ☐
   Trade press advertising ☐
   Others (specify)——————————————————— ☐

   ——————————————————————————————

4. Do you sell your products through dealers?   Yes ☐   No ☐
   If no, thank you for your co-operation. Please return the questionnaire.

5. If so, how are they maintained? (Tick all boxes that apply)
   By your company ☐
   By the dealers ☐
   By a third party maintenance company approved by you ☐
   By third party maintenance companies not approved by you ☐

6. Do you have special contract options for servicing dealer-sold equipment?

   Yes ☐   No ☐   Thank you for your co-operation.

Figure 7.2 Customer care multiclient study

From the guests' point of view, all these are basic features of a check-in service. The service performance requirement relates to *how* these services are delivered. For example, are they delivered quickly, through a person with a pleasing and friendly manner? Are any special requirements handled well? Are queries resolved promptly? Are complaints handled effectively? Are changes in requirements dealt with well? These are service *performance* requirements, rather than features of the service product.

The most important activity in researching customer needs for service performance is to define customers' general perceptions, wants and expectations in relation to the type of service. This means finding answers to questions such as:

(a) What are the principal dimensions which the customer uses to measure service performance (eg speed, accuracy, pleasantness, flexibility)?

(b) How do customers perceive current levels of service performance?

(c) How do customers perceive staff behaviour?

(d) When do customers believe that the service episode starts and finishes?

(e) What are the minimum levels of service customers will tolerate while staying loyal?

(f) What is the maximum level of service that customers believe that it would be reasonable for the supplier to supply?

(g) What are the main areas where customers see the need for improvement?

(h) How strongly do customers feel about service performance?

(i) How important is service performance in customers' decisions to buy the core product or service?

(j) Where does the customer wish the locus of control to be?

(k) What benefits do customers receive from being cared for?

(l) What images do customers have of service performance (of the supplier and its competitors)?

(m) What images do customers have of the staff providing the service?

(n) What changes in all the above are likely to occur during the period for which policy is being made? What will cause these changes (eg economic, social or demographic factors, competitive actions)?

(o) What image of the supplier would the customer like to have?

(p) Is it possible to identify particular groups of customers with significantly different care requirements?

(q) If there is a risk of certain types of customer not being "right" for the supplier in some way, what reasons for the supplier refusing to do business with them will be accepted by these customers?

The above information relates to what customers need in the way of service performance and what staff see themselves as providing. To this must be added information on:

(a) What level of service performance is actually achieved (as perceived by customer and supplier).
(b) What changes are planned in service performance delivery.

The result of the above analysis should be a comparison between current and planned levels of service performance and customer needs for performance. This will be fed into the next stage of the process.

Examples of market research questionnaires were given in Chapter 5.

The contact audit

Information about customer needs should not be interpreted in a vacuum. Customer needs occur in the context of contracts between supplier and customer. Now customers have a variety of contacts with suppliers. A supplier may not even be aware of some of these (eg failed attempts to telephone, chance encounters with the supplier's staff). With large organisations, an additional problem exists — that of the possibility of many contacts being made with staff in different parts of the organisation.

It may not be possible or even desirable to control all these contacts, or centralise information about them. However, it is important to understand how these different contacts affect customers' attitudes and perceptions in relation to customer care. Therefore, it is recommended that suppliers considering ways of improving customer care should first embark on contact audit. This begins with an enumeration of the different contact points. Managers are often surprised when they learn how many points of contact exist between their organisation and its customers. The audit shows the type, nature, frequency and quality of contact with customers. It should also show how these contacts affect customers' perceptions and attitudes.

An example of a questionnaire administered to customers as part of a contact audit is given in Figure 7.3. Figure 7.4 gives a format for summarising such an audit.

Truth and fiction

One problem customer care research uncovers is the inventiveness of some customers in finding reasons to demand high care levels. A good example occurs in public utilities (eg telephones, power). Customers whose accounts are about to be terminated for lack of payment can be very inventive in finding reasons why they should be allowed to continue enjoying the service despite not having paid. These often include severe medical distress. However, in some cases, this turns out to be pure fiction.

In one case, a woman was disconnected from service by a public utility because of the large amount of money she owed. She complained that her child had cancer and she had no money to pay. In fact, the child's growth was benign and she had money. The customer-oriented response to all such situations is to negotiate payment while asking politely for evidence (eg medical certificates). The damage that can be done by getting just one such case wrong will often outweigh all the saving of spotting several deliberate deceivers.

Feedback

In many organisations, the principal (and sometimes sole) source of information about customer needs and the organisations's performance in relation to those needs is feedback from staff who deal with customers. In some organisations this information is fed back formally, in others through informal reporting. This source of information obviously has high potential for bias. It relies upon:

(a) absolute honesty of staff
(b) lack of incentive to paint too rosy a picture!

However, such feedback is valuable, provided it is tempered by data provided directly by customers (eg customer satisfaction surveys). This ensures that problems are not covered up. This is important, because it is in the nature of large organisations to distort the feedback reaching top management. One large supplier cut out many service staff as part of an economy drive. Then, the consequent reduction in levels of customer care and rise in numbers of customer complaints was kept from top management until revealed by surveys. Also, if staff and customer attitudes are to be matched, it is vital for accurate information on both to reach decision makers.

Competitive Customer Care

This telephone questionnaire was designed to identify customers' attitudes to the main modes of contact used by an industrial equipment supplier.

DO NOT PROMPT UNLESS SPECIFICALLY INSTRUCTED

QUESTIONNAIRE No. _____   Interviewer No ._____

1. Good morning/afternoon. My name is _____. I work for ABC Research. I am carrying out a survey on behalf of XYZ. We should like to ask you a few questions. It will take about 5 minutes. Would you be prepared to help us in this way?
    If **"YES", GO TO 3**
    If **"YES BUT AT ANOTHER TIME", REBOOK CALL**
    If **"NO", TICK BOX HERE AND GO TO 2**

2. Can you tell me why you are not willing to help us in this way?

If reason given, **WRITE IT HERE**. If not, **TERMINATE CALL** by saying "Thank you very much for your help".

If reason is not suitable job/position, **ASK FOR AND ENTER DETAILS OF CORRECT PERSON BELOW AND ASK FOR TELEPHONE NUMBER**. If respondent offers to transfer you to this new contact, **ACCEPT OFFER**. If not, **ATTEMPT TO CALL THE NEW CONTACT**. In all cases, **ENTER THE NEW CONTACT'S DETAILS** on your list of customers to be contacted.

_____

_____

TERMINATE CALL by saying "Thank you very much for your help".

3. First, I should like to confirm your job title within your organisation. We have you listed as: **READ JOB TITLE FROM LABEL. IF JOB TITLE IS MISSING, ASK FOR IT.** Is this correct?
    If **"YES", TICK BOX HERE AND GO TO 4**
    If **"No", WRITE CORRECT TITLE BELOW, THEN GO TO 4**

Job title_____

4. I should like to confirm your position in relation to decisions for buying product X. I shall read you a list of possible positions and ask you to confirm which ones best describe you. It may be that more than one applies. Here is the list. Please say yes or no according to whether the description fits you. **PLACE Y OR N IN BOXES ON FORM**

a) Buyer
b) Manager of staff using product X
c) Recommender of product X
d) User of product X
    If buyer, recommender or manager, **GO TO 5**
    Otherwise, **GO TO 6**

5. When and where was the last time you bought product X? **ENTER DETAILS**

_____

Figure 7.3 Contact audit questionnaire

6. How did you hear of product X?   TICK BOX

    Mailing
    Catalogue
    Newsletter
    XYZ sales staff
    Telemarketing call
    Information from manager
    Information from colleague
    Press article
    Advertisement in press
    Advertisement on TV

    Other ――――――――――――――――――

7. Here is a list of sources of information about products such as product X. Please
    say whether you obtain no information from these sources, some information, or
    a lot of information. ENTER CODE 1 FOR NONE, 2 FOR SOME, 3 FOR A LOT.

    Mailing
    Catalogue
    Newsletter
    Sales staff
    Telemarketing
    Information from manager
    Information from colleague
    Press advertisements
    TV advertisements
    Press articles
    Other ――――――――――――――――――

8. I am now going to read you some statements about how XYZ tells you about its
    products. Please say if you agree (1), disagree (2), have no feelings either way
    (3) or partly agree (4). ENTER CORRECT SCORE

    a) I believe that a single catalogue containing details of all
        products is the best way to present information
    b) A regular newsletter containing product details and case
        histories is a good idea
    c) Mailings promoting individual products are a good way
        of drawing my attention to specific products
    d) I am happy to be telephoned to be asked if I am interested
        in buying a particular product
    e) The printed material that XYZ sends me about its products
        is high quality
    f) XYZ's printed material promoting products is better than
        that provided by other suppliers
    g) I would be happy to be mailed twice a year with details of
        new products.

Thank you for your co-operation.

Figure 7.3 Contact audit questionnaire contd.

TYPE	FREQUENCY	TYPICAL REASONS	AVERAGE QUALITY	TYPICAL OUTCOMES
Letter				
Invoice				
Catalogue				
Other mailing				
Telesales				
Other telephone				
Sales call				
Meet manager				
Receptionist				
Engineer				
Steward etc				
Advertising TV Press				
Exhibition staff				
Security guards etc				

Figure 7.4 Contact audit summary format

Behavioural requirement

The quality of service performance is closely related to the quality of the work of staff delivering that service. Research and analysis must therefore also be deployed in relation to the organisation's own staff. Two particular areas need researching, as follows:

(a) staff perceptions as to what happens in the service situation
(b) staff attitudes to performance requirements.

Staff perceptions

The commonest problem here is that staff may perceive their role as a technical one, not of serving customers. This may make them rather unhappy about carrying out actions which aim to make customers feel good about the service they have received, rather than actions which ensure that the service is efficiently delivered.

In many cases, the efficiency objective may seem to dictate that speed in processing a case is more important than meeting a customer's needs. However, if high speed in processing a case leads to the case returning for "treatment" (eg due to faulty diagnosis of a medical condition) or to the customer turning to another source of service, neither efficiency nor customer satisfaction objectives will be achieved. If staff do not see the world in this way, then even the best laid plans to achieve high levels of customer care may go astray. If research shows that staff attitudes are technically focused, then training and motivation action will be required to change that focus.

Staff attitudes to performance requirements

Whether or not staff already share the idea of customer care as a critical part of their work, attitudes to performance requirements can create another barrier to achieving high levels of customer care. For example, a hotel receptionist may be very highly motivated to meet customer needs, but strongly resistant to following "rules" for achieving it. The receptionist may prefer to "do it my way". This might lead, for example, to a situation in which devotion to the needs of one customer leads to the reception desk being unmanned for other customers. The receptionist's "own way" may consist of dropping everything until the needs of the initial customer are met (eg a request for more information). The hotel's performance requirements may be framed, for example, in terms of avoiding extreme delays rather than reducing the average delay. This would be achieved by finding out, as soon as customers come to or call reception, the nature of the query, and then asking them to wait a short time while the query is resolved by non-reception staff.

In this situation, the receptionist's way of dealing with problems will be deemed to be counter-productive. Finding out what staff's attitudes are to the kind of performance requirements likely to be necessary is therefore very important. Discovery of attitudes such as the above may indicate the need for training sessions designed to demonstrate the consequences of "doing it one's own way" rather than meeting company performance requirements.

Feasibility analysis

It would be nice if the only research required covered what customers need and what staff feel they should deliver or can be motivated to deliver. However, there are two constraints which warrant further research, as follows:

(a) technical feasibility
(b) financial or resource feasibility.

Technical feasibility

Technical feasibility is defined as levels of customer care it is possible to deliver at different resource levels. Here, levels of customer care should be translated into likely resulting customer behaviour, as the next step is to work out what levels of customer care it is worth providing, measured against the rewards to the provider in terms of changed customer behaviour.

Suppose a customer returns from a package holiday abroad and complains that the standard of accommodation was not as promised in the brochure. Suppose too that the key objective of the tour company is to retain customers. It might be that, for this customer, retention will only be possible by completely refunding the price of the holiday, or by crediting the customer with the price of the holiday for next year. However, the next level of customer care might be defined as "damage limitation" — keeping the customer at a level of satisfaction where loyalty is not retained but the customer speaks well of the company to others. This might be attained by refunding to the customer the difference between the class of accommodation promised and that perceived.

In a more positive situation, suppose an industrial equipment company wants to understand the feasibility of different levels of pre-sales service. At one extreme is a sales force calling according to a structured calling cycle or at the customer's request. At the other extreme is an occasional mail shot or telephone call, with the onus for the pre-sales relationship falling mainly upon the customer. The topic to be researched would be the effectiveness of the different degrees of closeness of contact. Here, effectiveness would be measured by the amount and type of sales realised by different methods.

In extreme circumstances, nothing may allow customer care outcomes in the range the company requires. For example, a problem caused by a customer may motivate him or her to denigrate the supplier, irrespective of the amount of compensation offered. For some customers, no level of pre-sales service will cause them to buy because they have a buying process in which they take on the tasks normally performed through pre-sales service (eg information gathering, analyses, etc).

In some cases there may be capacity constraints. For example, sustaining customer care may depend upon being able to produce a higher level of factory output. But the company may already be operating at full capacity and desperately short of inventory. What should it do? The answer to this question depends upon the type of product and customer. For example, if the product is an industrial one and essential to the production processes of its buyers, then the best solution is to have a very "transparent" queuing process, such that all customers know when they are going to receive their allocated output.

Financial feasibility

Once the alternatives that are achievable through customer care actions are identified, the supplier is in a position to research financial feasibility.

Customer care is an investment decision like any other and should therefore be subject to the same financial disciplines. This should ensure the provision of the right level of care. It is possible to provide too high a level of care, with no real return. For example, insisting on answering telephones before the third ring may be completely unnecessary. Customers may expect and tolerate a few rings before the call is answered. However, automatic return of money on merchandise (as practised by Marks & Spencer) is a sound investment. If the refund is cash, most customers spend the money before leaving the store. Also, over the lifetime of the customer with Marks & Spencer, he or she will spend many times more than the original sum. This also demonstrates the importance of segmenting customers by loyalty and lifetime as a customer. Unless these kinds of figures are known, it is very hard to justify customer care on financial grounds.

Assessing financial feasibility requires quantification of the costs of customer care policies and setting them against the benefits (eg reduced future costs of query handling, increased profit through increased sales). This is not always a question of simple calculations. In many cases, assumptions will have to made about financial and market factors which will apply in the future. For example, an industrial equipment company will have to make assumptions about:

(a) how customer needs will evolve
(b) what products customers are likely to buy
(c) what future costs of provision of customer care are likely to be.

Customer care sounds very good to the marketer but red lights flash for the financial manager when this term is used, for it can be a bottomless pit for hard-earned money. Hence the need to justify all customer care expenditure in terms of the financial objectives of the organisation. The best justification, for a commercial organisation, is increased business from existing customers, reduction in customer losses and more new customers.

Customer care does not come in large indivisible packages. Advocates of increased investment in customer care should be asked to justify not only the whole package but every individual element of it. This is the only way to stop the building-in of unnecessary costs.

Overall feasibility

Further constraints on the feasible range of customer care is:

(a) what customers consider to be reasonable
(b) what customers consider to be the highest priority
(c) what competitors are providing.

Summary

In this chapter, a process for managing customer care has been described. To get consistent and continued improvements, a proper planning cycle is required. This cycle should take into account how customers and staff perceive things and behave. Some aspects of the first part of the cycle were discussed.

Chapter 8

The Customer Care Plan

This stage of the process involves translating the results of research into a plan. This plan must cover objectives, policies and projects. Many topics will be addressed in this plan, such as:

(a) product and technical factors
(b) competitiveness
(c) service performance
(d) service behaviour.

The importance of strategy

Doing this properly depends on the supplier having a clearly determined corporate strategy. This allows the supplier to develop coherent and consistent plans about how this strategy will be translated into action through the different functions — marketing, finance, operations, personnel, etc.

Corporate strategy makes it clear:

(a) what the supplier wants to achieve

(b) which customers the supplier is interested in
(c) what the supplier wants to do with them
(d) what the value of these customers is to the supplier
(e) what resources the supplier is prepared to make available for managing different groups of customer.

Strategic focus

The key aim of the corporate plan is to generate focus for all who work within the organisation. This focus guides all subsequent policy making. The nature of the focus will, of course, be determined by the organisation's objectives, capabilities and environment. In care-intensive industries, there are many examples of such foci and the strategies created to maintain them. Here are two examples, one success and one failure.

(a) The focus of University National Bank & Trust of Palo Alto on high net worth customers led to a strategy of tough credit check before customers are accepted, full financial services offered and a tough rule on maintaining integrity of accounts ("two bad cheques and you're out").

(b) The initial successful focus of People Express on no-frills travel. The target market was mistakenly extended to business travellers to absorb spare capacity. This led to mismatch between service and customers, decline into losses and finally take-over by Texas Air.

The above are examples of focus on particular customers. However, any area of marketing policy can provide the subject for focus. One of the best examples of strategic product focus in planning is that of Procter and Gamble's focus on achievement of a "product delta" — the positive difference over competitive products. Another example is the McDonald focus on quality of service. For focus on service, the best strategy is usually to determine basic standards, conform to them and then surpass them when the foundations of performance are built. Figure 8.1 gives some more examples of types of strategic focus and their implications for customer care.

It is worth sounding a warning about focus. Too tight a focus can lead to marketing myopia. Focusing on one group of customers is risky if that group is diminishing in number or income. Focusing on

Focus	Customer care implications
Mass market clothing	Basic needs quickly fulfilled. Basic product range. No-questions-asked merchandise return. Quick payment processing. Clear displays. Personal service only when requested. Basic dressing rooms. No accounts other than store card.
Very up-market clothing	Attentive personal service. Spacious, well-appointed dressing rooms. Wide product range at higher prices. No-questions-asked merchandise return. Variety of credit facilities.
Family saloons	1 hour test drive. Credit card, hire purchase or cash payment. Instant trade-in price. Discounting. Junior sales staff. Follow up after sale by letter.
Super luxury cars	Full day test drive. Variety of payment methods. Trade-in price after checking. Discounting rare. Senior sales staff. Follow up after sales by branch manager.

Figure 8.1 Strategic focus and customer care

This figure demonstrates that customer care levels depend on a combination of customer needs and *affordability* — what the profit margin will allow.

excellence in one product is risky if the product is overtaken by technology. This is part of a more general warning against marketing myopia. The best way to avoid this is by staying closely in touch with customers and their needs. Customers will make it clear whether the focus is right.

Given the above, it is possible to develop the main lines of policy through which objectives will be achieved, with customer care objectives and practices built in. In this chapter, the main themes in determining objectives, policies and projects are identified. This chapter adheres to the framework described in Chapter 7.

Product and technical

At this stage, the aim is to determine:

(a) the customer care objectives the supplier wishes to achieve
(b) the main lines of policy through which these objectives will be achieved
(c) the main projects which need to be implemented for these policies to be delivered.

These will be determined by the corporate strategy as described above, together with the main strategies through which the supplier aims to achieve them. This requires working out:

(a) how the main policy areas affect customers
(b) what can be done to optimise care levels so as to maximise benefit to the supplier.

In a commercial company, policies which affect customer care will be adopted in relation to areas such as:

(a) products and services to be offered
(b) marketing channels through which they will be offered to customers
(c) how products and service will be physically accessed by individual customers
(d) how customers will obtain information about them — whether of the promotional kind or informative kind (before, during and after the sale)

(e) how they will be priced and what terms of trade will be offered (including customers' rights and obligations)

(f) which people will be involved in interfacing with customers, directly or indirectly.

The relative importance of customer care in these areas will depend mainly on the corporate strategy being pursued by the supplier and on its market and competitive position. For example, subject to public or political pressure, a supplier which has a complete monopoly (eg of a product market or of the right to administer something) may be able to afford a less customer-oriented position than one faced with fierce competition for every transaction. A supplier going into new markets, launching a new product or using new distribution channels may have to establish a different customer care position than for its existing products or markets. The more competitive the new situation, the more carefully tuned the customer care approach must be.

Research data should show whether there is a gap between the supplier's current offering and customer requirements. Feasibility analysis should show what prospects there are for reducing the gap between what customers want and what the organisation is providing.

Here is an example of specification of objectives, policies and projects. A machine tool company is launching a new product which is even more reliable than its previous product. With its previous product, visits by service engineers (typically once a month for high usage customers) created a close link between supplier and customers. Service engineers were also trained to deal with queries about the performance of the product in use. Their visit was therefore an opportunity for resolving many queries. With the new product, service engineer visit frequency is expected to fall to three or four times a year on average. Research has shown that the company's image is very dependent on the quality of query resolution. It has also shown that this produces a significant advantage over competition. The company had therefore established the objective of maintaining this kind of service and agreed to instigate a customer contact policy. This was to consist of a guarantee to customers concerning the speed and quality of query resolution.

At the same time, research had also shown that customers sometimes found it difficult to contact the company when they had urgent problems which needed resolving between service visits. This was due to congestion on the company's telephone switchboard. A project is therefore identified, aimed at evaluating different approaches to improving the customer's contactability. This is to include evaluation of the alternatives of:

(a) helpline provision
(b) pager provision to engineers, with personal numbers given to customers
(c) setting up a separate category of staff, to specialise in usage and applications.

Marketing objectives, policies and projects

In Chapter 1, the notion of seven Ps was introduced — product, price, promotion, place, people, process and presence. These are all tools for creating and managing relationships with customers. Through integrated planning, each can support the other, ensuring delivery of high levels of customer care. However, if they are planned separately, the different elements of the marketing mix can end up working against each other, for example:

(a) an excellent new product, designed without taking into account the skills of those who will be delivering it to customers or servicing it, could fail completely
(b) an advertising message which used an appeal based on an implausible picture of service staff (either humorous or exaggerating their competence) could alienate both customers and staff.

For this reason, all elements of the marketing mix must be determined taking into account customer care objectives and planned policies. In this way, the product's branding and the supplier's branding are likely to be strongly mutually reinforcing.

A supplier's corporate positioning and branding plays an important part in the buying process and in customers' perception of the care they are receiving. For example, many shoppers go to a Sainsbury, Asda or Tesco because they like the style and layout of the service environment. "Objectively" analysed, the products in each outlet are rather similar. The same applies to many other big service brands. Examples include IBM versus Digital Equipment or Unisys in computing; BMW or Mercedes in higher performance executive saloons; Marks & Spencer or BHS in women's clothes, or British Airways and Virgin in transatlantic air travel.

The consequences of weak corporate branding on customers' perception are all too obvious in the case of suppliers such as British Rail and National Health Service hospitals. Indeed, the emergence of trust hospitals within the National Health Service is already leading to great efforts on the part of such hospitals to distance their branding from that of the wider health service.

Marketing communication provides a particularly valuable set of tools for highlighting intangible aspects of customer care and creating expectations. Media advertising plays an important role in creating general expectations and attitudes, while direct marketing can do this and reinforce the experience of individual customers before and after service episodes.

Competitiveness

Particular attention should be paid to opportunities for winning customers through the use of customer care and threats of losing customers through inadequate customer care. This can be achieved through the whole range of competitive techniques, from competitive positioning through to competitiveness in delivery of the product or service.

An example will demonstrate how competitiveness applies to the determination of objectives, policies and projects. Southern Auto is a car dealer, holding a franchise from one of the major motor manufacturers, which has just introduced a new model, targeted at the luxury saloon market. Previously, the top model in the range was classed as a large family saloon. This model will take Southern and its supplier into direct competition with established luxury saloon suppliers and their dealers. Luxury car customers have different requirements from buyers of large family saloons, particularly when it comes to after sales service. Some employ chauffeurs either full or part time, or have an assistant of some kind who also helps with driving. Many do not bring their own cars in for service, either having them driven in or expecting the garage to collect. They are less sensitive to the price of the service, as many of these cars are run on the expenses of a business belonging to the owner. Such customers' key criteria in evaluating customer care include:

(a) the ability of the garage to deal with all problems within the day that the car is being serviced, including the supply of the rarest part
(b) no recurrence of problems

(c) the availability of a full valeting service, including special "touches"
(d) provision of a charge account
(e) completely professional customer handling, over the telephone and at the service location. Although direct contact between the customer and the garage is limited, failures will be relayed back to the customer.

Southern's problem is complicated by the fact that it is located in an area where there are several very strong dealerships for established luxury brands. Although some customers are highly brand loyal, a good proportion switch margins. This switching behaviour is sometimes stimulated by poor service performance. Southern therefore decides to set itself the service objective of surpassing the performance of its competitors. It commissions a small study of service perceptions of competitive customers. It also carries out a survey of the first customers to move away from a competitor to its brand.

Southern discovers that although its competitors have invested a great deal in ensuring that cars are treated well, less effort has been invested in customers. It therefore decides to identify whether customers have any neglected requirements. Research shows that competitors tend to neglect customers between services, except to remind them that a service is due. After calculating the costs and the likely increase in customer loyalty, Southern decides to introduce a policy of offering a free "quick check and valet" between services.

The risk of such a policy is that some customers will see it as an attempt to increase their service costs. However, some customers, perhaps those less sensitive to service costs, may see it as an attempt to minimise problems. The first project is therefore to identify which customers fall into which category. After further examination of the research, which shows that the free valeting is likely to prove attractive (particularly to chauffeurs or assistants for whom the task may be a chore), Southern decides to mail its existing customers with an offer of either a free valeting or a free valeting plus free check. In addition, new customers are offered two years' free valeting at specified intervals.

Service performance

As a result of decisions taken in relation to objectives, policies, projects and competitiveness, there will be a whole series of requirements which are specified in terms of service performance. This was defined above as what the customer wants to happen and what the supplier wants to happen in order that customer needs will be met. These include:

(a) the image of the service provider in the customer's mind
(b) the kind of relationship that should exist between the customer and the individual member of staff (if any) who provides the service
(c) the description of the details of the service from the customer's point of view. Examples of this include:
    (i)   what the content of the service is
    (ii)   issues relating to the frequency and timing of receipt of the service
    (iii)   waiting times
    (iv)   how queries and problems are resolved
    (v)   what the customer sees happening when there is a problem.

For example, a retailer might specify the following service performance criteria for a customer service unit for customers returning products which for some reason are unsatisfactory:

(a) When the customer appears in the store, the queuing time before the customer's problem begins to be dealt with should be a maximum of three minutes.
(b) The customer should be greeted courteously and asked the nature of the problem and for proof of purchase (normally a receipt).
(c) Information about the nature of the problem (product code number, date of purchase, nature of problem, reason for occurrence) should be recorded on the computer.
(d) In the absence of a receipt, the computer will confirm the price paid.
(e) The product will be checked according to the reason for the return (eg manufacturing or other defect).
(f) If the reason for the return is failure to fit (clothing) or inappropriateness for the task, the customer will be offered an alternative product, the choice of a credit or a refund. If it is because of a fault in the product, the customer will be offered a replacement.

The replacement will be brought by an assistant specially designated for the purpose.

(g) The exchange or refund will be completed.

Behavioural

Above, a number of examples of customer care objectives, policies and projects have been discussed. In each case, successful implementation rests on staff carrying out the policies and projects. This will depend upon recruitment, training, job definition, and motivation being set up correctly. This is discussed in more detail in Chapter 14.

Distribution channel management

Many suppliers only access their customers through third parties — their distributors. At one extreme, there is no control or influence over distributors' staff. This applies to large retailers. In this case, it is the retailers themselves who are responsible for customer care levels. At the other extreme, in highly controlled distribution outlets (eg franchises, some parts of the motor trade), staff can be trained and managed by the supplier to handle customers in particular ways. The main difference between this situation and the one in which the supplier's own staff deal with customers is that the costs of achieving particular levels of customer care may become totally explicit. This is because distributors may have to be provided with financial incentives to change the way their staff work, whether in the form of discounts or training.

Some suppliers find it helpful to apply the disciplines of distribution channel management to their own staff, by treating them as customers in their own right. This is consistent with another idea, that it is difficult to get staff to care for customers if staff themselves are poorly cared for.

This approach is often called "internal marketing". It applies all the principles of marketing — researching, need analysis, segmentation, targeting, communicating, motivation, etc — to an organisation's own staff. For example, any customer care policy should have clear benefits for staff. These benefits should be based on the needs of staff and be communicated professionally to staff. The rise in the use of internal marketing has made senior managers realise that communicating with staff cannot be left to personnel departments. As a result, many large companies have created an internal communications department.

Realism in planning

One problem faced by organisations of all sizes is the inevitable gap that opens up between plans and implementation. This gap may be caused by a number of factors, including:

(a) unrealistic situation analysis, in particular underestimation of customer requirements
(b) optimism about resource capabilities
(c) naivety about the extent to which staff dealing with customers are able to or motivated to follow centrally designed procedures.

In planning customer care it is wise to recognise the inevitability of this gap. One way to ensure that it is small is to test all new approaches in the field (ie in front of customers). This will ensure realism of data. However, if the test is given too much prominence there is a risk of a Hawthorne effect. This means that staff will work especially hard to get things right if they know they are in a test situation. The effort will die down once the task becomes routine.

The real challenge, however, is to implement what has been decided. This is the subject of the next chapter.

Chapter 9

Getting Customer Care Embedded in the Organisation

So far, this book has focused on:

(a) how customers and suppliers relate to customer service
(b) the main attributes of customer care that are important
(c) the importance of a professional marketing and planning approach
(d) the essentials of making customer care policy.

However, a supplier's ability to care for customers depends more on its capacity to *deliver* customer care than its ability to *analyse* requirements and make policy. There are several requirements a supplier must fulfil to be able to deliver customer care. There is little chance of sustaining delivery of customer care if only one or a few of these requirements are fulfilled. For this reason it is very important for the whole organisation, however large or small, to be committed to caring for customers. Otherwise, it is all too easy for the individual member of staff trying to keep a customer happy to come into conflict with the organisation's procedures or with other members of staff, or both.

This chapter briefly introduces these requirements, which are then analysed in detail in the following chapters. They are:

(a) the role of top management
(b) quality
(c) processes, procedures and systems
(d) marketing techniques
(e) people and organisation
(f) performance indicators and targets.

Top management (this chapter)

Given the need for a comprehensive, integrated approach, the role of top management is critical in the delivery of customer care. This applies in both large and small organisations.

Quality (Chapter 10)

The quality approach, both as an attitude of mind and as a systematic approach to improving the performance of the organisation, is closely related to the idea of customer care.

Processes, procedures and systems (Chapter 11)

In larger organisations senior managers tend to be responsible for setting overall objectives. They ensure delivery against these objectives by a series of processes and procedures. If these systems and procedures are not tuned to deliver customer care, then the result will normally be poor levels of performance in this respect.

Sometimes, meeting customer needs depends on the speed and accuracy of information flow around the organisation. Customers may require information about, for example, the stage of processing of their "case". Staff may require information about customer needs or behaviour that is located elsewhere in the organisation. It is not surprising, therefore, that large organisations dealing with very large numbers of customers have invested intensely in information systems. However, many mistakes have been made along the way, in particular in relation to the size and coverage of such systems.

Marketing techniques (Chapters 12 and 13)

The importance of a professional marketing approach was underlined in Chapters 2 and 3. However, there are many marketing techniques which can support the delivery of customer care. They range from branding, through account management, to tele-marketing.

People and organisation structure (Chapter 14)

Most customer care is delivered through people, either directly or at one remove (through backroom processing). Who these people are, what their skills level is, how they are recruited, trained, motivated and managed — these are all critical issues in relation to customer care. So much can be done to ensure that staff achieve high levels of customer care. However, large organisations also have the habit of putting many constraints in their way. One of the key issues in how staff roles are structured and how staff are managed is that of account-ability for customer care, in particular whether it is centralised or delegated.

Performance indicators and targets (Chapter 15)

The final component is the very practical one of targets and perfor-mance indicators. General motivation to improve the lot of customers cannot be relied upon to deliver results by itself. Most organisations cannot function just on general goodwill. They require performance indicators to be identified, targets to be set and performance to be measured and managed.

Top management commitment

In a small organisation, even a one man business, there is less chance for great variations in attitude between members of staff. If the owner or manager is not committed to caring for customers, this attitude will transfer quickly to other staff. There will be a close connection between staff behaviour and success according to the owner's or manager's criteria.

In a large organisation, staff working with customers can maintain standards of customer care which are not underwritten by the formal policies of their organisation. The more remote these staff are from the centre of power and the more freedom they are allowed, the longer such behaviour can continue. Eventually, however, resource pressures are likely to constrain this behaviour, unless staff are caring for customers using their own resources (eg outside work hours). However, staff in contact with customers may be totally unconcerned about them. They may believe that their task is to save the organisation money. Examples of this include:

(a) the supermarket check-out operator who economises on carrier bags to the discomfort of customers

(b) the bank clerk who tries to ensure that rules are followed irrespective of customer discomfort (the "it's more than my job's worth" character).

In such situations, the lead from top management is crucial. Without it, all down the line, managers will be faced with other priorities. These include short-term cost control or sales achievement, avoidance of risk by sticking to procedures and the like. For this reason, many large suppliers have dedicated much space in their in-house newspapers to repeated assurances of the importance of caring for customers. This may seem rather trite. After all, without caring for customers, most suppliers subject themselves to great risks. But the tensions between short-term financial success and long term success with customers are sometimes acute. Staff working close to customers need strong and frequent reinforcement if they are to stick to the principles of customer care.

As the previous chapter showed, strategic focus is essential to the success of customer care. But strategic focus by itself is not enough. Top management must also be committed to the role of customer care in achieving the desired focus and in contributing to competitive positioning. If customer care is considered as insignificant relative to return on assets, and as making only a marginal contribution to it, then there is little hope for its survival. The message will be clearly transmitted down the line!

Genuineness of commitment

Too much has been written and spoken about "top management commitment" for any line manager to suspend suspicion when hearing or seeing the phrase. It is a hack phrase and therefore a warning sign. Commitment means commitment to resources and to seeing policies through, particularly in adversity. It is easy to subscribe to slogans. It is more difficult to implement policies which require fundamental changes of attitude. It takes time as well as money. Therefore, when the term "top management commitment" is used in this book, it refers to considered commitment by top management. For this commitment to be true, top managers must have full knowledge of the time and resources that will be absorbed and the problems that will be encountered along the way — particularly those relating to staff attitudes and skills.

This implies that genuine commitment must be preceded by clear communication of the costs (financial and other) as well as the benefits of customer care. Where the situation allows, it should also be based on hard evidence as to the benefits (eg pilot studies).

Basing commitment on understanding

It is not sensible to ask top management to be committed to customer care unless they understand:

(a) their organisation's current relationship with customers
(b) how it can be improved
(c) the costs and benefits of improving it.

It therefore makes sense to involve senior management in some of the activities which usually form the "front end" of a commitment to customer care. It is not realistic to expect commitment other than on the basis of understanding. Ways to do this include involving senior management in research into customer and staff attitudes. This should not be just through presentation of results. Ways to involve top management include:

(a) attendance at discussion groups
(b) visits (to own and competitive sites)
(c) exposing them to the service provided by the supplier and its competitors
(d) involvement in research design and interpretation
(e) exposure to examples of successful and unsuccessful customer care programmes. The latter are important, as they indicate that such programmes are not easy to develop and run. Exposure should include performance indicators and financial results.

Continuity of commitment

The idea that commitment must be sustained has already been mentioned. Sustaining commitment to ideas which seem very attractive is a problem. New ideas come along and replace them. Consider the "management fashions" to which top managers have been committed in the last few years, and the possible outcomes of such commitment.

(a) Vertical integration — frequently nothing of the kind, with the integration often poor, creating a tied internal market which encouraged inefficiency.

(b) Synergy — a two plus two that all too often proved to be two and a half, not five.

(c) Strategic business units, which often turn out to be neither strategic nor coherent business units.

(d) Portfolio strategy — often a high level aspiration not reflected in policy "on the ground", or a rationalisation of haphazard moves made in response to competitive and economic pressures.

(e) Competitive advantage — often a justification for a policy which played to one of the (few) unassailable strengths of the organisation but did little to prevent competition making outflanking moves which made that strength irrelevant.

(f) Information for competitive advantage — often used to justify massive expenditure on information systems and information that became a white elephant with no relevance to current practice.

(g) Global branding — a good way for an advertising agency to get clients to spend even more, although it may mean exposing other markets to concepts which are irrelevant to them.

(h) Total quality management, which often proved to be neither total, nor quality, nor managed, but a veneer on tired old policies.

Of course, sometimes such concepts do prove to be valuable. But they, and customer care too, should always be approached with scepticism. Top management should treat all claims for the universal applicability of a concept with suspicion, demand hard evidence and insist on piloting. This is a solid foundation, and the only foundation, for customer care. Once such a foundation is built, it provides the basis for an enduring commitment.

Depth of commitment

Finally, the commitment must be deep, in the sense that it leads to the concept of customer care permeating all plans and delivery of those plans. This of course requires transfer of the commitment to those building the plans and implementing them.

This raises few problems when the drive for top management commitment has come from "the troops" — in this case middle managers. But it does raise problems when the commitment results from a top manager's own conviction, a private "journey to Damascus", perhaps stimulated by consultants. In such cases, a programme of communication and education may be required. In particular, the "seasoned operators" who form the core of the delivery apparatus may feel they have "seen it all before", as indeed they have. These operators, sales people, store or hotel managers, service engineers and managers, will have been subjected to many campaigns over the years. The situation will be worse if these campaigns were short lived, with no real benefit to the operators, disappearing like a will-o-the-wisp as soon as the environment changed.

To avoid this, customer care programmes must provide immediate and longer term benefits. This must be not only for staff responsible for implementing them in front of customers, but also for all staff in the line of command. The steady transmission of the philosophy and practices of customer care down the line is a much better solution than a quick blast of publicity with no follow-through. This implies that suppliers must pace their approach to customer care. The approach must be durable, with steady annual improvements in the quality of care and in resulting profitability.

Commitment without strain

It is not realistic to expect senior managers to live, eat and breathe customer care all the time. They have many other responsibilities. Their role in developing and supporting customer care must therefore be closely defined. In many successful service companies (Kentucky Fried Chicken, Kwik Fit, Marks & Spencer), the role of senior management is to:

(a) provide overall direction
(b) set customer care objectives and define quality standards

(c) support these standards by meeting regularly with staff to discuss problems and opportunities in relation to the standards

(d) create a style of teamwork which encourages staff to take responsibility for customer care and work together to improve it

(e) act as a role model (particularly through visiting company locations)

(f) accept responsibility for the quality of customer care

(g) help evaluate staff ideas on how to improve customer care

(h) help create a culture of orderly routine, within which customer care objectives can more easily be met

(i) spearhead customer care campaigns. Campaigns are sometimes needed to sustain motivation and interest. However, they do run the risk of making customer care seem peripheral rather than central to the business. It is therefore important for each campaign to build on the achievements of the previous one. Campaigns are a natural part of achieving higher levels of customer care. This must be firmly established in the minds of staff, through communication and motivation policies. Top management's role in this is critical, for they are in effect the leaders of present and past campaigns

(j) ensure that time is spent with new employees to introduce them to the supplier's culture and support them in their attempts to care for customers.

More than this should not be required. But in some suppliers this role would be a radical departure from the norm. In service industries the culture of customer care is readily accepted. But in industries which survive by selling physical products, particularly where contact with customers is infrequent, much of the focus of senior management is on current sales levels and the performance of sales staff. Customer care often takes a back seat, to the customer's misfortune. If senior management is to take on the kind of responsibilities listed above, it is all the more important for them to go through the kind of exposure to customer care outlined earlier in this chapter.

Performance indicators

In most organisations, if the commitment to customer care is not translated into the way staff are measured or managed, then little will change. If managers and staff hear messages about commitment but see no change in the way that their performance is judged, they will be deeply suspicious of the message. Some early move to change performance indicators in the direction indicated by the customer care concept is therefore recommended. Examples of such indicators are given in Chapter 15.

The acid test of these indicators, from top management's point of view, is how top management reacts when customer care performance indicators clash with others (eg financial). Of course, if the supplier is profit-oriented, and profits suddenly go deeply into the red, there is every excuse for focusing on indicators which relate to short-term profitability. Without survival, the supplier will not be able to satisfy *any* customers tomorrow. Despite this, however, there are different ways of reacting to a crisis.

For example, in a time of deep financial crisis, should customers be informed about what is going on in the organisation and how to manage relationships with it? Or should the supplier "batten down the hatches", keeping tight lipped until the situation is resolved one way or another. The customer care approach would indicate allocating a small amount of resource to maintaining a reasonable quality of communication. The profit maximising approach might say that it was best to cut all "unnecessary" costs. Some compromise may be necessary, but provided that it is a true compromise rather than a one-sided solution, belief of staff in top management commitment is likely to be sustained. Phrased in terms of performance indicators, staff who are measured on their ability to keep customers informed as well as on their ability to make money out of customers should not suddenly be assessed solely on the basis of profitability.

Integrating performance indicators

Top management has a particularly important role when it comes to integrating financial, technical and customer care indicators. One of the problems that many suppliers face is split responsibilities for achieving the following tasks:

(a) delivering quality according to specifications (ie technical performance)
(b) delivering financial performance (eg profits or satisfying a budget constraint)
(c) achieving appropriate levels of customer satisfaction.

For example in a large industrial equipment company:

(a) financial staff may be responsible for pricing, setting credit terms and chasing debtors (whether for equipment sales or after-sales service)
(b) engineers may be responsible for performance of installed equipment
(c) marketing and sales staff may be responsible for finding new customers and getting more business out of existing ones.

Each group potentially has a strong influence on customer care but can end up pulling in opposite directions. Financial staff may alienate customers by chasing debtors. Service engineers may create dissatisfaction by questioning customers' choice of equipment ("Who sold you this, then?"). Sales staff may respond to inventory shortages by selling equipment not suitable for the customers' use, raising service costs and creating customer dissatisfaction.

The lines of control through which these different staff are managed may only merge near the top of the organisation. Top management must insist that the performance of these staff is assessed partly on the basis of their help in achieving overall customer satisfaction, through their own actions or their impact on the actions of their colleagues in other departments. For example, attitude surveys should be used to provide information enabling the organisation to correlate treatment of debtors with later sales levels.

Resource allocation

A final test of top management commitment is whether it is translated into resources. Throughout this book, the view is that in the end, customer care pays for itself. However, in the short term, an investment may be required before a return is achieved. This investment may be in the form of training, systems, or even refunds to customers. Of course, it is only fair to top management not to demand allocation of resources without evidence of benefits. But once evidence has been accepted, then the commitment should stay.

Chapter 10

Quality

Introduction

In times of pressure, a stock British response was to batten down the hatches until better times came. In industry, this led British companies to fall prey to competitors who understood the need for continued efforts to improve quality in every aspect of industrial life from research and manufacturing through to customer care. The British would cut investment, lay off staff, fight tough battles on wage claims and reduce dividends.

This led to worse service to customers. British products were lower quality and often out of stock. They did not meet customer requirements. This guaranteed failure. Britain's competitors pursued improved quality. They created organisations focused entirely on delivery of quality to customers.

The service age

Public and private service suppliers throughout the word learnt these lessons. As advanced economies moved into the service age, the competitive focus moved to service suppliers. The spotlight is on the quality they deliver. Hotels, airlines, fast food outlets, educational and medical institutions, telecommunications and postal authorities and even government departments are using quality programmes to harness the power that lies within their organisations. They use it to give better service to customers or, as many quality programmes put it, *to meet customer requirements first time, every time.* Their quality programmes range from the superficial — customer surveys combined with broad, shallow staff training programmes, to the deep — wide-ranging changes of fundamental processes to ensure that the whole organisation is focused on achieving cost-effective delivery of quality.

The difference between customer care and quality

Many suppliers, large and small, have embarked on quality pro-grammes lately. Staff involved in such programmes might legitimately ask what the difference is between quality and customer care. The answer is — quite small.

However, there are some differences between the two. Quality programmes cover many topics other than dealing with customers, while customer care programmes are insistent on very deep knowledge of customers and how to improve care for them. However, this focus on final customers must be maintained from the beginning to the end of the quality process. It could be said that customer care should be the external customer's experience of the outcome of quality programmes when they are applied to the entire organisation.

In an ideal world, every supplier should focus on quality. One aspect of this focus should always be customer care. In practice, this is rarely the case. Many managers involved in improving customer care will stumble on the lack of a quality approach in their organisation. For this reason, it is vital for all involved in customer care to understand what quality programmes are, what they can do, and how they affect customer care.

Quality management

The aim of quality programmes is to ensure that customer needs are satisfied while company objectives are met. This means providing products and services with the right:

(a) quality
(b) availability (launch and after)
(c) service
(d) support
(e) reliability
(f) cost /value for money.

Quality programmes must be comprehensive. In industry, they usually extend backwards into suppliers and forward into distributors. There is little point in, say, an engineering company having high quality work processes if the components it buys in are low quality. If its distributors work in a low quality way with their customers, the product's virtues will be dissipated.

Quality management has played a key role in the turnaround of many companies. One of the most well known examples of this is Jaguar. A survey of XJ6 owners found 150 recurring faults in the car, 60 per cent of which could be traced back to component suppliers. The resulting quality programme included installation of testing systems with suppliers and many quality studies and audits. Customers benefited from a much higher level of reliability in their cars.

Approaches to quality

There are two main approaches to quality:

(a) the technical approach, where quality is defined by performance to specification (of product, of launch programme, etc)
(b) the customer approach, where quality is defined by customers' perception of the extent to which the product or service meets their needs.

Of course, in a competitive world, the two must merge. For if technical specifications do not match customer requirements, the supplier will be working hard to deliver unrequired quality. However, in engineering and other technical environments, the technical approach is often a good starting point for a quality programme. This is for the simple reason that technical people are sometimes suspicious of the "marketing language" that surrounds the customer approach. But even the technical approach requires the use of information from customers (in this case, their perceptions as to the technical quality of the product). This information is almost certain to reveal whether there is a gap between technical specification and customer needs.

Suppliers of services rather than physical products usually take more quickly to the customer-focused quality approach. For them, it is often hard to define quality of output in technical terms. Quality is achieved by matching output with customer expectations. However, manufacturing companies often start with the technical approach and gradually merge it with the customer approach.

It is important not to confuse the modern meaning of quality of service with an older meaning of the term, personal service. It is now clear that many customers want care in other ways than through personal service. Cost is also an element of care. Many customers cannot afford to pay the high price that personal care implies. The quality approach is particularly valuable in helping companies deliver high levels of customer care while minimising high cost personal service. It achieves this by single-minded focus on customer requirements and on what staff need to do to meet them.

One aspect of this focus is identifying:

(a) which aspects of care customers want
(b) which aspects the supplier is providing.

In many cases, it turns out that organisations are providing what customers do not want and not providing what they want. This leads to waste of resources. Hence the importance of researching and prioritising customer needs.

What does a quality programme entail?

Successful quality programmes have these characteristics:

Total involvement

They require *all members* of an organisation to improve quality. This is because, with the right techniques and within the right framework, those best qualified to improve things are the people doing those things. Also, if the programme is not all-embracing, attempts to improve quality in one area will stumble on absence of quality in another. A group of staff trying to improve the quality of care delivered to customers will be frustrated in their work if those responsible for, say, service or product design, are not trying to improve quality. A key implication of this is that the responsibility for improving quality should not be delegated to subordinates or consultants.

Customer-orientation

They are *customer-oriented*. Each internal group is considered a customer and/or a supplier to other internal groups and/or to the market. However, quality programmes can start at any point. Even if the quality of supply to a group is low, it should improve its own quality before turning to its suppliers to ask them to improve quality. Unless it does this, it is not sure what to ask for.

Identifying customers, their requirements and obligations

Strong emphasis is placed on this. Customers may include external customers, employees, shareholders, top management, government and regulators. Requirements should be "reasonable", given resource constraints, objectives, etc. Obligations must be identified, as relationships between customers and suppliers are mutual. A customer must help, by specifying requirements clearly and by co-operating where necessary. Requirements are always quantifiable. They must be agreed by *both* sides as being reasonable. This is particularly important for the customer care area.

Measurement

Quality programmes thrive on measurement. They wither when data on quality is unavailable, hushed up, or political. The first step in measurement is clear specification of required output. The next step is installing mechanisms which provide clear evidence of achievement of output. Quality programmes rely upon openness and honesty about problems, and on concerted attempts being made to quantify problems and opportunities. Just developing reliable quality measurement and control systems can take a long time, and this must precede steps to improve quality. For a service supplier, this data is a mixture of:

(a) customer surveys (internal and external)
(b) customer behaviour (are they buying?)
(c) "production" data (eg turn round times, meeting output targets within quality specifications).

The measures should lend themselves to classic techniques of financial management (eg analysis of key ratios and trends). They should also form part of the classic financial assess–plan–implement–monitor cycle. Kodak's quality programme is couched in these terms.

Leadership from the top

Senior management is visibly committed to achieving quality and ensuring that the programme delivers in *hard* terms (cash, increased sales, better service quality).

Strong process

They are not left to the whim of individual staff or groups. They are driven through a strongly administered process, covering timing, ownership of action areas, gathering and interpretation of data, etc. Each quality improvement project is run according to a structured process and the results are recorded in an agreed format and learning is transferred.

External customer objectives

The context of the quality programme is always the organisation's objectives in relation to external customers. All analyses are referenced back to these. Examples include:

(a) increased sales, higher profitability
(b) lower price provision of service
(c) improved perception of service quality
(d) more balanced or smaller waiting lists.

These should in turn be closely related to the organisation's mission and values. Otherwise, the quality programme becomes irrelevant to the main thrust of the organisation.

Quality and competition

In the previous chapter, the idea of measuring competitors' customer care achievements was discussed. The same applies to quality. In the 1970s and 80s, many American and European companies were being hit by Japanese competition. The former made great efforts to identify what levels of quality were being achieved by their competitors. Customer surveys proliferated. Competitive products were bought, tested and stripped down. A competitive quality gap opened up.

The quality gap

Western companies also made great efforts to identify how these higher quality levels were being achieved. This was not difficult, as Japanese companies were very proud of their quality achievements. They also knew that if they tried to be secretive the cries of "unfair competition" and "dumping" would be raised. They were almost forced to prove that their advantage lay in higher quality, not lower cost.

Most important of all, because they knew that they were trying to hit a moving target, Western companies also tried to find out what quality targets were being set for future years. This was particularly important in industries where quality had become a key dimension of competition.

The idea of a quality gap can be usefully translated into customer care gap — the gap between a company's level of customer care and that provided by its competition. The best position is to be ahead of competition with the gap widening. Failing that, the gap needs to be closed.

Few surprises in quality problems

Quality programmes produce few surprises. Most of the areas singled out as requiring attention come as no surprise to customers, staff or suppliers. They are usually particular instances of more general causes, such as:

(a) poor specification of objectives (eg in a design, a process)
(b) lack of clarity in accountability

(c) poor communication between different staff

(d) lack of focus on strategic need

(e) slackness on cycle times — not focusing tightly enough on the time it takes to carry out operations. This is particularly important for customer care where the customer is closely involved in service delivery.

Quality processes

Quality as defined by performance to specification and quality as defined by meeting customers' needs must, in the final analysis (as was suggested earlier) be combined. Most customers want performance to specification and more. So most quality programmes combine the two and achieve their results by following a number of key principles. None of the principles is innovative. They are all part of good management. The difficulties lie in implementing them thoroughly. These principles are:

(a) determination of which customers are relevant

(b) understanding of needs and perceptions of customers

(c) measurement of the extent to which existing procedures lead to customer needs being met

(d) determination of objectives to be achieved with those customers, ie what the supplier wants customers to perceive

(e) determination of company objectives, ie how the supplier's products and services need to perform to achieve customer and company objectives

(f) clear specification of how these objectives are to be achieved

(g) clear specification of resources required to achieve them

(h) allocation of accountability for achieving them (including ensuring availability of resource)

(i) specification of processes and methods to achieve them, in particular clear specification of work stages, review stages and feedback points

(j) identification of interfaces between staff, work groups, suppliers, etc, where quality transfer is critical

(k) measurement of individual and group performance against objectives

(l) verification that technical and customer objectives are being met

(m) correction of processes and methods
(n) continual review of validity of objectives, resource needs, etc
(o) involving staff in determining how principles are applied to their work.

Involving staff

The latter principle has received much attention, particularly when it goes under the label of "quality circles". This consists of groups of staff, perhaps also involving internal and external customers and suppliers. The staff on the team are those who have accountability for particular tasks. They work to identify opportunities for improving quality and to determine what actually should be done to improve it. They use a variety of techniques for identifying problems and opportunities, measuring their impact and solving the problems or capturing the opportunities. The objective of each team is to identify and capture the most important quality opportunities in their work area. The process is therefore not simply analytical. The teams are trained and where necessary provided with specialist support. This support may include statistical analysis, survey research, process development and computer systems. The teams meet at short, regular intervals, progressing their projects to implementation through an agreed quality methodology. British Airways has used this kind of approach with its "Customer First" teams.

This approach is particularly valuable in situations where customer care depends upon the quality of service delivered by staff (ie in a served environment). Here, the staff are likely to have much knowledge and experience relating to the standard of care delivered to customers. They are therefore likely to be in the best situation to diagnose causes and effects.

The importance of commitment

Quality programmes require a commitment of time by all staff, and budgets to carry out surveys and to train staff in quality techniques. However, quality programmes are not just quality circles or quality surveys. They require a highly structured process. The aim is to capture the main quality opportunities facing the organisation as a whole or the work group which is pursuing quality. These opportunities must be identified at the beginning of the programme. This may be done through a quality workshop involving staff in the group and representatives of customers and suppliers.

Way of life

This process (or similar) should be part of the "way of life" of the supplier or work group. That is, the natural way of capturing opportunities or tackling problems is a quality way. This is why quality programmes may have milestones, but should have no end. Quality is definitely a culture, not a veneer.

One way in which this approach has been implemented is to build the idea of "benchmarking" into planning. The idea is that quality standards are set according to the best levels currently achieved, whether by competitors or parallel organisations. These benchmark levels are established on the basis of competitive research. The approach is therefore closely related to the idea of a quality gap. The research identifies:

(a) which companies perform the best (from the customer's point of view)
(b) which are the key performance variables
(c) what standards should be set.

The benchmarks are recalibrated frequently. Closing the gap is set as a task for the different business functions. In cases where the company finds itself to be a leader, maintaining the gap becomes the objective. This approach has been used successfully by companies such as Ford, Kodak and Xerox, in areas from product design to customer care.

Motivation

Most quality experts believe that staff should not be given financial incentives for achievement of team quality goals. Rather, these goals should be regarded as an essential part of the job, satisfying in themselves. This is partly because they improve the quality of the individual's working life. However, it is considered helpful to give small awards which increase the visibility of quality achievements and prizes for individual suggestions. Of course, contribution to achieving quality should be a major factor in appraisal, promotion and determining longer term remuneration.

The internal customer

This idea has already been introduced. Many quality programmes use this principle — that *within* the company, staff are customers for each others' work. For example, anyone receiving a piece of work from someone else is a customer for that work. This seems to put a great onus on those whose work is furthest downstream (ie closest to the final customer). This is counterbalanced by reversing the principle. For example, the downstream person who received the work was the supplier of the specification by which it was produced, the customer for the specification being the upstream person. This helps cope with the fact that many problems with quality are due to downstream needs and problems not being communicated back.

Figure 10.1 gives some examples of internal and external customers, their requirements and how they relate to each other.

Quality systems

Robust quality management systems are particularly important in companies which produce, launch and support complex technical products and services. These are usually the outcome of a long design and development process, which has been broken down into many parts, each the responsibility of a different individual or team. In such processes, it is critical that everyone knows what their job is, everyone knows how to do it and meet quality requirements, and everyone actually does it.

Customer type

Requirements

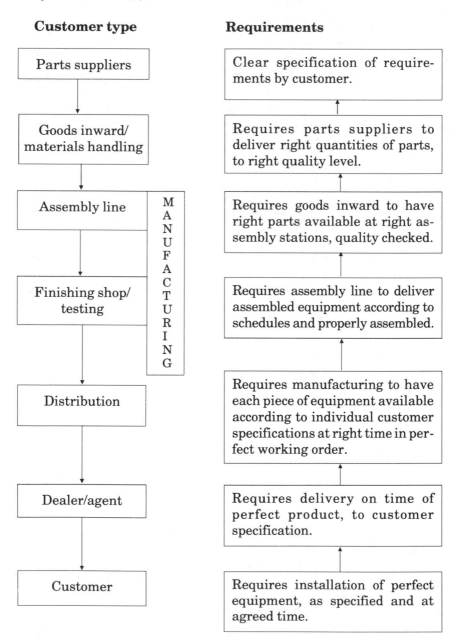

Figure 10.1 Internal and external customers

Three levels of documentation may be required in a quality management system:

(a) Specification of general business objectives which relate to quality.
(b) The detailed procedures and specifications, often called procedures. Examples of procedure documentation include instructions, manuals, handbooks, flowcharts, standards, specifications, drawings, diagrams and check lists. In customer service environments, these often need to be trained into staff, so that they do not need to refer to them in front of customers.
(c) The linking documents which ensure that the detailed procedures reflect the general business objectives, often called the *quality plans*. These relate to a particular area of work or to the achievement of a defined sub-set of objectives. They are often represented in project management flow charts or programme stage definitions.

There is a British Standard (5750) which can be applied to any operation or function. This standard exists for marketing too and can provide an excellent basis for a customer care programme.

The responsibility for quality cannot be delegated or allocated to selected individuals. Many companies have found it helpful to appoint a quality manager. The latter's task includes:

(a) helping management introduce quality processes
(b) ensuring that all functions and workgroups are adopting them
(c) ensuring that specialist support is provided where needed
(d) helping sort out problems
(e) identifying training needs
(f) implementing training programmes
(g) ensuring high visibility for the programme as a whole.

In many cases, quality managers are needed to achieve the introduction of new business disciplines, such as:

(a) statistical quality control
(b) quality circles
(c) quality costing.

They may also need to reinforce the use of existing disciplines (eg project management, standard checklists).

A quality management system is all-embracing but not a substitute for other business procedures. Many quality disciplines are, after all, only basic management disciplines. But they derive their added value when used in quality systems by the coherence of the overall quality programme.

What does a programme cover?

The broad coverage of the programme is influenced by the outcomes of surveys and workshops, but no areas are excluded. This is because every quality team has the remit to identify, prioritise and capture opportunity areas.

What does a quality programme cost?

Eventually, quality comes free, because the organisation saves the costs of failure, rectification and checking. Initially, funding is required for training (staff and trainer time), staff time spent identifying opportunities for improvement and how to capture them and for specialist support.

What benefits does a programme bring?

A successful quality programme brings these benefits:

(a) better service to external customers (improved quality in existing products and better attunement of product range to needs), leading to more customer satisfaction and increased demand
(b) more efficient utilisation of existing resources
(c) improved staff motivation
(d) higher pay because staff spend more of their time doing what customers want (and what they pay for)
(e) quicker response to change and more active anticipation of change
(f) stronger defence against competition.

What are the risks?

The main risk is partial commitment, resulting lip service and eventual cynicism and demoralisation. This is best avoided by all grades of management having their performance on quality built into their management processes, appraisal and reward systems.

Another risk is that people might not be prepared to "open up". They may remain defensive, closed to change and obstructive of the quality programme. The risk of this can be reduced by ensuring that early projects are highly visible and successful.

Setting too aggressive objectives for a quality programme can be dangerous. It took the Japanese twenty years to sort out their manufacturing quality (late 1940s to late 1960s).

What are the risks of not having a quality programme?

Conventionally, the costs of quality are analysed in three categories:

(a) cost of measurement
(b) cost of failure
(c) cost of prevention.

The same applies to customer care. The more suspect its quality, the more needs to be spent on measuring and prevention and the more that is lost through failure (typically customers failing to return to buy more and even persuading others not do so too).

The main risks incurred by not having a commitment to quality in customer care are increased costs of failure, incurred by:

(a) continued reductions in the quality of customer care
(b) increased customer dissatisfaction (internal and external)
(c) more severe competitive inroads
(d) falling sales and revenues
(e) increasing staff demoralisation
(f) difficulties in recruiting staff
(g) financial problems.

How long would a quality programme last?

Quality programmes are never ending. But a reasonable planning horizon for delivery of major benefits in the area of customer care would be two years — one year for immediately realisable improvements to quality that do not depend on strategic or structural change, two years for those that do.

Chapter 11

Processes, Procedures, Systems and Organisation

It is common to distinguish between the "hard" and "soft" factors that characterise an organisation. Hard factors include:

(a) formal statements of objectives and strategies
(b) the formal plan
(c) formal organisation structure
(d) formal information and communication systems
(e) the formal rules people follow in carrying out their work
(f) the formal management processes which are used to ensure that people channel their efforts into the "right direction" (eg formal review processes).

These are contrasted with the "soft" factors, which cannot be described so simply and may leave room for argument concerning the state of play. Examples include:

(a) the skills possessed by individuals
(b) organisation culture

(c) shared norms and aspirations
(d) the style in which people work
(e) the informal networks of communication and influence which modify the way that information flows and that policy changes occur.

The activities involved in ensuring that policies are properly applied "in the field" are called *operations* or *implementation*. Successful implementation depends on staff:

(a) knowing *what* they are supposed to be doing
(b) knowing *how* to do these things, which may involve training
(c) receiving the right support and help from managers
(d) having the right tools for the job. This includes everything from computer systems and the design of the service location to clothing
(e) having the time to do all the things they need to do.

Smaller organisations are more flexible to changes in workload, especially if they are owner-managed. People will just work harder or longer, or take time off. In a large organisation there is much more specialisation. Here, the main implementation problems relate to the efficiency and thoroughness with which individuals carry out their tasks. Larger organisations are less flexible to changes in workload. Resources have to be formally reallocated as needs change. This takes time (to plan) and money (to hire, fire, train, etc). So small companies tend to run on lists of tasks, often carried around in the managers' heads. Larger companies tend to run on formalised procedures, based on form-filling, computerised work processes, measurement and formal review.

Processes

The need for management processes

Growing organisations need gradually to add processes at a rate which matches their size. The main determinants of the need for a more procedural approach are the number of staff and the number of branches. A single branch operation with two or three staff needs only task lists. Once two or three branches exist, with some degree of delegation taking place, then those at the receiving end of delegation need clear instructions and procedures start to emerge.

What is a management process?

A management process is simply an organised way of going about things. More simply, it is a clear specification of how different tasks are to be performed. The elements and visible signs of a process include the following.

Formalised planning and decision making

Typically, in a large service company there will be a periodic planning cycle (usually yearly). Decisions will be taken about what is to be done. The tasks, goals and milestones arising will be formally allocated. Once the plan is in force, the progress against it will be reviewed at predetermined intervals, more often if there are problems!

Information flows

The process for managing operations will be visible in the information flow that takes place between branches and HQ, between different divisions in the HQ, and between staff within branches. These information flows include regular and exception reports on a variety of topics. These are likely to include:

(a) enquiries received from customers
(b) sales material dispatched (eg brochures)
(c) orders taken, confirmed and fulfilled
(d) flow of payments
(e) levels of credit outstanding
(f) average price achieved
(g) additional purchases made by customers
(h) capacity availability and usage
(i) use of particular facilities
(j) supplies inventory levels
(k) customer profiles

(l) staff productivity
(m) profit — by staff group, facility, service type
(n) sales/communications campaign results.

Exception reports will normally be required for problem situations and for one-off events (eg non-routine campaigns, new market research).

All this information will normally flow as a result of form filling and computerised data entry. Computers reduce the need for form filling and document filing. Staff are thereby allowed to focus more on giving improved service to customers. Indeed, computerisation allows staff to give data to customers more quickly.

People processes

Service industries work through people. This means that in large companies achieving target levels on the items being reported above depends on someone having accountability for the achievement of each item. Staff must also be motivated and managed so that they do achieve their targets. For example, if customer care is an important item, it is no use just training staff to be "nice" to customers if their performance in this respect is not managed properly and then measured. This means motivating staff, monitoring their performance and rewarding them for achieving target levels. The reward does not necessarily have to be financial. It may be through recognition by management or peers or special benefits. Measurement may be formal, eg through customer questionnaires or informal — the manager's judgement.

Defining tasks by time period

In developing processes for handling customer care, it usually helps if tasks are divided by the kind of time horizons they involve (eg whether they are daily, weekly, monthly, quarterly, yearly or special).

Daily work is the everyday job of managing individual tasks. Daily work for managers tends to differ from the daily work of non-managerial staff. The work of supervisory staff tends to be a mixture of the two. For management, daily work may include:

(a) filling forms and data entry
(b) filing
(c) diary management
(d) back-up provision
(e) people management
(f) problem solving
(g) meeting management.

At the human level, the focus is on such items as checking that things are proceeding properly, managing problems, helping people complete tasks, supporting and giving them lift through motivation.

For non-management staff, daily work includes:

(a) serving customers
(b) backing up the service of customers (eg maintenance, safety monitoring, preparation, etc).

The focus here is on individual tasks and balancing between them on a daily basis.

As the period of analysis gets longer, management routines start to dominate. Weekly routines tend to relate to issues such as:

(a) staffing rosters
(b) handling typical weekly workload changes (especially between weekday and weekend)
(c) collating daily results and reporting them.

In capacity-driven businesses, capacity utilisation is likely to be reported and acted upon each week. Weekly meetings with staff for communication, motivation and performance review are common, particularly in customer-facing work situations. This is because the quality delivered to customers must be properly managed.

Monthly and quarterly routines tend to relate to slightly longer term activities or projects. These are often seasonal. They include:

(a) putting together plans
(b) implementing sales and communication campaigns
(c) briefing agencies
(d) recruiting, developing, communicating with and motivating staff
(e) measuring performance against budget.

Annual routines tend to relate to major activities and very important projects. These include:

(a) launching a major new service
(b) development and implementation of a strategic communications campaign
(c) production of a business-wide plan.

Also included here are longer term people activities such as:

(a) appraisal
(b) long term development
(c) promotion of key staff.

There is a strong tendency in all businesses for shorter term tasks to dominate the longer term ones. Planning often gets displaced by the demands of the moment. This may result in a company dealing very well with the needs of today and neglecting those of tomorrow. For example, existing customers may receive a very high level of service, while nothing is done about recruiting customers for tomorrow.

For this reason, larger companies create strong processes for all their main tasks. Each task is broken down into its elements. Then responsibility is assigned for each element to specific people. Assigning is usually in great detail — what is to be done, by whom, by when, in what form any results are to be presented, how results are to be measured, who is to supervise and so on.

Figure 11.1 gives an example of this approach.

Defining standards

Once tasks are properly defined and responsibility for their achievement allocated, it is possible to define the standards that apply to the performance of those tasks. These standards can be drawn from many areas. The kinds of standard that can be applied to customer care have been best described by A Parasuraman et al, in their "Conceptual Model of Service Quality" (Journal of Marketing, Fall 1985). They list the following as potential standards:

Receive customer call.
Take details of claim.
Check status of insurance policy.
Find out when customer is available for damage assessment visit and arrange time.
Give customer names of approved repairers.
Check customer understands next steps.
Customer arranges for repairers to visit and quote for damage repair. Sends quotes to insurance company.
Inspector visits to assess damage.
Inspector evaluates quotes against damage and makes decision.
Insurance company sends letter instructing customer how to proceed with repair.
Customer receives letter and carries out instructions. Repair receipt sent to insurance company.
Insurance company issues cheque, sends it to customer, and records claim.

Figure 11.1 Breaking down a customer care task

Example — processing an insurance claim

(a) Courtesy — consideration for customers, their property, cleanliness, neatness, honesty.
(b) Competence — knowledge and skill of contact/support staff.
(c) Service reliability — accuracy, good records, performing services at the designated time to published standards.
(d) Security — physical and financial safety, confidence.
(e) Credibility — trustworthiness, believability, honesty, strength of company name, reputation, personal character.
(f) Process — easy, reasonable waiting time, convenient opening hours.
(g) Understanding the customer — needs, giving attention and recognition.
(h) Communication — explaining the service, its costs, trade-offs and how problems are handled.
(i) Responsiveness — speed, updating the customer on progress, giving prompt service.
(j) Tangibles — physical service facilities, uniform, tools or equipment, documentation. This is equivalent to the "presence" of the seven Ps.

Not all of these standards are immediately amenable to quantification but they can all certainly be assessed through customer feedback. This means that tasks can be defined so as to have these kinds of measured output.

Here are some examples of how such standards are translated into actionable items. Thomas Cook defines its standards for handling customers in its travel agency offices in this way:

(a) acknowledgement that the customer is waiting
(b) high standard of appearance (staff and offices)
(c) well defined offices
(d) customer to be called by name
(e) good telephone service (measured partly by time to answer)
(f) quality correspondence handling
(g) good customer documentation
(h) good after-sales service.

British Telecom uses (amongst others) these standards:

(a) faults cleared within a defined time
(b) proportion of calls completed

(c) proportion of orders fulfilled

(d) speed of answering telephone enquiries

(e) proportion of payphones working.

Note that the British Telecom standards are of a higher order of generality and require much more complicated sets of standards to achieve them. For example, fault clearance requires complex sets of engineering tasks to be carried out and standards to be set for each task.

Running a process

Some processes can be self-administered. This applies particularly if tasks are simple and routine and all involved in doing the tasks know exactly:

(a) what the tasks are

(b) why they are necessary

(c) the consequences of not doing them.

For example, staff taking bookings know that they have to make certain kinds of check on availability and capture certain information on a form. All that staff need to carry out this process successfully is the training, a telephone and the forms. They do not need a checklist or a computer to ensure that they carry out the right steps. However, staff handling complaints over the telephone may need a more formal process, given the immense variety of complaints. Such a process, using checklists, might be necessary to protect the legal position of the company.

Self-administered processes also work well if managers concentrate on managing the exceptions. This should be by strong positive reward for successes *and* for working to the process, and by negative reinforcement for staff not observing agreed processes.

But if tasks are not simple or required only occasionally, if understanding about the need for them is not widespread, and so on, then a hands-on-approach to management may be required. In some cases, a document-intensive process may be used to ensure that people think what they are doing and communicate it to each other. This is the case, for example, for most planning activities.

Making customer care work

If a procedural approach is taken, for it to work, these conditions must hold:

(a) Staff must understand and be committed to the process. This means that they should be trained in the process as part of their normal training programme. This ensures that conformity to the process comes naturally and is not seen as an additional burden.

(b) Roles must be allocated clearly, and staff must understand them and have the skills, time and resources to do them (eg what they are accountable for, what they can decide or influence). There are few things more demotivating than being disciplined for not carrying out something that one was never told or trained to do.

(c) The process should produce clear benefits for staff (eg help them work better, reduce tension or conflict, or give them clear standards by which to judge their own performance).

(d) Staff commitment to the process must be reinforced by management action (via involvement by management in implementing the process, setting clear priorities, administering rewards and sanctions). Appraisals must take into account contribution to the process.

(e) Management must know when someone is or is not carrying out their role, otherwise individual reinforcement cannot take place. A good process ensures that the right information is available at the right time to the right people. This means that the process should produce routine reports which indicate who is succeeding and who is not.

(f) The process must be designed to support marketing objectives and allow staff to work more effectively to achieve it.

Workload planning

The quality of operations in service companies depends critically on proper work design and workload planning. A visit to a well-managed service outlet will demonstrate this point. Although staff are busy, they are not frantically so (unless there is an emergency). They move speedily from task to task. They may talk to their colleagues but only while working. They deal with customers politely and kindly, but efficiently.

Behind this ideal situation, when it exists, is usually an immense amount of attention to detail. Jobs have been built up from detailed task descriptions. Staff performing those tasks have been measured and timed. Staff with less routine jobs have completed time diaries, to allow identification of wasted time or tasks that should be reallocated. Technology has been deployed wherever possible to minimise time not spent serving customers and to maximise efficiency in front of customers.

Front office and back office

The split between customer-facing (front office) and company-facing (back office) tasks must be considered, and systems designed to support each of these functions so that each can concentrate on the task in hand. Figure 11.2 gives an example of this arrangement.

Front office procedures should be designed with the prime objective of serving customers cost-effectively. They must be:

(a) able to handle variations in the rate at which customers arrive for processing. If the tasks do not have to be completed while customers are waiting, then a process is required to extract from customers all that is required (information, money, etc) to enable the processing of the case quickly. If the tasks must be completed while the customer is waiting, then processes must also cover how the customer is to be treated while waiting

(b) inclusive. They must deal with both the company, the customer and the interaction between them. Put another way, they must work from the point of view of both the company and the customer

(c) allow for the different requirements of customers and the different types of customer. Types of customer will vary from highly experienced to inexperienced, loyal to "cherry-picking".

The reason for the distinction between front office and back office is that it is in the back office where more complex processing of cases takes place. This may include:

215

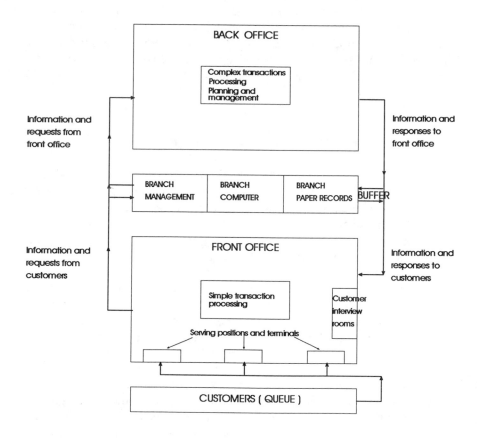

Figure 11.2 Front and back offices — simple outline

(NB The buffer may be bypassed for simple requests and in urgent situations.)

(a) assessment of insurance claims
(b) preparing quotations, statements and clarifications
(c) reconciling data

and the like.

In principle, all these can be done in front of customers. But if they can be organised into a "production" environment, they can be carried out more quickly and reliably than if they are carried out by staff whose attention has to switch between customers and complex case processing. Also, different skills and personalities may be required for the two types of operation. The focus of back office management should be on cost-effective and accurate case processing. The focus of front office management should be on meeting customer needs while staying within cost constraints. Buffers may be required between the two to ensure optimum allocation of effort. These buffers may consist of:

(a) orderly queuing arrangements for case processing
(b) information systems to ensure rapid availability of data on cases on line, in such a way as to prevent back office staff being disturbed
(c) escalation procedures for problem handling.

Where the volume of front office contact is very high, it can be centralised into an environment in which some of the tasks are confined to a kind of back office. The national or regional telephone enquiry service, as used by AT&T, US General Electric, General Motors, Polaroid and Digital Equipment, centralises enquiries and maintains a telephonic front office for dealing with the calls. However, it is supported by a computerised back office for providing information customers need. The GE system, which is open 24 hours a day, 7 days a week, has over 200 staff and handles millions of calls a year. It would simply be too expensive to have this volume dealt with locally. It also provides a much higher level of customer care.

Planning and managing tasks

Attention should be paid to the speed and accuracy with which information gets transferred and processed. Information flowing up from operations should be processed quickly and problems isolated soon after or even as they occur. Planning processes should be structured so as to fit the culture of the organisation. If it is centralised, information and decision requirements and accountabilities should be clearly specified. The processes of communication and decision making should be facilitated by the use of standard formats. Diarying of the time of important staff should be closely controlled and meetings properly managed. Computerised decision support systems should be used to analyse results and project manage major changes.

Unfortunately, this professional approach to day to day management is not as common as it should be. The focus is more on immediate results than on improving the way these results are obtained. However, the advent of quality programmes in many companies has brought home the message that it is not possible to divide neatly between how work is carried out and the end result of that work (sales, customer care, etc). So, for example, if customer handling is not being carried out effectively, then other operating parameters start to deteriorate.

Work design

Quality programmes have also taught managers in many industries the importance of the discipline of specifying every action required to achieve particular tasks. In some cases, there will be branching from the main task sequence (eg if the required service is not available). The work must then be designed from the point of view of all those involved in the work situation.

If customers are to be cared for, work design must include the customer. For example, at the moment of purchase, the customer will typically be either waiting at a counter or on the end of a telephone line. Anyone who has experienced the frustration of waiting while an inexperience member of staff consults a complex brochure or an unintelligible computer screen will know what the problems are. The best solution is to simulate real service being given. This will provide all the information needed to optimise the service from the customer's point of view. In particular, it is likely to reveal information about how the customer sees the process.

Work layout

In many organisations, customers are "processed" in the manufacturing sense of the term, in that they physically move through the location of service. Too often, the design of these locations maximises back office space, puts barriers between staff and customers, or causes customers to wait for a long time in uncomfortable situations. As retailers have focused on more productive (and more pleasant) treatment of customers through design-based solutions, their influence has happily spread into other parts of the service sector. The design of environments in which customers are processed is often tested, with staff at their "work stations", to see whether customer needs are met.

Information systems

As the need for higher productivity combined with more customer-oriented treatment has intensified, many organisations have looked to computerisation to cut through this Gordian knot. Once service information systems only carried information on capacity availability, prices and customer debiting. Now, they cover customer histories and customer requirements too. This means that customers and services can be matched more quickly. With proper management processes, information and measurement systems, recruitment and training of staff, and control systems, the service operation should be as good as planned

Systems, processes and procedures

Processes and procedures include ways for:

(a) transmitting orders and communications to staff
(b) handling of incoming commands
(c) motivation
(d) payment.

These are used to structure the environment of staff working with customers and to ensure that the former manage the latter according to the organisation's objectives. Their focus is usually on how the department or individual should perform in order to play the right role for the rest of the organisation.

Take for example a department which has the responsibility for preparing cost estimates for use by other departments. Its procedures and systems are likely to focus on the requirement for getting figures of the right type, accurately and on time to the "customer" departments. Suppose the department is working under pressure, and cannot meet all the requirements. Suppose too that the organisation does not have the resources to recruit more staff to the department. Some tasks will have to be delayed or deferred. Which? The commonest rule for prioritising is "who shouts loudest gets first". This is not acceptable as a professional management approach. There are two obvious candidates for prioritising rules, as follows:

(a) cost minimisation or profit maximising, ie which delay will be the least costly in terms of cost incurred or revenue foregone
(b) which delay will be least damaging to customer care.

The extent to which the second rule is used will indicate how far the organisation is prepared to lean in the direction of customer care.

Processes and procedures — definitions

These terms can be defined in many ways. In this book, a *process* is defined as a structured way of handling a series of connected tasks. For example, the process for handling a customer's complaint may involve a set of defined steps, with different options to follow according to the type of complaint and how the customer reacts to each step. A *procedure* determines the detailed actions which should be followed to ensure completion of a task within a process. For example, if one of the steps in handling a customer complaint is to obtain precise information about the complaint, then the associated procedure might be to complete a specified form.

Of course, the use of these terms is relative. There may be several layers of process. For example, an organisation may have a planning process within which there are further processes (eg a marketing planning process). A procedure to support a high level policy might be considered a process seen from the perspective of someone involved in day to day operations.

Process analysis

Once customer care strategy has been determined, one of the first steps in ensuring its implementation is to develop a very clear picture of the processes and procedures currently followed in those parts of the organisation whose actions affect the quality of customer care and then to determine how these need to be changed to improve the quality of customer care.

The tool used here is called "process analysis". It is nothing more than its name implies — a thorough analysis of all the tasks involved in delivering policy. More detailed analysis can go down to the procedural level.

The first thing that process analysis shows up is how confused the "real life" situation is. There may be a corporate view on "how things are done", but this view is unlikely to be sustained by reality. For example, a complaints handling process may stipulate that certain steps are followed before a customer is given or refused a refund. Practice may show that these steps are only followed exceptionally because of the time pressures on the staff concerned. This will indicate the need either to simplify the process (ie less major tasks), to make the procedures for delivering each step in the process more simple (eg less information collected), or to change the objective of the process (eg from minimising refunds to maximising customer loyalty).

Customer care-oriented processes

How an organisation handles complaints is one of the best tests of the extent of customer care orientation in its processes. A customer oriented process is one which has as its main objective the satisfying of customer needs, with a subsidiary requirement being that of checking the validity of the claim and ensuring that meeting the claim causes minimum disturbance and loss to the organisation. An internally-oriented process reverses these priorities.

As processes are the main method by which management makes the organisation move, they are critical in determining whether customers are cared for. If processes are internally-oriented, then staff will continually have to fight against these processes to meet customer needs.

The two approaches to process design can be summarised as follows:

	Customer-oriented	**Internally-oriented**
Step 1	Determine customer needs	Determine organisation's needs
Step 2	Identify areas where meeting customers' needs may also offer opportunities for meeting organisation's needs	Identify areas where meeting organisation's needs may also offer opportunities for meeting customers' needs
Step 3	Develop strategies to meet customers' needs, while satisfying constraint of organisation's needs	Develop strategies to meet organisation's needs, while satisfying constraint of customers' needs
Step 4	Develop processes and procedures to meet customers' needs, while satisfying constraint of organisation's needs	Develop processes and procedures to meet organisation's needs, while satisfying constraint of customers' needs

In a customer-oriented organisation, processes and procedures are naturally developed with meeting customers' needs as a prime objective. But most organisations are not like this.

Here are examples of customer- and internally-oriented procedures for handling complaints.

	Customer-oriented	**Internally-oriented**
Step 1	Welcome customer, let customer express feelings as well as facts, and identify nature of complaint and appropriate style for handling it.	Identify the customer and verify status.
Step 2	Check details of complaint.	Determine nature of complaint.
Step 3	Establish how to meet customer's needs.	Check details of complaint.
Step 4	Review options with customer.	Identify solution preferred by organisation.
Stage 5	Customer chooses option.	Offer preferred solution to customer.
Stage 6	Customer status verified.	If offer refused, offer next best solution from organisation's point of view.
Stage 7	Solution implemented.	If offer not accepted, defer complaint. Otherwise implement solution.

If an organisation's procedures are similar to those on the right hand side, then the level of returned complainers is likely to be higher, and the rate of loss of customers is also likely to be higher.

If an organisation is starting with many processes and procedures of the right hand side kind, then it needs to review them, particularly if it is under threat of losing customers.

Complaint handling processes

The complaints example is a simple one, where the problem is easily identified and rectified.

However, the problem with complaints handling is that complaints vary so much. There are some general procedures for complaints handling which should always be followed in designing a complaints handling process, as follows:

(a) Always let the customer express emotions. Failure to accept the customer's emotions is a common reason for persistence of complaints.

(b) Help those handling the complaints deal with their own emotions too, by training them to see the customer's point of view and not to feel responsible for the complaint, only for the solution.

(c) Make sure that the information required to identify the reason for the complaint is gathered accurately and politely.

(d) Recognise that often what is apparently a complaint is a request for more information.

(e) Ensure that where the reason is a request for information, the information likely to be requested is at hand.

(f) Recognise that many complaints are a confirmation of customer need, and therefore present an opportunity for deepening the relationship with the customer by selling more.

(g) Give the customer details of the process for handling the complaint, including who will be responsible for resolving it.

(h) Keep the customer informed of progress and solution.

(i) Keep records of complaints and complainers. This information helps identify customers who experience persistent problems (and "over-complainers" and persistent problems). This information should ideally be computerised at source to speed up the reporting process.

Most suppliers' complaints follow the 80:20 rule. For the 20 per cent of topics which produce 80 per cent of the complaints, processes for dealing with the complaints need to be designed just like any other customer care process. For the 80 per cent of topics which produce 20 per cent of the complaints, flexibility, staff-empowerment and quick resort to senior management decision is the right answer.

Of course, it goes without saying that the best complaints-handling mechanism is a policy process which continues to investigate the reasons for complaints so as to anticipate and forestall them by removing the source of the complaint. This can be dispiriting, in the sense that new sources of complaint continually pop up. But persistence with this approach is the hallmark of the customer-oriented supplier. Irrespective of the volume of complaints, the supplier should be committed to removing the source of the complaint and then hunting for new complaints and removing their sources.

Feasible processes

In some areas of policy, the commitment to care for customers may be more difficult to translate into feasible processes. Take the example of a product development process in a "high technology" company. Suppose that the company is operating in a field in which most new products are the result of genuine innovations, and that in general customers are educated by suppliers as to the virtues of new products. That is to say, although customers have a general need for products of the type being developed, these products could take many forms, any one of which would satisfy customer needs. Customers needs are, in a sense, ill-formed.

In such a case, the difference between the customer-oriented and the internally-oriented process may not lie in their initial stages. It is more likely to lie in the extent to which potential customers are researched in relation to the details of product features, distribution channel and after-sales service requirements, and the like. The more customer-oriented process is likely to result in a total offering (product, distribution channels, after-sales service, problem resolution process, etc) which meets customer needs.

Problems with feasibility

All this sounds good in theory. However, the experienced manager may object that too much caring for customers, particularly in day to day operations, can result in staff simply "not getting through the work". Long queues of customers may build up and many of them may want to transact more important business than have a complaint dealt with. Staff will come under pressure and start to depart from customer-oriented procedures in order to reduce queue lengths.

Two points need to be made in response to this.

(a) Procedures must of course be designed to operate quickly as well as fairly. Problems and customer status must be checked quickly. This is why modern information systems and policies which empower frontline staff are required. Also plan B procedures are required. These identify in advance the kind of problems that are likely to occur less frequently and the options available to staff for dealing with them. Plan B procedures must also be designed for the unspecified unexpected! Plan B procedures prevent staff having to break rules or "get around the system" to meet customer requirements. They also save costs, as the optimum way of meeting customer needs is worked out in advance.

(b) Failing to handle customers properly may lead to worse problems, in particular absence of customers. So resources may need to be invested in handling customers.

Organisational Structure

Organisational structure is a complex issue. It is easy to fall into the trap of assuming that decentralisation is somehow a close cousin of customer care. Many writings on customer care use the concept of "empowering staff to care for customers", usually in relation to staff who deal directly with customers.

However, this view is a little superficial. In large organisations many staff apparently quite remote from customers have an influence on the extent to which customers are cared for. Product planners and even technical researchers or scientists can have an influence, for the extent to which they empathise with customers' needs while planning, creating or designing products will determine whether they produce products which make it easier for the organisation to care for customers. Information system specifiers and designers can have a dramatic influence on an organisation's ability to care for customers. They can make it easy or hard for staff dealing directly with customers to access information the organisation already holds on customer needs, or to transmit information "commanding" the organisation to deliver something that meets customer needs.

Growth and organisational structure

Many of the debates about how organisational structure can influence customer care turn on the issue of centralisation or decentralisation of different types of decision. In a growing organisation these issues come to the fore quickly.

Take, for example, a one man business which imports a manufactured product and sells it to other businesses. The volume of business becomes too great for the owner to manage, so a sales person is employed. The sales person proves to be very effective and is soon involved in negotiations with a quite large customer. In the course of the negotiations, the latter asks for a discount. The sales person is not empowered to make the decision, so tries to contact the owner. Unfortunately, the latter is on holiday (one of the benefits of having an additional member of staff is the ability to take a holiday). So the customer has to wait until the owner returns. Meanwhile a competitor knocks on the door. . .

If the owner had thought ahead, a policy on discounts could have been worked out and used as a foundation for devolving authority to the sales person. However, this is not the only solution. An information system could have been installed, allowing the sales person to communicate the details of any proposed deal to the owner, anywhere in the world. The customer could have had a response within, say, two hours. Or some combination of these two approaches could have been developed, with local authority to discount up to a certain level and central authorisation required for greater discounts.

This shows that caring for customers does not necessarily require decentralised authority. Rather, it requires *clarity* on the limits of authority at each level and *clear, fast communications* when reference to higher authority is required. It would be nice to say that the optimum situation is complete delegation, but many a good sales person has bankrupted a business in this way! The ideal is therefore clear allocation of accountability in job definitions, while maintaining flexibility to meet customer needs. Of course, provision should also be made for creation of an alternative approach (plan B) for the occasional unusual customer request.

Here is a summary of the strengths and weaknesses of centralised and decentralised approaches to management, from the perspective of customer care:

Centralised approach	Decentralised approach

Strengths

Centralised approach	Decentralised approach
Ensures consistency of treatment of customers	More easily allows variation in treatment of customers to meet individual needs
Allows achievement of economies of scale	Allows staff to marshall local resources flexibly
Facilitates recording of outcomes for future reference	Facilitates use of purely local information
Makes it easier to call upon resources of entire organisation	Low overall visibility of concessions makes unfavourable precedents less likely

Weaknesses

Centralised approach	Decentralised approach
Possible inflexibility and slowness of response	Local staff may not have skills to deliver right solution
Information on customer needs possibly less available to local staff	Possible problems in accessing centrally held information on customer needs or on possible solutions

Awareness of strengths and weaknesses will take an organisation a long way in the direction of being able to make either approach work. In the end, the choice of approach is less likely to be dictated by customer care requirements than by the culture or style of an organisation. An organisation which has been strongly centralised or decentralised for a number of years is unlikely to be able to switch to the opposite extreme quickly and without cost. The skills required to implement the opposite approach are likely to be scarce.

Which approach is right for the organisation?

This is not easy to answer generally but there are a few key indicators. From the customer care point of view, centralised organisations tend to work well when:

(a) there is a high volume of customers in frequent contact with the supplier
(b) customers have a well known set of needs and these vary little between customers
(c) the same kinds of problem tend to occur and these problems tend to be easy to resolve
(d) the importance to the customer of each transaction is relatively low.

This does not imply that in these situations caring for customers should be entirely centralised. It does imply that policies should be laid down centrally and implemented within tight but simple guidelines.

Decentralised organisations work well when:

(a) there is a lower volume of customers, in contact with the organisation at greatly varying intervals
(b) customers' needs vary greatly and there is little commonality between the needs of different customers
(c) problems vary widely in their nature and significance to customers
(d) each transaction is very important to customers.

Functional issues

The second major issue concerning organisation structure relates to functional issues. Once an organisation grows beyond a certain size, it needs to create a number of lines of command to deal with the variety of its activities. The main approaches are:

(a) Geographical area — setting up branches to operate at particular locations or to cover customers in particular areas. The most obvious examples of this are retail outlets, but public authority administrative branches and private sector sales branches are also examples of this. This approach is most common where demand for the services of the organisation is widely distributed and needs to be dealt with at or near the point of demand.

(b) Customer type — setting up departments to cover particular types of customer (eg large businesses, small business and consumers). This is most common where these different types of customer have greatly differing needs which cannot be handled by the same kind of people and/or processes.

(c) Function or discipline — setting up departments which carry out specific kinds of task (eg marketing, finance, production, research and development). This is most common where the function requires specific sets of skills and where performance criteria vary greatly between the different functions.

(d) Activity or product — setting up departments responsible for part or all of the process of delivering particular products or services to customers (eg in a motor vehicle company, one department for commercial vehicles, one for family cars and one for luxury saloons).

An examination of the structure of most large organisations will reveal that these approaches are usually combined. For example, a large area branch office may be organised by function or customer type within the office. Combinations of approach usually lead to an approximation of the matrix organisation structure. In this example, branch finance staff might report to the branch general manager,but have a "dotted line" report into the finance director of the whole organisation. The approach may vary according to the stage in the production process. For example, in a manufacturing company, research and development might be organised by activity or product. Production might be functionally organised (ie according to the different activities within production), marketing might be organised by customer type and distribution by area.

The reason why these different approaches to organisation pose problems for customer care is that responsibility for meeting customer needs normally cuts across lines of organisation. The processes that connect the different departments will often be designed to meet the needs of those departments for smooth operation rather than to meet the needs of customers. For example, in our manufacturing company, the process of transfer of products from R and D to manufacturers may focus entirely on ensuring the smoothness of the transition and the speed of transfer, rather than on ensuring that subsequent customer problems are minimised.

The more complex the organisation, the more likely it is that its processes and procedures will focus on smoothness of operation rather than effect on final customers. For this reason, process analysis must seek to identify each process that has been defined according to this criterion and revise it to ensure that customers' needs come first.

Systems

The importance of systems has already been mentioned in this chapter. Irrespective of the degree of centralisation, two forces are increasing the needs for systems support to customer care. They are:

(a) the need for higher quality in customer care. Systems are increasingly being used to marshal the resources of the organisation (including information) to meet customer needs

(b) the need for greater productivity in customer care, where information systems carry out the job of automating work that was done by humans (eg record keeping).

The major development in information systems that relate to customer care are customer information systems, in particular customer database systems. Many large organisations have invested in systems which enable them to call up very quickly details of every customer's relationship with the organisation — sales, service calls, promotions received, etc. However, these systems can be very expensive and liable to information overload. Their performance slows down dramatically as they get larger and searches for details of customers take longer. The need to prioritise has become paramount. This means that:

(a) information about customers should be automated in strict order of priority, measured by the importance of the customers to the organisation. There is little point in having lots of information available about customers with whom the organisation is rarely in contact

(b) where particular customers are attached to particular locations (eg if they are managed by a particular sales or service office), it is usually better to decentralise the information to these locations. The corporate mainframe keeps updated copies of this information for corporate purposes (eg invoicing, analysis)

(c) the same applies to the kind of information that customers are likely to require from the organisation. There is little point in having a great deal of information available of the kind that customers rarely need

(d) the information supplied by the system to policy makers should allow them to identify customer needs; it should not just be a record of a few aspects of the relationship between the organisation and its customers.

Additional points are that:

(a) systems need to be thoroughly tested for the integrity of their data and of their communications links

(b) staff operating such systems need to be thoroughly trained before they operate them in front of customers. Very few things are more frustrating than confused operators. The customer immediately suspects that the transaction will fail or be incorrectly recorded.

An example of a configuration of a customer information system is shown in Figure 11.3.

The integrity and usefulness of such systems depends critically upon the quality of the data. This has led to a strong emphasis by systems designers on data capture at the point of contact with the customer and at other points. This applies to everything from sales transactions, through engineer service calls, to public utility meter reading, telemarketing calls and complaint handling. For example, the systems used by Federal Express capture bar-coded data on parcels at a large number of points in the handling process. This enables them to keep their promise of a half-hour response time on any enquiry (particularly those concerning the location of a given package).

Information systems and performance measurement

In many cases, information systems provide the data through which staff are assessed for their success in meeting customer needs. For example, together with sales data, information from customer satis-

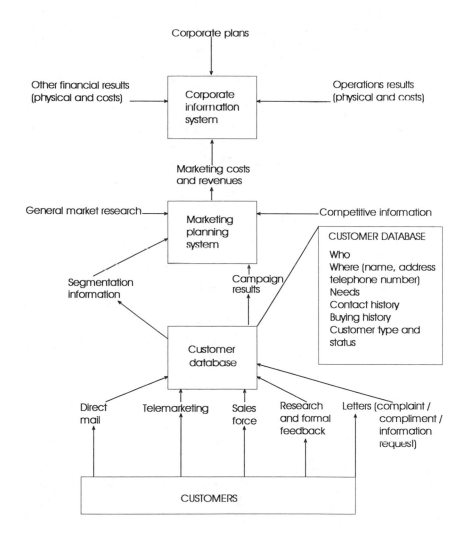

Figure 11.3 Customer information system

(NB the arrows show the flow of information from customers. Flows in the reverse direction maintain the customer relationship.)

faction questionnaires may be used to calculate a sales person's bonuses. This carries risks as well as benefits. A significant risk is that, if money depends upon it, staff will try to influence what goes on the system and, in the worst case, try to alter it. Hence the need for very clear system security provision.

On a more positive note, information systems can make a major contribution to the clarity and speed with which performance measures are made available. The variety of measures which can be used is discussed fully in Chapter 15. However, the sooner measures are available and the more clearly they are presented, the quicker action can be taken. Also, computer systems can ensure attributability. They can show which member of staff is most successful in dealing with customers and which the least.

Too often, when such systems are designed, the emphasis in designing reports is on the needs of middle and senior management. From a customer care perspective, the key need is for staff dealing with customers and first line management to have fast, clear reporting — ideally immediately or at worst at the end of the working day. In telemarketing, where much of the data is recorded as part of the normal business process, this frequency of reporting is the norm. The standards of telemarketing can be extended to most areas where there is daily interaction with customers, provided that these requirements are programmed in from the beginning.

Legal and regulatory issues in systems

Data protection — a caution

The more that an organisation knows about a customer, the better able the organisation is to serve that customer. However, there are limits to information gathering. One limit is the commonsense one of avoiding over-intrusiveness. This is the kind of limit that is best identified in face to face transactions. But the law also imposes limitations.

In the UK, in the last decade, regulation of business gave way to deregulation and freedom to compete. The effects have been seen almost everywhere in the UK economy. For example, the deregulation of the financial services industry has had a significant impact on that industry. Many financial service companies turned to direct marketing as the most cost-effective means of penetrating new markets and launching new products. This led to the accumulation of large amounts of data on individuals. This data was then used to design new products and then to target sales campaigns. Privatisation of the telecommunications industry created a competitor to British Telecom, increased the latter's use of direct marketing, and made it a more aggressive competitor in the provision of data-related services. British Telecom has one of the largest customer databases in the world.

The liberalisation of media has witnessed the arrival of new terrestrial television channels, cable and satellite channels and local radio stations. Many of these are now used in conjunction with direct marketing methods, which have the common characteristic that they involve addressing customers individually, whether by post, telephone or through a face to face encounter. All these developments have considerably enhanced the opportunities for improving customer care. But at the same time they have increased the risk of error. Large databases are never 100 per cent accurate. The direct marketing industry abounds with tales of poor addressing, the wrong pack being sent to the wrong type of customer and multiple letters arriving at the same address. Fears have also arisen among consumers about information gathered as the result of one transaction being misused to stimulate another.

Prompted by these developments, there have been major changes in the legislative framework of marketers who use data on individuals. The Data Protection Act 1984 is perhaps the most significant piece of legislation.

The Act states specifically that personal data should be:

(a) obtained and processed fairly and lawfully. This means that people who give data should know why they give it and should not be deceived into giving it
(b) held for one or more specified purposes. In other words, it is not legal to collect data without a specified purpose
(c) only disclosed for the purpose held. For example, data collected for the purposes of checking creditworthiness should not be disclosed for the purpose of marketing products. So if the intention is to use it for both, the individual from whom it is being collected should be told so at the time of collection
(d) adequate, relevant and not excessive. In other words, the company collecting the data should be able to justify every element of it in terms of improving its ability to meet customer needs

(e) accurate and updated. It is not enough to collect it and continue to use it, even if it becomes outdated. The company should ensure that it budgets for updating — often very expensive

(f) retained only as long as necessary for the stated purpose or purposes. Provided the company is using the data as a foundation for building a relationship with the customer, this should not pose a problem. But it would be illegal to collect the information, use it once, and then keep it in case it could be sold

(g) accessible to individuals at reasonable intervals and without undue delay or cost. It must also be corrected or erased as appropriate. A charge for access to personal data has been fixed by the Registrar

(h) appropriately secured against unauthorised access, alteration, disclosure or destruction and against accidental loss or destruction. These are commonsense provisions.

The Data Protection Registrar has already issued a number of rulings relating specifically to the use of personal data by the direct marketing industry. Guidance Note 19 (October 1988) requires computerised prospect lists to be compiled and used only with the prior notification (and consent) of data subjects on those lists. A company sending a mailshot to someone who has not given consent to receive it may be subject to criminal prosecution and a large fine. The effect is such as to end third party mailings to names selected from lists of catalogue buyers unless at the time of data collection the use is foreseen and explained.

A similar approach in Germany had a profound effect on the availability of lists. It reduced 2500 lists five years ago to only 250 lists today. Ironically, companies rent fewer lists, target less well and therefore produce *more* "junk mail" rather than less!

The German position on data protection contrasts sharply with the US experience. In the United States there are still no federal laws governing data protection although some states do have their own rules. The major piece of legislation remains the Privacy Act of 1974. But the Mail Preference Service, which dates from 1971, was lauded in the Privacy Protection Study Commission report. This service has provided consumers with an opportunity to be removed from (or added to) large numbers of mailing lists. Interestingly, three times more people have asked to have their names *added* than have asked to have their names *deleted* from lists!

The Mailing Preference Service

The aim of the MPS is to "promote with the general public the Direct Marketing Industry in the United Kingdom by providing facilities for the consumer to exercise a choice in regard to the receipt of direct mail". The emphasis is very much on encouraging the continued growth of direct mail by ensuring that customer alienation is minimised.

With the MPS, consumers may add their name to the register of those not wishing to receive unsolicited direct mail, free of charge. Many add their names in several different formats, according to the formats they are addressed by, so there are many duplicates on the list. The MPS is paid for by the subscribing companies, who include users, agencies, bureaux and list brokers. In order to maintain quality standards, many bureaux and list brokers are insisting that clients' lists going into deduplication are MPS-cleaned beforehand.

Financial services

The Financial Services Act 1986 was enacted to provide a fairer framework for the conduct of investment business. The Department of Trade and Industry delegated its regulatory powers to the SIB (Securities and Investments Board) which in turn established the SROs (Self Regulatory Organisations) to police the various branches of the investment industry. For marketers a key clause focuses on polarisation, which requires sellers to be either wholly independent intermediaries selling a range of products or to sell only the products of the parent institution to which they are tied. This requirement has increased the use of alternative channels of distribution, notably direct mail and telemarketing.

The Building Societies Act 1986 gives building societies much more freedom to behave as banks, competing more freely across a wide range of financial services. Again, this has given rise to more direct marketing activity as building societies build databases and cross-sell a wider range of services through different media.

The various privatisations of large state corporations led to massive lists of shareholders being created and then used as a prospecting list for further financial service marketing.

All these developments, and the prospect of more, means that organisations intending to deliver some of their customer care through the use of marketing databases need to be particularly careful to observe the law and, just as importantly, the growing number of guidance notes arriving from the Data Protection Registrar.

The role of marketing techniques

This chapter has focused mainly on the hard factors involved in delivery of customer care. But without the right elements of the marketing mix in place, and the right marketing techniques, few of the approaches described will work. These subjects are covered in the next two chapters.

Chapter 12

Branding, Products and Positioning

Integrated marketing through the brand

The elements of the marketing mix are not separate in their effect but build upon each other. Customer care is delivered through combinations of different elements of the mix and implementation procedures. The softer Ps of the mix, people, processes and presence, perform a vital role in the delivery of customer care.

The marketing mix must be determined according to the supplier's target market. In turn, a supplier's approach to market targeting and the marketing mix is determined by its marketing objectives and the conclusions it has reached through analysis of the market, as described in the earlier chapters of this book. The marketer's aim is to combine the mix so as to achieve the desired effect in the organisation's target market.

Focus and branding

The marketing concept which integrates the mix and makes the organisation's relationship with the consumer more coherent is *branding*. This is defined as the complete set of values which the customer derives from the supplier's offering. These values are created by the operation of the marketing mix on the customer's perceptions. The problem facing most suppliers is that it is not just the *current* marketing mix that matters. Customers have memories. Successful deployment of the marketing mix over a period of years leads to very strong and positive branding.

The brand is therefore an asset which remains valuable even after investment in creating it is reduced. A strong brand can survive weak marketing for a period. However, like any asset, a brand has a tendency to depreciate. This tendency is accelerated if the brand is poorly maintained. Investing in a brand usually requires:

(a) maintenance of the value added by the product range
(b) continual reinforcing of positive messages through promotion.

Well maintained brands have a value which can be measured. Owning a brand gives a supplier the opportunity to make more profit. Some companies therefore value their brands on their balance sheets.

Whatever a supplier's size, creating a brand is considered one of the best long term routes to survival and growth. But creating a brand is not easy. It may take years of hard work. From the point of view of suppliers with strong brands, branding is one of the most effective barriers to entry by new competitors. It is a psychological barrier in consumers' minds that makes them less willing to try other experiences. This barrier also makes them more willing to pay higher prices. A brand strongly associated with good customer care is an excellent barrier to competition.

Brand values

Branding a product is therefore not just a question of a particular set of product features. Nor is it created by a particular advertising campaign. It is something that exists in customers' minds. The supplier's aim is to get *brand values* associated with its *brand name*. This means that whenever the consumer sees the brand name, the values are recalled. When a brand name is strongly established, it makes it much easier for a supplier to get its promotional messages over. This is because when the consumer hears or sees the brand name, a positive frame of mind is created. The consumer is then more receptive to further messages.

Branding and the service experience

Branding is not created solely, or even principally, by promotion. In most service markets the most powerful weapon is experience of the service itself. This is because of the high degree of emotional involvement that consumers have with services, in most cases. In fact, if advertising makes branding claims which are not sustained by the *perceived* product experience, it is usually worse than if the claim had never been made. This is because expectations have been raised and then dashed. For this reason, suppliers wishing to establish strong branding must pay careful attention to *every* aspect of the service they provide. For example, the US General Electric advertising theme "We don't desert you after we deliver it" must be backed up by the kind of investment involved in the GE Answer Centre.

Determining brand values

The brand's values are sustained by the marketing mix. In making marketing policy, a supplier should:

(a) determine what set of values it wants its brand to have
(b) find out what set of values it actually has
(c) make plans to change the actual values to the required set.

Finding out what a brand's values are is done through market research. Usually, consumers are given a list of products, services or organisations, and asked what statements come to mind in relation to them. They may be prompted with suggested statements or asked to suggest their own. The list of products, services and suppliers will include close competitors, but also other products and services which the consumer might consume with the service in question or as substitutes for it. Also included might be other companies or products whose brand values the organisation in question might want to emulate or avoid (eg parallel suppliers).

The same type of research can also be used to establish what sort of values consumers would *like* to derive from a product or service. Here, it is not reliable to ask consumers directly what they would like to have.

This leads to the production of "wish-lists" — long lists of things that would be impossible to deliver. It is better to ask consumers what values they are experiencing through what they have already chosen. Reports on behaviour and the reasons for it are considered a more reliable guide than statements of desires.

Branding is supported by a variety of other concepts. These are discussed below.

Positioning

This is an important concept for translating desired brand values into promotional and packaging concepts. It describes how the brand should fit into its competitive market. Figure 12.1 shows how a positioning diagram demonstrates the relative strengths of different brands.

In such positioning analysis it is critical to focus on those aspects which consumers say are most important to them. The aim of positioning analysis is to determine the positioning that consumers want and move the product towards it.

Positioning is closely related to the *benefits* of the brand — what the customer will get out of buying it (see Chapter 2).

Brand proposition

In the world of advertising, benefits and values are often translated into the brand proposition. These are the words that express the values and benefits of the brand most succinctly. This is what the supplier wants to occur in customers' minds when they see, hear of or buy the brand.

Brand personality

This is a term that refers to the embodiment of the brand's values in personal attributes. It gives advertising agencies a great deal of help in determining how the product is to be presented.

Competitive presentation of customer care branding

One of the problems facing marketers of customer care is how to present the care they deliver in a way that stands out from competition. Customers are subject to so many influences that it is hard to make a

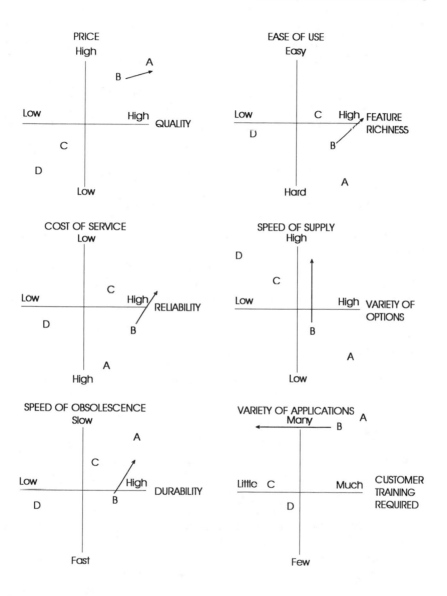

Figure 12.1 Positioning diagrams

These show positioning as revealed by market research. The arrows show where managers of product B would like to take it. Product A is the market leader, C and D are lower cost alternatives.

real difference stand out. The best way is of course the experience itself, but this assumes that the customer has already bought or experienced the service. It is hard to steer a course between:

(a) a simplistic claim that is just like the one every other supplier is making
(b) a complex claim, which lists every feature of care and service, and confuses the customer.

Figure 12.2 describes an analysis of the brochures that computer companies use to promote their customer service. It also draws some conclusions about how companies should present care in print.

This study of the presentation of customer service through brochures was undertaken especially for this book. The brochures of a large number of companies were obtained and analysed. Here, their characteristics and quality are summarised, with recommendations for any company trying to position complex customer care offerings through brochures.

Brand support

This refers to the features of the service and the promotional methods which support the branding. As was stressed above, the brand must be supported by both the service itself and the way it is promoted.

The big well-known national or international brands provide the best examples of branding as an asset. They include Coca Cola, Mars, Jaguar, Rolls Royce, IBM, Givenchy, Marks & Spencer and so on. In service markets, whether national or local, there is plenty of opportunity for the development of branding. Indeed, the more focused the marketing, the easier and cheaper it is to develop branding. In very large markets, finding the branding which stands out and making it stick in customers' minds, is an expensive business. This is because it is not cheap to create a service which appeals strongly to a large number of people and then promote it extensively.

Supplier and product brands

It is important to distinguish between company brands, which apply to an entire organisation, and product brands. The former are important

BULL
- Emphasis on the total approach of service: TOTALCARE
- Clear, simple and very comprehensive
- General information — Support Service for each item of equipment
- Several brochures
- Good quality print
- Restrained brochure, but with good use of colour
- Inspires confidence

CONTROL DATA
- Presentation: one brochure + several data sheets detailing each support package
- Clear and simple — very comprehensive
- More or less the same basic services as competitors
- Case studies as references (eg Volkswagen)
- The last page of the brochure is reserved for "customer comments"
- Picture of men and women working — "human faces" as opposed to IBM's image, which is robotic

DIGITAL EQUIPMENT
- Same system as Hewlett-Packard. Data sheets — practical
- Sometimes two separate brochures, eg DECsite
- More detailed, more complex, due to number of different programmes and agreements. Some services could have been summarised on one data sheet instead of several.
- Full service — inspires confidence
- Good quality print except some data sheets too thin

GRANADA
- Brochures general but good
- Very clear and well presented
- Good quality print and excellent colour photos
- Case-studies plus list of key customers

HEWLETT-PACKARD
- Several brochures; one for each service — very practical
- Clear documentation; always in "3 steps" — planning, implementation, operation
- Clear, concise positioning statements
- Simple and not too technical
- Very comprehensive
- Consistent emphasis on importance of planning and strategy, help in case of problem, education and training of future users/managers

Figure 12.2 Analysis of computer companies' customer service brochures

- Well illustrated and good quality print
- Use of case studies
- Inspires confidence because customer-oriented and full service, from planning and installation of computer systems to recovery service

IBM

- A total approach to service. IBM covers every service
- Several data sheets and brochures for each service, plus guide covering all IBM activities and services
- Good quality print, well organised
- Clear explanations through "highlights" at the end of each brochure
- Too much writing, print too small. To find out about IBM's services, too much reading is required
- Uniform writing and page-setting, not very clear, boring
- More complex than the competitors
- No examples or specification of precise, detailed agreements (eg different levels of support)

ICL

- Bound in one volume
- Very clear and organised (framed highlights, insistence on customer benefits, good page-setting)
- Comprehensive but not over-technical
- Inspires confidence. No description of detailed agreements but states the essential

PRIME SERVICE

- Style of writing not as "aggressive" as the competitors
- Simple description of the services offered
- No illustration except on the front page
- Restrained style, black and white

CONCLUSIONS

The most successfully presented services had these characteristics:
- Clear corporate image and branding coming through all brochures
- Clear general methodology applied to all services
- Service branding stated clearly in words
- Detail only when essential
- Use of case studies to bring offer alive and add human face
- A single brochure or page for each service
- Simple, clear layout, with use of graphics to steer customer through

Figure 12.2 Analysis of computer companies' customer service brochures contd.

where the buyer makes a separate decision on the organisation and the product. This is true in many markets, particularly mature ones.

Product policy

The aim of product policy is to determine:

(a) how the organisation's offer is going to be made to the customer, in terms of the "bundles" of features which make up products
(b) how these products are to be named and packaged.

Many elements of service products are customised to the needs of individual customers (sometimes on the spot). However, the main features within which this customisation takes place normally have to be specified in advance.

Dimensions of service

Service products are defined along a number of dimensions, such as:

(a) information exchanged during service delivery — what information is given to the customer and by the customer. This may include facts, advice and other help
(b) environment(s) within which the service is given
(c) relationship with staff giving the service. This covers aspects such as:
   (i)   the physical distance between customer and staff
   (ii)   separation by barriers
   (iii)   amount of time dedicated by the member of staff to each customer
   (iv)   the role of each member of staff
   (v)   the attitude of staff
(d) the range of different services offered. Customers generally like to have a choice. The service supplier has to compromise between the large range of choice that customers would like and the small range that can economically be provided
(e) degree of control by the customer over the service situation. In most mass service situations, customers feel that they are being processed

(f) consistency — whether the service meets or exceeds the required standard each time it is experienced. Note that the over-enthusiastic member of staff can be as much of a problem as the under-enthusiastic one. Giving too high a level of service may create expectations which cannot be fulfilled next time

(g) timing — how long the service takes, including waiting time

(h) cost of service — how much the customer pays and what other costs are entailed in using the service

(i) availability — whether the service is available at the time required

(j) quality — whether the service meets the specification. Although few suppliers deliberately supply services which do not meet the specification, many do not take enough steps to ensure that the services do (eg by training staff, securing the right facilities). This is tantamount to not offering services which meet the specification

The service product depends heavily on service delivery by people. In most cases, staff operate within a particular physical environment. Part of this environment is shared with customers. Therefore, much of the product policy process in some service industries focuses on the environment, the people and how they work together. The customer care element of the package can be treated in many respects as just a very important feature, offering opportunities of achieving quality through good design and standardisation like any other feature. However, it is clearly not a "stand alone" feature, as it affects the customer's perception of all other features and of the brand itself.

The design environment

The environment should be designed to handle customers so as to achieve two objectives:

(a) to create the right impression on customers

(b) to allow the efficient and cost-effective "processing" of customers through or in the service location.

In some cases the design of the environment is the main way of differentiating the service from other services offered by the same supplier (eg first class versus second class accommodation). In other cases the aim is to differentiate the total offering from competitive offerings. Here, the aim is often to ensure that customers are naturally pulled towards the service and enjoy it.

Design is one of the most important inputs that turns good marketing ideas into operational reality. Like many marketing inputs, it is often supplied to larger organisations by external consultancies. Many such inputs take the form of recommendations contained in reports. But design inputs are more "tactile" — they consist of designs for places. They share much in common with the copy of advertisements. In particular, they are subject to intervention by managers who understand little about them. However, with design, there is good reason for this. Many managers have worked their way up through the operating side of their organisations. They have an intuitive sense of what will work for customers. It is therefore vital to channel their input into the design process as early as possible. It is very wasteful to evolve a fully-fledged design concept and have it rejected at the last moment by experienced operators on the (correct) grounds that "it won't work".

Some would argue that the design of many service facilities is allowed to evolve, often without the right inputs from experienced managers. This leads to many poorly-designed facilities. On the other hand, if design were planned from the start, based on sound customer-oriented marketing principles, organisations could be sure that their designs really would meet customer needs.

Design suffers because it is one of the most easily manipulated elements in the service equation. If one design does not work, the temptation is to reject it out of hand and try another. But this ease of manipulation should not be an excuse for slackness of management.

Design covers a variety of different topics, as follows:

(a) *Space planning*

This includes quantifying the space requirement and then making the best use of the space available. In some cases, the amount of service to be provided is the target. This may be specified in terms of the number of customers to be served, frequency of service, timing of service, type and quality of service to be delivered and so on. Space has then to be bought and a design created for it in order to yield the right level of service. In other cases the space may be a constraint. In this case space planning is used to optimise the level of service, given the space constraint. In either case, note that using modern techniques of movable interiors, it is possible to vary space planning to meet the needs of different times of day, week, month and year.

(b) *Architecture.*
This covers the internal and external look of the facility and the structural support for it.

(c) *Graphics.*
This refers to the way colour and shape are used on the surfaces of the facility, to create different impressions.

(d) *Location.*
This mean the siting of the facility. Although this factor does not belong entirely to the design category, it may affect space planning, architecture and external graphics.

These four factors need to be combined to support the creation of successful service facility. The kind of characteristics which they can support include:

(a) Visual excitement — the creation of a sense of excitement, of anticipation of a different experience.

(b) Consumer appeal — drawing of customers into the facility by the strength of the concept that the facility represents, encouraging them to sample the different options available within the facility, creating a sense of regret when they leave and motivating them to return to benefit from its attractions again, and encouraging them to recommend the facility to others and (in consumer services) bring friends with them when they come next time.

(c) Quality — ensuring that the quality of the service provided by staff in the facility is supported by what the customers *see* and *feel* in the facility.

(d) Branding — conveying the brand values of the supplying organisation. The aim here is to ensure that customers perceive consistency between the communications they receive inviting them to come to the facility, the messages the staff give them (overtly or implicitly) while serving them, and the messages the physical environment gives them.

(e) Benefits — so that customers get from the facility what they wanted, in terms of the total experience, rather than a series of disjointed features.

(f) Durability — sustaining the appeal with the passing of time.

(g) Differentiation — here, the aim is to set the facility above its competitors, so that it is seen as not just better of the same kind, but of a different and better kind.

(h) Productivity — helping the supplier function more cost-effectively (eg design for maintainability, optimal space usage).

(i) Flexibility — the ability to alter different aspects of the facility to meet shorter and longer term changes in customer needs. In situations where customers' needs change frequently, there is a tendency to go for the lowest common denominator in design, rather than go for a design concept which allows frequent change.

All these kinds of characteristic are best supported if the design is properly planned in an integrated way. This means that every element of design should support the required characteristics.

The design environment has received considerable attention as companies with long pedigrees in product and retail outlet design (eg Fitch) have been invited by service companies to examine their offerings. This has produced considerable improvements in the way service outlets are designed. Of course, design is to some extent subject to fashion. So even if customer needs were unchanging (which is rarely true), design must to be reviewed every few years.

People

This involves recruiting, training and managing staff to deliver the service within their environment. Large companies in labour intensive service industries normally have well established recruitment and training procedures, to ensure that:

(a) staff are of the right quality
(b) they receive the right behavioural training (how to handle customers)
(c) they receive the right procedural training (how to carry out the role assigned to them)
(d) their performance is monitored
(e) they are rewarded for success in carrying out their roles and in handling customers well.

Smaller suppliers usually achieve the same effect by close team work, often based on family. A full analysis of how people factors affect customer care is given in Chapter 14.

251

Determining product specifications

The first step in determining what range of services are to be provided is to determine the target market and understand the needs of its customers. Only then is a supplier in a position to determine desired service specifications. Note the use of the word "desired". This is because there is a large leap between describing service specifications on paper and achieving them in practice. Beyond this is the very important step of ensuring that what is delivered still meets the customer requirements which justified the specification in the first place.

In some cases it may be possible to research service specifications before committing too much money to development. However, the unreliability of data on "wants" extends to this topic. Asking consumers how they would react to changes in service provision will not usually yield reliable data. If testing is a viable option, it should be used.

In cases where the change is more radical a different procedure might be required. Extensive market research will be needed to identify who the target customers are and what benefits they require. This might be followed by a full scale pilot of the concept before it is launched nationally.

Degree of newness of service

The approach to new service development depends partly on the degree of "newness" of a service. Is a new service simply a variant on an existing service, or does it satisfy a need that no other service has satisfied before? According to the answer to this, the service is likely to require very different approaches to development, testing and marketing. The degree of change to marketing policy required by a new service concept can often be determined using a very simple matrix (see Figure 12.3).

Of course, many ventures are not easily classifiable in this way; services may be partly new, markets may be extensions of existing markets. But the further down and to the right an organisation goes, the greater the change. The organisation has to put more effort into understanding the target market, developing concepts to meet the needs of customers and devising the marketing mix which will cause customers to buy.

	Existing customers	**New customers**
New product	• Ensure new product meets quality and performance standards of customers. • Monitor any new needs of customers satisfied by product. • Ensure rest of marketing mix supports new product. • Focus on monitoring customer feedback concerning new product.	BOTH OF THESE
Existing product	• Monitor and maintain product quality. • Monitor customer needs and satisfaction, to ensure product continues to meet needs and that customers are happy with relationship with supplier. • Adjust pricing, promotion, distribution and three Ps of customer care to maintain and strengthen competitive position.	• Identify customers. • Research and understand their needs. • Research and understand newly encountered competitors. • Put in place procedures to measure and monitor needs and behaviour of new customers. • Adjust pricing, promotion, distribution and three Ps of customer care to ensure new customers are happy with relationship with supplier.

Figure 12.3 New Product matrix — marketing and customer care implications

(NB The degree of newness of products or customers does not always change so abruptly. Products can proliferate into variants. Customer targeting may add customers, many of whom are very similar to existing customers.)

Service evaluation

There are two main ways of evaluating new services. The first is financial evaluation, when the anticipated financial flows related to the new service (development costs, construction, materials, staffing, distribution, revenues, cash flow, etc) are analysed to determine the rate of return or payback period. This is likely to be used where an organisation has a great deal of experience with the market and where the performance of services is highly predictable.

The other approach is factor weighting. This involves listing the factors considered important for success, weighting them by their relative importance, giving each service concept a score for how it rates against each factor, multiplying the scores by the weights and totalling the result. This approach tends to be used in more uncertain situations, where markets are less forecastable. Typical factors included in the evaluation list include:

(a) estimate of financial return
(b) fit with the existing operations situation (ie could the new service be operated on a day to day basis without prejudicing the delivery of other services?)
(c) fit with marketing skills and strategy (including SW/OT analysis against market conditions, fit with target market, extent to which it meets customer needs)
(d) fit with management skills and resources.

Figure 12.4 gives an example of the use of this evaluation approach.

In many cases, evaluation is undertaken to decide not whether a change in service policy should take place, but *what* that change should be. Evaluation against existing resources and skills is undertaken partly to identify whether additional resources or skills should be brought in. The financial implications of this should be built into the financial evaluation. Management time and effort involved in making the new resources productive should be included under management skills and resources.

The more basic message of this chapter is that new services should be launched as part of the rational process of business development. The decision to develop and market a new service should be based on:

(a) a clear statement of the supplier's branding

| Factor | Weight | Service A | | Service B | |
		Score (out of 10)	Weighted score	Score (out of 10)	Weighted score
Return on capital	0.4	8	3.20	7	2.80
Distribution channel fit	0.05	7	0.35	9	0.45
Fit with supplier brand	0.05	9	0.45	9	0.45
Support to existing products	0.05	8	0.40	9	0.45
Match to customer buying patterns	0.15	9	1.35	9	1.35
Advantage over competitive services	0.15	10	1.50	8	1.20
Match to supplier human resources	0.1	6	0.60	8	0.80
Similarity of operating procedures to existing services	0.05	7	0.35	9	0.45
TOTAL			8.2		7.95

Figure 12.4 Weighted evaluation of two services

Note that the weights add up to 1 and the scoring is out of 10. This makes it easy to compare the final score with a key factor (eg return on capital). The factors listed are those which the supplier has found to be critical in the success of past service launches.

(b) a good understanding of the resource requirements of the change
(c) a good understanding of customer needs and how the new service will meet them
(d) a properly planned procedure for developing and launching the new service
(e) full integration of the product with the rest of the marketing mix.

The marketing mix — a reminder

In examining the marketing mix for a particular product, service or supplier, remember that no element of the marketing mix is independent of other elements and the whole marketing mix is tightly connected to market targeting and strategy. Investing time in developing sound strategy and targeting usually pays great dividends in the long run. However, it is also necessary to deliver that branding through appropriate and efficient marketing techniques which sustain and improve customer care; this is the subject of the next chapter.

Chapter 13

Techniques of Selling and Marketing

Suppliers reach their customers in many ways — retail outlets, direct marketing, a calling sales force and so on. Most ways of getting to customers require a professional approach to marketing and sales. In this chapter some of the concepts are described and their implications for customer care identified.

These concepts are:

(a) account management
(b) selling
(c) channels of distribution and communication
(d) database marketing
(e) telemarketing.

Account management

A young, fast growing supplier usually focuses on increasing its customer base as quickly as possible. If it has a direct sales force, it tries to get sales staff to contact as many good prospects as possible. Prospecting, finding new customers, is the major focus of sales activity. Caring for existing customers tends to be a low priority, as there are few of them.

As the supplier grows it may reach a situation where most of its business comes from customers who have already bought from it or are using its services. The number of products and services offered by the supplier may increase to meet customer needs. Managing customers becomes a complex business. They have many needs and the supplier has many products to meet them. In industrial markets the responsibility for buying, recommending or using products may be spread very widely in the customer organisation. Competitors will complicate the situation.

When this situation is reached companies often appoint account managers to look after some of their customers. The role of account managers differs between customers. Account managers' job descriptions might include the following elements.

(a) Manage the commercial dialogue with the customer and resulting transactions.

(b) Act as the main interface between supplier and customer. In many suppliers the account manager has principal responsibility for the sales interface but may work with other sales staff (eg specialists). The account manager may also have general responsibility for service, support, customer administration (eg invoices) and any other function that comes into direct contact with the customer.

(c) Identify all relevant customer needs (now and in the future). This covers which products and services are needed, what they are used for, the benefits that are obtained from using them and so on.

(d) Understand the business situation and organisation of the customer and how they influence the customer's need for products and services, and ability to pay for them!

(e) Understand the process by which the customer decides to buy relevant products and services (budgeting, decision making, etc).

(f) Become part of the process and act as a consultant to customers. This includes helping them deal with problems and capture new opportunities through using the supplier's products and services.

(g) Present the benefits for the customer of doing business with the supplier.
(h) Identify competitive threats to the supplier's position within the account.
(i) Provide information about the customer to the rest of the organisation.
(j) Provide the customer with information and with a channel for influencing the supplier.

And, by all the above, to maximise customer satisfaction, sales and profitability.

The account manager must be the supplier's representative to the customer and the customer's representative to the supplier. A good account management system has the effect of tying the customer and supplier closely together. It does this by ensuring that both derive great benefit from their relationship.

The depth of the relationship varies with:

(a) *The degree of market maturity*
As customers learn more about the product or service and how to use it, they may require the services of the account manager less. They develop the ability to act as their own consultants. However, if customer needs, applications and product or service technologies are evolving fast, the account manager continues to provide a useful service by educating and supporting the customer.

(b) *The type of product or service*
The more essential the product or service is to the customer's own business, the greater the potential for a close relationship and the greater the desire of the customer for such a relationship.

(c) *The level of potential business in each customer*
If it is very small, then the supplier may find it uneconomical to invest in developing a close relationship. However, by using telemarketing and other direct marketing techniques and carefully planning the contact frequency, a supplier can extend the principle of account management a long way down the market.

(d) *The range of needs to be covered*
Simple needs met by a few products and services do not need deep relationships. Complex needs and great product and service variety do!

The account managing "type"

Many types of people succeed in account management. Some are very aggressive individuals who command customers' respect through the ability to manage complex sales and implement projects authoritatively. Some are the "softly softly" type. They are strong on listening skills and expert at getting customers to devise their own solutions — using the supplier's products and services. But not all customers expect the same approach. Nor do all users of the account management approach require the same style. If anything is certain, it is that the really good account manager deploys many skills differently according to the type of customer and selling task, the stage of evolution of the market and customer needs, and the type of product or service.

What sort of abilities and skills does the account manager need? Here is a list of those generally felt to be necessary:

(a) Skills of questioning and listening, so as to build up a picture of the customer's needs. So are skills of sorting out relevant information.

(b) Analytical skills — the ability to make sense of customer information, and to put it together with information about company products and services to identify opportunities.

(c) Product knowledge — not necessarily in technical terms, but in terms that make sense to the customer.

(d) The ability to express what the company offers (its products, support, commitment, etc) in terms of benefits to customers, not just features and functions. Benefits express how a product meets a customer's needs, in the language the customer has used to define these needs. Benefits are the answer to the question the customer asks — "What will it do for me?".

(e) The ability to devise relevant options, so that the customers consider they have a real choice, and to match them to different benefits.

(f) Negotiating and influencing skills — knowing how to win people's hearts and minds, when to give and when to take, and the ability to handle problems and objections.

(g) A steady and strong activity rate combined with diligence and determination. This does not necessarily mean calling many customers, as they may not be good prospects. It does mean working hard and preparing thoroughly so that every call is an effective one. It also means maintaining a frequency of contact with the customer that the customer perceives to be right. It means determining call objectives and pursuing them thoroughly. However, the smaller the customers are, and the lower their average potential, the higher the calling rate required.

(h) Self-management skills — presentation, time management, organisation of information, etc.

(i) Consultative skills, which include the ability to see things from the customer's point of view, to identify tasks that need to be done, to recommend how they should be done, and how to use the supplier's products and services to ensure that they will be done. This is "solution selling". It forms a particularly important part of account defence. Consultative skills are used to show customers how their business problems can be solved by the supplier's products and services. Promotional material that customers receive should focus on benefits, not features, and provide account managers with keys to improve their consultative selling performance.

(j) The ability to foresee problems that might arise, before or after the sale and neutralise them.

(k) The ability to handle rejection positively.

It should be clear from this description of the role and skills of the account manager that in situations where a customer is in close contact with the supplier, account management is almost a necessary condition for customer care. Without it, there is high potential for failure to orchestrate the relationship between the customer and the supplier in such a way as to meet customer needs. Figure 13.1 summarises the relationship between the account manager and the customer and highlights the customer care opportunities provided by account management.

Selling

Selling is an integral part of marketing. It is defined as how a company:

(a) targets individual customers

261

Task	Opportunity
Diagnosis of needs	Prioritising needs. Making unexpressed needs explicit. Resolving conflicts of needs. Unearthing unidentified needs.
Analysis of buying process	Identifying all relevant users, influencers, advisors, etc. Identifying and managing conflicting forces. Ensuring supplier is ready to meet needs of different people in buying centre.
Consulting with customer	Summarising customer's total requirement in relation to customer care. Putting together proposals which cover whole relationship with customer. Advising different members of buying centre as to how their needs can best be met.
Identifying and presenting benefits to customer	Matching benefits to needs (product, service, control). Ensuring all elements of package meet customer needs.
Orchestrating supplier's policies	Ensuring locus of control is where it should be. Where necessary, intervening in management of service episodes.
Providing customer with channel to influence supplier	Gathering feedback on supplier performance. Showing customer round the supplier's organisation. Keeping customer informed about what is being done with feedback.

Figure 13.1 Example of how account management opens up customer care opportunities

(b) identifies their needs

(c) motivates them to buy standard or customised versions of products and services that have been designed to meet the needs of the market of which they are part.

Marketing cannot succeed without selling and selling has a hard time without marketing. The sales process is usually described as multi-stage. The simplest model is a three-stage one, as follows:

(a) *Identifying suspects*

Finding out which people or businesses seem most likely to want the supplier's products and services. If prospects are not identified or the supplier's market coverage is weak, the door to competition is opened. However mature the market, the supplier may still need to identify opportunities to turn its existing clients into customers for its newer products.

(b) *Identifying prospects*

By qualifying suspects according to factors such as the intensity of their need, timing of likely purchase, presence of competitive threat, availability of budget and so on.

(c) *Turning prospects into customers*

By proposing products and services to customers in a form which meets their needs, by giving them real options from which to choose, by negotiating, handling objections and closing the sale, and by managing the process after the sale. These are the real "sharp-end" sales skills, possession of which quickly sorts out the wheat from the chaff.

An account manager usually has a defined group of customers, but still has to identify which of them are good prospects. In other words, even account managers have to go through the full sales cycle.

Just as there is no such thing as a perfect account manager, there is no such thing as a perfect salesperson. The skills required for a good salesperson are similar to those required for account management. Typically, the new business representative, responsible for opening new accounts, needs to be high on activity and time management skills. He or she needs the activity rate of a new business salesperson combined with the skills of the account manager.

Figure 13.2 summarises the idea of the sales cycle and the customer care opportunities that occur during it.

Status	Customer care opportunities
Suspects	Encourage suspects to get closer to supplier. Provide information to help suspects get closer. If appropriate, help customer control sales process. Identify aspects of relationship which are particularly important. Keep in touch with customer.
Prospects	Identify relationship needs in detail (product benefits, control, service episode management, communication, etc). Build package to meet relationship needs. Negotiate deal which satisfies customer and supplier which is deliverable and sustainable.
Customers	Keep listening to customers, to get quick notice of changes in needs or problems in relationship. Identify additional areas for satisfying customer needs. Provide feedback to supplier to ensure customer needs continue to be met.

Figure 13.2 Customer care opportunities within the sales cycle — some examples

Channels of distribution and of communication

One symptom of increased customer orientation is the highlighting of how a company manages and communicates with its customers. One aspect of this is the channel through which it deals with those customers. This may be a direct sales force, a distributor, dealer or agent, a sales office, telemarketing unit, or a retail outlet.

Formally defined, a *channel of distribution* is the method a company uses to get its products and services to customers and to manage relationships with them before and after the sale.

Channels can be defined *physically*. This covers:

(a) the way a product is transported to a customer, perhaps via a third party

(b) how the product is stored while it is waiting to be bought

(c) how the customer comes in physical contact with the supplier.

Channels can also be defined *commercially*. This relates more to the business process at work and covers:

(a) how customers are identified or how they identify themselves

(b) how they come into commercial contact with the supplier

(c) how transactions take place

(d) how they are completed

(e) how customers are managed after the sale

and so forth.

Suppliers use different channels of distribution to manage different sizes and types of customer. In some cases it may be the type rather than size of customer that is important. For example, some companies use channels which are specialised in the needs of particular industry sectors. However, in all cases, the type of channel chosen should be closely supported by the marketing communications policy.

Figure 13.3 summarises the functions of channels of distribution and highlights opportunities for enhanced delivery of customer care through distribution channel management.

A *channel of communication* is closely related to a channel of distribution, but is not the same. It is a combination of:

(a) the means used to get information about the supplier and its products and services to its customers

(b) the means used to receive information about what customers' needs are and how customers would like to be dealt with.

The main challenges in communication channel management are:

(a) what mix of communications media to use (eg television, radio and press advertising, direct mail, business centres, exhibitions, seminars, etc)

(b) who the supplier should be communicating with (two-way)

(c) what messages to send via these channels (eg about individual products, or about ranges of products and services that meet identified needs)

(d) how often to send these messages

Function	Opportunity
Identifying customer needs	Staying close to customers — even observing them. Monitoring customer buying patterns. Taking customer suggestions.
Providing information on needs to supplier	Collating customer information. Following through to ensure satisfactory supplier response.
Receiving product, displaying it or making service available	Providing customer-oriented display/service facilities allowing customer required degree of control. Ensuring that people, processes and presence are in tune with customer needs.
Making the sale	Setting terms and conditions (including delivery and credit) which meet customer needs. Effective and non-bureaucratic sales process.
Taking payment	Quick and friendly processing. Variety of credit terms.
Handling returns / complaints	Customer orientation, not bureaucratic, in processing. Friendly management of customer during process.
After-sales service	Staying close to customer to monitor needs. Providing variety of cost-effective service options. Managing transition from sales to service smoothly.

Figure 13.3 Distribution channels — functions and customer care opportunities

(e) what information should be received from customers via these channels
(f) how to ensure that the different messages do not clash but are consistent with each other and properly sequenced
(g) how to co-ordinate the different channels of communication so as to support distribution channels in their work. Several channels may be used to influence a particular kind of customer, each channel playing a specific role at particular stages in the "contact strategy"
(h) how to ensure that the supplier's overall brand is properly developed and supported, while promotions for products and services are as effective as possible
(i) how to do all this cost-effectively.

Figure 13.4 shows communication relationships between customer and supplier and how communication can enhance customer care.

Database marketing

Database marketing is an interactive approach to marketing. It uses computer technology and a process-oriented view of marketing management to extend professional marketing into managing direct relationships between a supplier and a large number of customers. It uses individually addressable communications media (such as mail, telephone and the sales force) to:

(a) extend help to a supplier's target audience
(b) stimulate their demand
(c) stay close to them by recording and keeping an electronic database memory of customer, prospect and all communication and commercial contacts
(d) help improve all future contacts
(e) ensure realistic planning of all marketing.

The central idea of database marketing is to ensure that a supplier is driven by customers' needs. This is the opposite of much selling, where customers are driven by the supplier's need to sell them products. But to be driven by individual customer needs, a supplier must know who its customers are and establish direct communication with them.

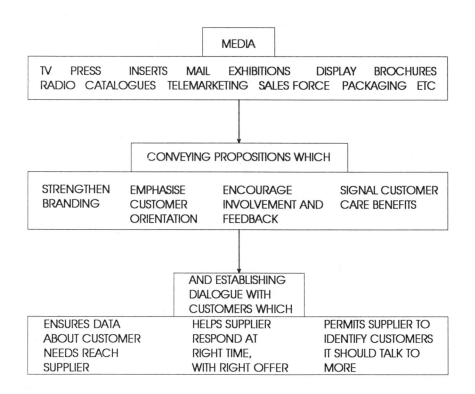

Figure 13.4 Customer communication and customer care

This diagram stresses that, for customer care to benefit from marketing communication, the latter should be managed in an integrated way, to deliver propositions which support customer care and encourage dialogue with customers.

The dialogue with customers

Database marketing improves the relationship with customers and prospects by:

(a) reaching them
(b) informing them
(c) conditioning them
(d) selling to them
(e) listening to them
(f) helping them communicate back.

A good marketing plan will normally contain a number of plans for communicating with customers, each constituting one or more campaigns. A campaign consists of a period of structured communication. During a campaign a customer receives one or more communications and responds to them. The end result, usually a sale, is achieved. After a time, when all expected responses are in, the campaign is closed.

However, the relationship with customers should not just be a series of campaigns, not connected with each other and interrupted by long periods of silence. Suppliers should talk to customers not only when they want to sell them something. This would reduce the chance of selling to them. It would also ensure that customers are not very satisfied with them.

The relationship with customers should be a true relationship. In this relationship, a supplier should manage customers to achieve mutual benefit and satisfaction. The campaign is just a tool to focus communications effort. This includes media advertising, direct marketing, public relations, exhibitions and sales force visits.

From a database marketing perspective, the dialogue with customers must be seen as a continuous series of campaigns which form a relationship. Campaigns aimed at selling particular products and services start with identification or confirmation of customer needs. They end with a series of contacts which yield profit for the supplier and satisfaction for customers. Every distribution and communications channel plays a key role in this. Each channel used in a campaign should move customers closer to the purchasing decision. Each should also yield information to help handle the customer better.

Information from customers

Database marketing depends on the collection, maintenance and regular use of information about customers. In database marketing, the response sought from customers at each stage of the relationship varies. It may be a move to the next stage in the sales cycle. Responses sought at different stages include:

(a) placing an order
(b) information enabling qualification of a respondent as a prospect
(c) commitment to an appointment with sales staff
(d) commitment to attendance at an exhibition, showroom or a sales seminar
(e) assurance that a prospect has received all relevant information about a product or service. This enables the sales person to concentrate on selling
(f) indication of a favourable disposition to buy
(g) acknowledgement of receipt and acceptance of messages which deliver branding information or support.

Customers benefit from a well planned sales dialogue with a supplier because:

(a) they have the information they need to take decisions
(b) their problems may be solved before they occur
(c) they can make buying decisions with the confidence that they have obtained the right information and developed a good relationship with the supplier, which will ensure that the purchase goes smoothly.

Data quality

Database marketing requires high quality information about customers. This information may have been collated from other company databases — sales order entry, customer service, sales people's files, responses to marketing campaigns, etc.

The database must support tracking of contacts with customers and allow campaign modelling. It should be the *sole* marketing database. It should contain information (provided by *all* marketing and sales groups) about customers, the types of marketing action taken with them and how they have responded. This is critical in managing relationships with customers proactively.

A proper customer marketing database also allows marketing staff to assess the effectiveness of previous campaigns and to target future ones more accurately. The more the customer database is used, with customer information and dialogue information being keyed back into the system, the more accurate the data becomes. The more accurate the data, the more able are the sales and marketing teams to address relevant sales and marketing activities to the customers (right time, right offer, right place). If this happens, the more the system will be used . . . and so on. This should result in better, more lasting business between customers and suppliers.

Some suppliers use several different distribution channels to manage customers. In this case, the marketing database may be fed by a variety of operational systems used by different channels to run their daily activities. But the feed must be frequent (ideally on-line or at least over-night processing). A modular approach to operational systems ensures that operational integrity is not compromised by marketing needs.

The idea of the *contact strategy* is used to manage the customer relationship. A contact strategy is a particular set of steps used in handling a customer. It starts with the initial contact and goes through to the conclusion of the particular phase in the dialogue, when the customer has either agreed to meet the supplier's objective (eg a purchase) or decided not to.

Different contact strategies are used to manage customers through to the sale (eg a letter followed by a telephone call, or a telephone call followed by a sales visit). Contact strategies are formalised, by having well prepared options to deal with different turns which the dialogue with customers might take, to produce:

(a) clearer options for customers. For example, not "Do you want more information?" but "May I send you our brochure?" or "Would you like our salesman to call or to come to our next sales seminar on topic X?"
(b) economies of scale — eg standard brochure or sales seminar where a dialogue with several customers can be conducted at once
(c) control over the company's next step (eg if there is a standard brochure or regularly scheduled seminars, the process of informing the customer can be handled fairly automatically).

The campaign process

The elements of campaign design are usually summarised as:

(a) targeting
(b) timing
(c) the offer
(d) creative.

"Targeting" relates to who is contacted. Even the best designed campaign will yield bad results if it is aimed at the wrong customers. "Timing" relates to when the customer is contacted. This can reduce customer satisfaction if it ignores the customer's buying cycles (eg replacement demand, business expansion or moving, seasonality or personal availability — freedom to take a call). Targeting and timing, taken together, are "customer-side" variables. They relate to the ability to identify the market.

The "offer" is the product or products being promoted to the customer together with the packaging of the product and incentives to buy. These elements are combined into an overall offering designed to meet customer needs. The offer is a critical factor in encouraging the customer to buy. Sending the wrong offer can be extremely alienating. The "creative" is the way in which the offer is expressed, eg the telemarketing script or the copy of the letter and brochure. The offer and the creative, taken together, are "supplier-side" variables. They relate to ability to put together the right package for the market.

Campaigns are in a sense temporary phenomena. They can conflict with the ideology of a permanent approach to customer care. However, if campaigns are blended together carefully, so that they are seen as a continuing process of finding new ways of meeting customer needs and caring for customers, they can be a powerful addition to the armoury of customer care. Figure 13.5 shows an approach to achieving this.

Enquiry management

The ability to respond to customer needs at the time they are expressed is called *enquiry management*. When customers enquire about a product, their interest in it is usually more than transitory. The interest will not disappear if the response takes time. But the customer may be making similar enquiries of competitors. If the response is quick

Campaign no.	Media	Objectives
1	TV	Create and reinforce awareness of customer service aspect of product.
	Press	Show practical benefits of high care levels through case studies.
2	Mail	Promote enhanced service levels.
	Telemarket	Identify unmet care needs and follow up mail responses.
3	Sales forces	Sell enhanced service contracts.
	Customer service staff	Draw attention of customers to enhanced service contracts.
4	Telemarket	Follow up leads from customer service staff.

Figure 13.5 Communication campaign

This shows how a supplier of office equipment to small businesses might use a sequence of campaigns to promote contracts embodying higher levels of care.

and appropriate, a company stands a better chance of making the sale.

Fulfilment

The term fulfilment refers to the process by which the enquiry is managed to the point where the customer is satisfied with the conclusion. Fulfilment may consist of a number of further steps. These include sales visits, telephone calls, invitations to a showroom, sales seminars or exhibitions, or an order for the product. There are many different routes an enquiry can take.

Testing

To get the best response, different approaches are tested. Because database marketing techniques allow quantification of the results of every campaign, testing provides a low cost way of getting the details of the campaign right and maximising customer care.

Targeting

The ability to manage dialogue with customers depends on two kinds of targeting:

(a) *market targeting* — identifying the kinds of need which the supplier can satisfy
(b) *individual targeting* — selecting individual customers who have these needs.

Good targeting depends on the information on the database being high quality and on using the right criteria for selecting customers for a campaign. When the database is used to select customers for a campaign, a target customer profile is defined. This indicates the kind of customer the supplier wants to attract with the campaign. It gives criteria by which to select customers from the database. Selection is facilitated by the ability to control the target precisely. Controlling selection criteria enables the supplier to test the responses of different types of customer to different approaches.

Management disciplines

All database marketing activities require tightly controlled, systematic measurement and management. Database marketing is often justified by its accountability. It can genuinely claim to know when a campaign is cost-effective, because all inputs and outputs are measured. It can also be used to match information on marketing performance and on customer needs and satisfaction. Figure 13.6 summarises the database marketing approach. Figure 13.7 shows how it can contribute to enhanced customer care.

Telemarketing

What is telemarketing?

Telemarketing involves using the telephone as a properly managed part of the marketing, sales and service mix. It differs from telephone selling, which is aimed at getting sales over the telephone. Teleselling is usually used as a stand-alone strategy rather than an integrated element of the marketing mix. In business-to-business marketing, telemarketing has been used for many years. In consumer marketing teleselling is still very common, but telemarketing is beginning to be adopted.

Many businesses and consumers find teleselling a nuisance. Consumers have a ready set of excuses to deal with poorly targeted calls: "I've got one already" or "We had it done last year" must be the commonest. In business, such calls are often barred by secretaries, acting on their manager's instructions.

Telemarketing is a discipline in the full sense of the word. It involves use of telecommunications equipment and networks by highly trained staff. Their aim is to achieve marketing objectives by carrying out a controlled dialogue with customers who need the benefits provided by the supplier. In so doing, they are supported by systems which allow the company to manage the workflow, measure it and follow through the outcome of the dialogue.

Telemarketing requires systematic management, measurement and control of every aspect of its operation. Without this, the relationship between the inputs and outputs of a telemarketing operation will not be known. This information is essential for effectiveness.

Customers find the telephone one of the best ways of conducting their relationship with their suppliers because:

(a) *It saves their time.*
    They do not have to handle the formality of a sales visit or travel to see the product.
(b) *It allows them to feel they control the relationship.*
    They can say when it is convenient to call and call their suppliers when convenient to them. They can terminate the call when they want.
(c) *It gives them information when they need it.*
    They may find it frustrating to wait for information to come in the post or during a field sales visit. They can call and the supplier can respond immediately or quite soon after.
(d) *It gives them a direct dialogue with their supplier.*
    This gives them confidence in the relationship.

Key concepts in telemarketing

Telemarketing is best employed as an aspect of database marketing. A key principle of database marketing is the need to be in constant dialogue with customers. This ensures that their needs are being met

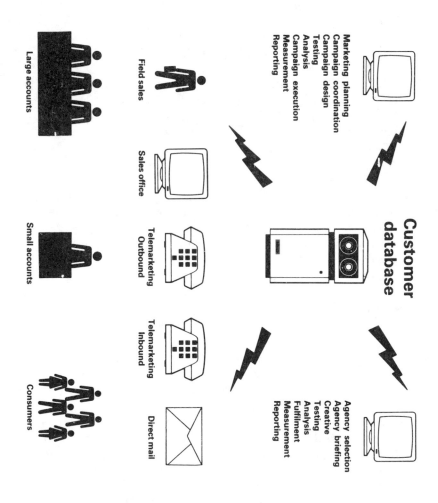

Figure 13.6 The database marketing approach

Reproduced by permission of Gower Publishing Group (from *Database Marketing* by Merlin Stone and Robert Shaw)

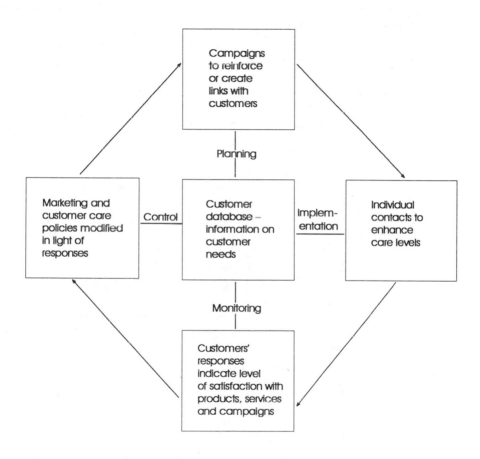

Figure 13.7 Database marketing and customer care

and that the information on the database is kept fresh. In a dialogue information flows both ways. This dialogue lasts as long as the customer stays with the supplier. It will consist of a series of "conversations", conducted over the telephone. Letters, brochures and other material confirm or add to what is said. A sales visit or visit to a showroom takes place where necessary.

Telemarketing in context

Telemarketing helps achieve many objectives. They may be fundamental "coal face" objectives (ie what particular "customer facing" staff should do with individual customers). Or they may be higher level, more strategic objectives. Here are some examples:

1   *"Coal face" objectives* may include:
    (a)   Progressing the relationship with the customer
          (i)   *Call handling*
                Answering customer calls on any matter, whether enquiries about products, requests for service, handling complaints or problems.
          (ii) *Moving towards a sale*
                Lead generation, appointment creation, order taking, seeking or closing, selling up or cross-selling, converting non-sales related inbound or outbound calls into sales opportunities.
          (iii) *Cold calling*
                Normally as part of a campaign.
          (iv) *Building loyalty*
                By meeting needs and by just listening and remaining in contact.
    (b)   Obtaining or providing information
          (i)   *Enquiry screening*
                Obtaining information to confirm whether a customer is a prospect for a product or how serious a particular prospect is.
          (ii) *Customer and market research*
                Gathering information to use in making business decisions. This includes screening of lists of customers or prospects to be used in particular marketing campaigns.
          (iii) *Delivering customised advice*

2. More strategic objectives may include:
   (a) *Account management*
       Improving the quality of account management so that certain groups of customers benefit from a better relationship with the supplier. This may include finding new purchasers within existing accounts, preventing competitive inroads into customers and reactivating lapsed customers.
   (b) *New business*
       Identifying and developing new customers and new markets, extending coverage of existing markets or launching a new product or service.
   (c) *Quality*
       Improving the effectiveness, professionalism and economics of the sales force and other channels.
   (d) *Customer care*
       Improving customer service and satisfaction.

Figure 13.8 summarises the telemarketing approach, while Figure 13.9 shows how it can enhance customer care.

Summary

Here is a summary of how the ideas covered in this chapter can enhance customer care:

(a) Account management provides the key to customer care for individual customers in the sales relationship.
(b) Channels of distribution and communication require the customer care dimension to be catered for right through the channel.
(c) The wrong sales approach to the wrong customer can be very damaging to customer satisfaction. The first job is to get the customer on board.
(d) Database marketing is the key to customer care at high volumes.
(e) Campaigns require tight management but can deliver increased standards of customer care.
(f) Telemarketing provides a highly effective way of personally managing customer care for large numbers of customers.

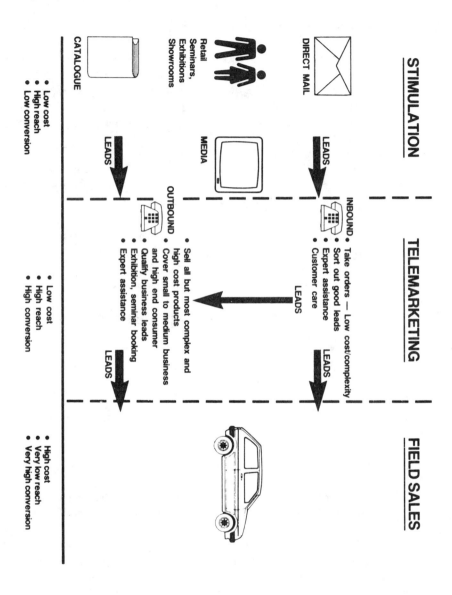

Figure 13.8 How telemarketing works

Reproduced by permission of Gower Publishing Group (from *Database Marketing* by Merlin Stone and Robert Shaw)

Telemarketing task	Customer care benefit
Call handling	Provision of information. Reassurance. Complaint handling.
Enquiry handling and order taking	Ensuring customer needs are met.
Customer research	Identifying customer needs.
List cleaning / research	Ensuring correct customers are targeted.
Lead generation	Ensuring customer is managed through correct channel, and that handling is professional.
Cross-selling	Meeting customer needs more completely.
Servicing marginal accounts	Preventing customer neglect.
Order progress chasing	Ensuring that customer follows correct procedures (script).
Account management	Cost-effective way of giving customer benefits of account management.
After-sales follow-up	Ensuring that customer remains satisfied.

Figure 13.9 Telemarketing and customer care

Chapter 14

Customer Care Through People

Customer care is about getting the right people, motivating and training them well, putting them in the right situation (organisation structure, systems, etc) so that they can manage customers well. Even if the contact with the customer is not face to face, but by letter, telephone or through a machine, people still have an important influence. In the case of machine contact (eg an automated teller machine in a bank), the influence of people comes through in the design of the interface and the messages that are displayed on the screen.

The hidden potential

Despite the great importance of people in caring for customers, most organisations, particularly larger ones, seem to do their very best to *restrain* their staff from helping customers. Outside work hours many people have responsibilities which are much greater than those they are permitted to exercise at work. Irrespective of their backgrounds and education, people can be found outside work hours in duties which involve dealing with people, often in difficult situations. These include:

(a) running a household (the family, the property, etc)
(b) running a charity
(c) being a sportsman
(d) coaching or managing sporting teams
(e) performing (acting, playing, singing)
(f) producing or directing performances
(g) being school governors
(h) renting property
(i) owning a part-time business or helping their spouse with their business.

Managers are very often surprised to find that staff whom they have treated as being incapable of exercising responsibility have these kinds of background. What is more, managers often ignore evidence of this under their own eyes. When a crisis occurs inside the organisation, people usually rally round in ways that are considered quite exceptional. The phrase commonly used is "the Dunkirk spirit". When the crisis is over, people sink back into their unmotivating regime. Their well-practised skills in handling people are no longer used or trusted. This is often what lies behind the belief of many staff that they care for customers more than managers do.

Restrictive roles

In some respects, senior managers of large organisations are *afraid* of their own staff. They manage them according to an outdated interpretation of the military model. According to this model, each person is only capable of and asked to do certain tasks and no others. One reason for this is that suppliers which employ large numbers of staff tend to take rather a technical approach. They focus on ensuring that staff are recruited, graded and paid correctly, and work within the right organisation structure. What staff actually do day to day is often left to the line manager, who tends to have a rather strong task orientation.

System maintenance

In this situation, senior management tend to focus on maintaining the system and achieving the prime objective (usually profit). They also expect staff to focus on this system maintenance objective. This situation used to be particularly common in labour intensive service operations such as retailing, hotels and transport. Fortunately, realisation that staff deal with customers as well as maintain systems has now dawned. The management approach is changing.

Most managers now realise that asking staff who deal with customers to focus entirely on system maintenance will lead to customers being highly dissatisfied. The end result will be a vicious circle, as shown in Figure 14.1. This will apply even if staff are highly motivated by their task of system maintenance. Their positive feelings as they force customers to stick to difficult procedures are unlikely to be matched by positive feelings on the part of customers. A balance between customer needs and system maintenance must therefore be struck. Without this balance, staff will feel highly frustrated, lack confidence in their organisation and experience role stress. This requires managers who are service enthusiasts rather than service bureaucrats. They can create a virtuous circle of customer care, as shown in Figure 14.1.

Empowering staff

As has been shown, staff who manage customers are usually capable of much more than they are asked to do. That is why policies which empower staff to give customers better care work so well. It is also why giving the responsibility for improving quality to those who do the work seems to produce the best results. On the other hand, if staff are not given responsibility commensurate with their ability, their attitude towards customers may become negative. This will be communicated to customers, usually unconsciously. It is therefore much better to take an optimistic, even aggressive, view of staff's role in dealing with customers.

This is not an argument for radical change in the way large suppliers ask their staff to manage customers. People seem to rise best to progressive challenges. Asking staff to find ways to make radical improvements quickly may destabilise them and wreck their confidence. Staff need to learn what works and what does not by experience. They may also need some training to help them.

If this approach is taken, staff can take on more, and more can be taken on with existing staff. The latter is important, as people cost money.

The cost of people

In most western economies, people are becoming more expensive.

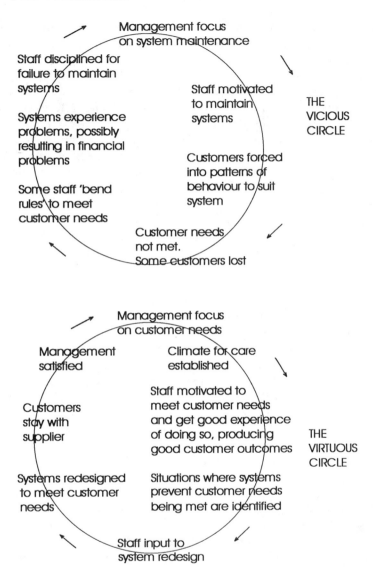

Figure 14.1 Circles of customer care

Rising productivity leads to rising wages, and therefore rising costs of employing people. Added to this, in some countries difficulties in recruiting are being caused by demographic trends, in particular a scarcity of younger people. For these reasons, there is strong pressure to automate and reserve people for where they really add value to care. These trends have been visible in consumer markets for many years in supermarkets. But they have also had a dramatic impact in industrial markets, in such areas as after sales service (where remote diagnostics and service are becoming increasingly common for advanced technical equipment) and field selling (where telephone prospecting and follow-up are being used to reserve the field sales person for the most difficult tasks, such as gathering sensitive information about customer needs and behaviour and closing complex sales).

In areas of activity where face to face management of customers seems to be indispensible, automation has been introduced to shorten the time it takes to process individual cases. Today, a visit to a building society to withdraw cash from a current account compared to a visit for the same purposes several years ago will reveal the following changes:

(a) The customer no longer completes the form, but gives verbal instructions, which the counter assistant keys directly into the computer. The customer then signs the form.
(b) For some accounts there is no longer a pass book to be updated. The account is operated entirely via a plastic card. Computerised statements can be printed out whenever required. The same card can be used to withdraw cash from an automated teller machine.

This allows staff to spend more time selling the higher value-added services.

Managing, leading and educating customers

The idea that the job of customer facing staff is just to process cases is not conducive to customer care. The term "processing cases" is used to focus on the "production" elements of customer care situations. It also recognises the fact that many organisations which serve customers do not see them as customers, but more as cases. Many public sector bodies (eg courts, benefit and tax offices) are (or were) like this. Also, a fundamental condition of customer care is that cases *do continue* to be processed, but to a higher quality and more to the satisfaction of customers.

Staff are also involved in managing, perhaps leading and sometimes educating customers. This is the very opposite of the "laissez faire" attitude, which would be characterised by the statement:

> I'll meet customers' needs when they come to me, but I won't encourage them to come to me, and when they come I won't tell them what else they can do to get better service.

The opposite approach has these characteristics:

(a) customers are encouraged to make use of all opportunities of receiving better care
(b) customers are led in that direction during every transaction (particularly if unfamiliarity causes them to hold back)
(c) customers are educated about new standards of care that they can benefit from.

This may seem expensive in the short run but is vital in the long run, for customer retention.

The facilities which enable staff to provide this enhanced level of service may be provided, but unless staff are trained and motivated to work with customers in this way, a supplier will not derive long term benefit from it.

The unstructured situation

In some service situations, the idea of processing cases is inappropriate. Take the example of a large international airport. There are may cases to be processed — the large numbers of passengers checking in. But there are also customers who do not present themselves as simple cases. They may wander around lost or be unsure where to go. From a particular airline's point of view they may even be a competitor's customers, though they will still be potential customers for next time. In such situations, it can be productive to employ staff in a trouble-shooting role. Their job is to look for customers with problems and help them. An American acquaintance of one of the authors switched from

Pan Am to British Airways because a BA"helper" got him through check-in and on to his Pan Am flight quickly when he arrived late at Heathrow Airport.

Looking for trouble

The above example demonstrates another customer care principle, that looking for trouble is better than waiting for it to happen. But to deal with the discovered trouble, staff need to have:

(a) plan B to deal with the situation if it is uncommon
(b) the authority to implement plan B on the spot.

In some cases, pleasant but low cost gift packages are an ideal solution. In others, authorising staff to spend up to a particular limit helps.

Role analysis

In analysing how staff relate to customers, it may be helpful to use the ideas of transactional analysis (TA). One of the central ideas of TA is that particular transactions can be analysed in terms of whether participants are playing the roles of children or adults. New and/or experimental customers often act as dependent children, and require parental escorting through the complexities of receiving service. Experienced customers prefer to deal on level terms with suppliers (adult to adult), but may be (and want to be) in the position of parent vis-à-vis junior supplier staff (eg telephone operators, receptionists, secretaries, junior managers). The role the customer desires to play should not be resisted. Instead, customer management should conform to these principles in terms of the language used, without deserting the objectives of the transaction in question.

Emotional labour

One of the reasons why it has taken so long for management to come to terms with the potential for staff to help in managing customers is that many of the norms of people management have their origins in the management of manual, technical and clerical workforces. Their jobs consist of dealing not with people but with things, such as:

(a) laboratory equipment and pilot plants
(b) product designs and prototypes
(c) manufacturing and administrative equipment
(d) paper.

When jobs in service organisations were first designed, the focus was on the task, not on the person being served. Yet both needed doing. The task had to be completed and the customer served. As automation has made the task easier to perform, the focus has moved to the customer to be served. This requires a different kind of labour. It is termed "emotional labour" by sociologists.

Defined in a commonsense way, emotional labour is work in which the emotions of the worker interact with the emotions of the customer. Like any other work, emotional labour can take place with varying degrees of skill. At the peak of the emotional labour pyramid come people who work almost completely at the emotional level — performing artists. These include comedians, actors, musicians and dancers. At the bottom are workers whom customers see only briefly and with whom the transaction is almost automatic. But in the middle lie most service staff, as depicted in Figure 14.2. Their emotional labour skills are amenable to improvement by training, and are subject to diminution if not sustained by training and motivation.

Surface acting and deep acting

The distinction between these two types of acting corresponds, again in a commonsense way, with the distinction between high and low involvement of the customer and the worker. Most everyday contacts between staff and customers only involve surface acting. There is no creation or continuation of a deep relationship. But in some situations, the relationship goes beneath the skin, to one of trust, or mistrust. For example, a financial advisor and client build up a deep relationship over time. However, it may be positive and then become negative if the advisor gives the client catastrophic advice.

Research carried out by Dr Stephen Lloyd Smith produced the following findings.

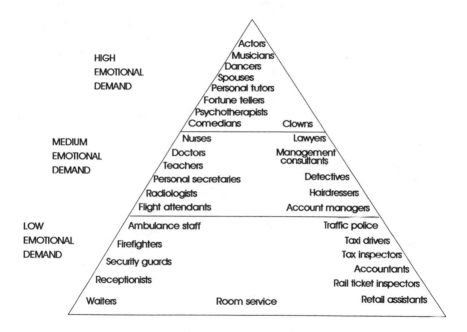

Figure 14.2 The emotional labour pyramid

This is merely a suggestion as to the extent of the emotional demand. Individual workers may improve their relationship with "customers" by raising their emotional commitment, but going too far may cause customers to react adversely. Conversely, too low a level of emotional commitment my cause customers to react adversely (eg doctors).

(a) Emotional labourers definitely do like contact with the customer. Customers can be very unpleasant. But on the whole, emotional labourers positively value having customers. The main exception to this were a few police officers. They complained of being in a state of considerable emotional distress for extended periods of time. This may be due to the rather special nature of their "customer" relationships!

(b) Most emotional labourers are surface actors most of the time. Less than 15 per cent were deep actors. This is not simply a function of job definition, however. A "good" worker can develop really close and helpful relationships with customers, while others might fail to do so. In the survey, a sex shop manager and a children's theme park guide were shown to be excellent at this, while others in similar jobs failed.

(c) Virtually none of the workers was given any training in emotional labour. Only a minority had been given formal training at all. None had been helped by their employers into deep acting.

One of the problems with emotional labour is that although it is possible to select staff for their ability to work at a deep emotional level with customers, it seems difficult to train them to do so. This may be because staff feel that this is a private domain. Also, customers may feel intruded on if staff are poorly trained and try to take a relationship beyond its "natural" emotional level.

Staff attitudes

In circumstances where productivity and quality underlie the organisation's policies, staff are being given messages which can conflict. Process more cases in the same time, but care for customers more. Of course, the systems and processes discussed in the previous chapter provide the solution to the problem — better care is not inconsistent with less time and cost per case.

With the right systems and processes, and in particular clear objectives in handling customers, many companies have shown that automation not only maintains but improves customer care. As was stressed in the chapter on customer behaviour, many customers actually want to be *more* in control of the situation than they have been allowed in the past. If *they* are controlling the machine, with staff assistance where necessary, the outcome may be better for them.

Service simplification

An additional policy area where changes can be made so as to reduce the perceived conflict between care and productivity is simplification of the service. Perhaps the best example of this is fast food restaurants. A restricted product range, with several variations on a few simple themes, allows operators the time to deal with customers in a friendly way while serving them within minutes and sometimes seconds. The till is one of the clues to how this is done. If operators press product buttons instead of price buttons, their job is made much easier and the chances of error greatly reduced. This takes a lot of stress out of the work situation.

A similar situation can be seen in supermarket check-outs. Once, the idea that the till operator might talk to the customer while keying in prices was disliked by some customers, as it increased the chances of error. With scanning of bar codes, it is not unusual to see till operators chatting happily to their customers while processing what is in effect a highly complex transaction. Similarly, electronic funds transfer cash cards have eased the processing of payment, taking the stress out of receiving large sums of money and getting the change right.

So, there are many positive forces at work to reduce the stress that might be caused by the conflict between care and productivity. The fact that this is so is most evident when analysing operations in which these kinds of change have not been made. For example, in many areas of the public sector in the UK, staff are being asked to deliver, with less resources, not fewer but more products, which are not simpler but more complex. Added to this are complicated sets of ever-changing objectives.

School education — an example

School education is probably a good example of this, and it is not surprising therefore to learn of the high stress levels being caused to staff by these changes, and the rising rates of resignation from the service. All this is combined with decreasing levels of service and reduced customer satisfaction. In such circumstances, talk of customer care programmes is not likely to be welcome, and rightly so. For if management do not understand and make use of the connection between productivity, product and process simplification, and customer satisfaction, there is little that the individual can do to improve customer care, at least within the bounds of normal work hours. In such cases, management relies, rather immorally, on the good will of service staff, who work more hours than they are paid for or experience inordinate levels of stress, in order to keep their customers happy.

This example emphasises the need for customer care programmes to be integrated with overall policy, as per the framework of Chapters 7 and 8. Without this, attempts to address the problem through "charm school" methods are likely to backfire badly.

Own needs versus customer needs

The perceptions and attitudes of frontline staff are critical to the delivery of customer care. The role stress induced by trying to achieve high standards of customer care is caused by attempting to suppress the natural tendency to focus on one's own needs and instead focus on those of customers. The more complex the service situation, the more stress is caused.

This problem can only be solved when a clear understanding of staff needs is achieved. In most cases, the need is very simple. It might be expressed as:

> If I don't own or control the area in which service is given and the process through which it is given, I feel worried that things might get out of control. It may take a very long time to process a case. Or it may prove impossible. So I want to be in charge.

Not surprisingly, this kind of attitude is almost certain to cause problems in an age when productivity pressures are forcing organisations to give customers more control over the service area and process. Self-service restaurants, petrol stations and grocery stores are perhaps the best example.

The solution to this problem is to redefine:

(a) the area which staff are formally asked to control
(b) the process so that staff are asked to control (and be responsible for) only those elements which are absolutely essential.

Counter service and territory

Take a situation in which there are several service counters, each offering a wide range of services of varying complexity and average service times. If customers queue at individual counters, some queues may move very slowly, others very fast. Servers feel responsible for the length of queue at their individual counter. A case which takes a long time to process adds to stress levels, as people in the queue behind start to mutter their disapproval and peer anxiously over the shoulder of the customer being served to see how much longer it will take. This situation is unsatisfactory for both customers and staff.

If the queues are merged into one, with the first customer in the queue going to the first available counter, this not only reduces the variation in waiting time, but takes the area of the queue away from the perceived responsibility of individual operators. The whole team is now responsible for the length of the queue, and the team manager (if one exists) can open or close counters to regulate its length. Customers are happier and stress is reduced.

Lecturing and the service process

Where control over elements of the service process is concerned, take the example of a college lecturer. A lecturer prepares material, teaches using it, sets assignments and then marks them. As productivity pressures grow, teachers find it difficult to manage the whole process but feel that they ought to do so. An alternative might be to move to:

(a) standardised material, shared between many lectures
(b) student-centred learning, in which students move through material, at their own pace, assisted where required by the lecturer
(c) standardised assessment material, shared between many lecturers
(d) computerised marking of assignments.

This approach enables lecturers to focus on the areas where they add value most — in helping overcome individual problems of understanding. It is already in use (for productivity reasons) in distance learning (eg the Open University), but is likely to permeate all higher education in the next few years. Interestingly, it usually results in higher quality customer care, as:

(a) poor quality teaching is identified sooner
(b) students receive higher quality material to work on
(c) students learn more from material with the assistance of lecturers than from being lectured to
(d) there is less variability in the assessment process.

The problem of the rogue case

The situation in which personnel face the most stress is in the handling of the rogue case. This may be:

(a) a customer who refuses to pay
(b) a customer who has experienced really severe problems in getting service
(c) a customer who *claims* to have experienced severe problems, but in fact has not
(d) a case which is very difficult to deal with because it genuinely extends the organisation's capability to handle it
(e) a customer whose manner is offensive, irrespective of whether the case is being processed properly.

In all such cases, the organisation must give the member of staff the feeling that support is available. Support can be of many forms:

(a) training to handle such cases — which questions to ask, how to compose oneself, how to admit responsibility without feeling demeaned, how to avoid a defensive reaction
(b) procedures to follow — steps to follow, who else to involve if necessary
(c) benefits that can be offered to the customer on the spot, to defuse the situation (eg refunds or credits).

Personnel management of staff who care for customers

From the above, it should be clear that people who care for customers are a special category of staff. They may not be rare but they are very important to the organisation. To ensure that staff will maximise the customer care opportunity, the following rules should be followed.

(a) When staff are being recruited, special emphasis should be placed on their openness to attitude change. People with deeply held views about the status of different types of people, or about the roles that they should play, should be avoided.

(b) Training programmes should be constructed so that they provide continuous reinforcement to the objective of caring for customers as well as the techniques staff require to do their jobs better. A single blast of customer care training at the beginning is not enough. Training programmes should contain a strong role-play element, covering in particular the problematic customer.

(c) The ergonomics of their work situation should support their role. For example, if there are likely to be many situations in which customers do not want to discuss their situation in public, screens or separate rooms should be provided. The tills in a fast food chain are another example of physical design supporting customer care.

(d) Staff should be cared for as the organisation wishes to care for customers. Here, the rule is "do as you wish them to". Organisations which mishandle their staff find it difficult to deliver high standards of care.

(e) Distinguish clearly between the definition of a job on the one hand and the mission or essence of the job on the other hand. It is the latter which should guide staff, not the former. If a job-holder has to step outside the formally defined job to perform the mission (eg serving customers), then this should be encouraged. Management should act as supporters of the mission, not monitors of the job function.

(f) Reward staff for caring for customers but in ways which are consistent with the culture. In some cases congratulations and encouragement may be enough. If financial reward is required, do not make the reward exceptional, as caring for customers should be routine. Exceptional rewards will encourage customer care, by exception. Often, visibility within the organisation (and to customers) is reward enough in itself. However, it is important to ensure that staff who care for customers receive pay that they consider decent, given the norms of the industry.

(g) Where appropriate, help staff create an appearance which is conducive to positive customer attitudes. Provide image wear, or at least set standards of dress. If appearance is important and one member of staff "lets the side down", the attitude may be contagious.

(h) Give staff an identity (even a name tag) and a personality, rather than a cipher.

(i) Create the frontline management role as leader, helper, coach and motivator, not just as controller. The latter role is by itself unconducive to customer care.

(j) Ensure that middle managers do not become isolated in relation to customer care. Middle managers, one of whose major roles is to provide the connection between plans and implementation, can make or break customer care policies. If they place too many burdens upon customer facing staff, and do not see the consequences in terms of customer care, the result may be very destructive. So involve them in all training and communications about customer care. Ensure that their role is defined as much in terms of supporting customer-facing staff as senior management.

(k) Carry out regular audits of staff attitudes, needs and skills, and ensure that they match to customer care requirements. Make sure that they are detailed and specific, as the customer research should be. Whether through group discussions or staff questionnaires, they should cover all the key areas of customer care (eg courtesy, competence, adequacy of staffing, administration, technical service, convenience, staff turnover, sales requirements).

The need for a comprehensive approach to personnel management is confirmed by the view of McDonalds' management that without outstanding employee relations, good customer relations are impossible. Their personnel programmes include:

(a) initial and continuing training
(b) clearly defined roles of managers and supervisors
(c) reward and recognition for service
(d) quantitative methods for monitoring achievement of service levels
(e) continuing reinforcement of success.

The role of training

At the beginning of this chapter the idea that staff are much more capable of dealing with customers than most managers realise was put forward. However, this does not negate the need for training. The companies with the best reputation for customer care normally achieve it partly through continuous and widespread training.

Perhaps the most famous programme in this area was British Airways' suite of training programmes which were initiated when the company began its efforts to become customer-oriented. The first major programme was "Putting People First". All 37,000 employees went through this. It was followed by additional programmes. "Day in the Life" highlighted the company's dependence on cross-functional working. "To be the Best" asked all participants to examine what they needed to do to deliver the company's promise of supremacy in customer care. Other programmes followed, all of them involving hard work on the part of the participants. The Avis "Service Leadership Programme" is similar in content and achievement and puts special emphasis on empowering staff.

Internal marketing

In recent years, there has been a development in employee communications which can transform the way staff are communicated with and motivated. *Internal marketing* simply applies to staff all the disciplines of marketing. The rationale for this is that many staff are internal customers. Hence the Scandinavian Airways statement "If you're not serving a customer, you should be serving someone who is". In terms of the quality issues discussed in Chapter 10, staff are seen as customers in the fullest sense — for information, policies and indeed anything that the organisation wishes them to do.

Internal marketing follows the usual marketing disciplines of:

(a) understanding the market (in this case what kinds of staff there are, what their needs are, right through to segmentation by factors such as need, attitude and so on)
(b) setting objectives (eg in relation to delivery of customer care)

(c) creating policies (eg to help staff deliver customer care effect-ively)

(d) marketing them to staff (using all the required media and communication disciplines)

(e) measuring results of the marketing, in terms of attitudes and delivered performance

(f) improving plans and implementation next time round.

Many ideas that contribute to an organisation's ability to deliver customer care have arisen from this approach. They include:

(a) setting clear objectives about what to communicate and measuring the effect of the communication in terms of these original objectives

(b) costing communication as an important input into the management process, and setting the cost against the measured benefits (to staff and customers)

(c) the need to identify the difference between the languages of internal and external customers, and match or merge them

(d) the need to segment the internal audience according to the type of tasks they are required to do and the benefits they derive from doing them, so that the right messages can be sent to the right people (targeting)

(e) the need to carry out regular staff surveys so as to measure the effect of internal marketing (and not just to hear the good or bad news about attitudes)

(f) using a greater variety of media to get messages over, from print and video to team briefings (the equivalent of face-to-face contact)

(g) the need to use professional communications agencies (if the budget stands it!)

(h) the importance of creative concepts, compared to pedestrian instructions

(i) the need to control the frequency and reach of internal communications, so that the right communications are sent out, to the right people at the right time. Otherwise, there is a severe risk of drowning staff in information and exhortation

(j) the importance of mobilising all staff, wherever they work, as they nearly all have an influence on customer care.

Measuring performance

Performance measurement and staff management are inseparable. The connection between the two is most clearly visible in British Airways' definition of the role of Director of Marketplace Performance. The holder of this post sets performance standards in most areas that involve customers. But these standards can only be achieved through intensive training programmes. Staff are also given the opportunities to interrogate senior managers about their policies in "hot seat" sessions.

If everything is well planned and implemented, the right levels of customer care should be created. But organisations must be sure that the effect is as intended, hence the need for monitoring, measurement and control, the subject of the next chapter.

Chapter 15

Performance Indicators and Targets

The best, and some would say the only, reason for customer care is that it is an investment which pays off, in terms of the objectives of the organisation. Customer care must be managed, using quantitive data on the extent to which it is being achieved and on the benefits arising from it. Although precise measurement may not be possible in every situation, it must be attempted. This is because good management depends upon following a simple cycle of plan – implement – monitor – control. This applies as strongly to customer care as to the most technical of management actions.

In earlier chapters, the idea that in the short term financial success and customer care seem to pull in opposite directions was explored. It was shown that, properly implemented, customer care, productivity and efficiency go hand in hand. Proper implementation requires including in the scope of customer care projects *all* aspects of the relationship with customers, not just face to face treatment, but systems, procedures, products, the management practices of every function, and even strategic plans. In this way, a virtuous circle of care, simplicity (and variety within it), clarity and effectiveness can be established. Where functions do not work together, where organisational structure and processes are not planned taking into account customer needs, there is more likely to be a vicious circle of customer dissatisfaction, increased costs of quality (in handling disaffected customers), reduced overall effectiveness, followed by even worse treatment of customers.

The fundamental financial premise of customer care

The fundamental financial premise of customer care is that any direct costs of customer care can be set against a variety of benefits. These include:

(a) higher revenue and profit from increased customer retention and more business with retained customers
(b) revenue from new customers, attracted by the company's reputation (word of mouth or other means) or resulting from (in business-to-business markets) buyers moving between organisations
(c) reduced costs of quality (eg handling queries, disaffected customers)
(d) reduced costs of complexity (as ways of meeting customer needs are found which involve less complex processes and policies)
(e) reduced direct costs (as customers are allowed to take over those parts of the process that they themselves want to do anyway).

An example of costs and benefits

Consider a simple example. A business-to-business mail order company is experiencing a downturn in its business. It identifies that one of the reasons for this is a falling customer loyalty rate. Its customers are placing a higher proportion of their business with competitors and some are leaving outright. Market research is commissioned. This shows that the reason for customers becoming less loyal and leaving altogether is that its finance director decided to tighten up on debtors. Payment terms were reduced from 45 to 30 days. Customers who had not paid within 30 days were first chased. If they then had not paid within 45 days no further orders were accepted from them. The company had thought that its competitive position and branding were strong enough to achieve this change. It was wrong. However, the company's profitability had started to fall in a time of rising interest rates, so just being lax on debtors was not an option.

Instead, the company decided on a more complex policy. As 90 per cent of its business came from 10 per cent of its customers, it decided to negotiate individual payment terms with its customers. These were based on a notional payment period of 30 days. Earlier payment was rewarded with a bonus (a larger discount against list prices than the normal one), subtracted from the cost of the next order, and late payment by a reduced discount, which was debited to the next order.

The overall change involved:

(a) some investment in software development and changed management practices. This ensured that payments were credited quickly, that information on orders requiring debiting or crediting was available more quickly to account managers, and that customers were provided with clearer statements of their position and summaries of their performance over the year

(b) reduced numbers of staff involved in chasing individual payments

(c) increased sales force time spent on badly overdue accounts.

The result was a stabilisation of the customer loss rate and a rebuilding of business among existing customers. In addition, because negotiations usually involved direct long term liaison with the financial function of customer companies, there were opportunities for longer term contracts with some customers, with increased discounts but lower handling costs to the company.

Such benefits take time to pay off. Strictly speaking, one should carry out a net present value calculation to work out whether the action is likely to be worthwhile. The problem with such evaluations is that they involve forecasting the likely outcome of the change. Although market research can give some indication of the benefits that will arise, in terms of the likelihood of customer remaining loyal or buying more if practices are changed, such intentions data are notoriously suspect. However, an organisation which is committed to customer care will be continually making changes and should therefore develop a sense of the kinds of change in customer behaviour that are likely to result from alterations in policy.

Testing policies

It is possible to test changes in customer care. Any organisations with branches for dealing with customers, or which deal with customers mainly through direct marketing techniques (mail, telephone, direct sales force) can test an approach on one group of customers. If it works, it can be extended to others. For example, a major airline followed a policy of keeping one group of customers very fully informed of every offer it was promoting and of a variety of other activities it was engaged in. Another group of customers were given the bare minimum of information. The loyalty and ordering rates of the latter started to fall relative to those of the former. The profit yielded by the additional sales more than outweighed the costs of sending the extra information. In addition, the more informed customers recommended the company more often, so additional benefits accrued through word of mouth.

Target levels of performance

It is very difficult to predict the returns to customer care, so it is hard to set targets. However, targets based on testing have the dual advantage that they are likely to be more realistic and that staff will *perceive* them as feasible, and therefore make more efforts to surpass them.

Customer care targets are of three basic kinds:

(a) work-flow targets, which measure the flow of work through the customer care process (eg more cases processed to quality standards, reductions in queue lengths)
(b) output targets, which measure the results of customer care in terms of what customers do (eg stay loyal, buy more, complain less, say they are more satisfied, write more complimentary letters) or perceive (as revealed in surveys)
(c) intermediate measures, which relate to what happens to the customers during the processing of their cases (eg spend less time in queues).

The best practice is first to identify the relationship between work-flow, intermediate and output measures. This may not be a very tight one. The uncertain and probabilistic nature of the relationship affects the way staff should be targeted. Staff achieve output successes through their work. They do not "control" customers, so assessing staff on the basis of output measures is not fair. It also presumes that management knows precisely how to improve customer care. If work-flow measures improve, but output measures do not, this is a good indication that management's wisdom does know a bound!

Setting standards

To ensure that operations are delivering as planned, service standards must be set. Where customer-facing or front office activities are concerned, these should be based on:

(a) financial targets — these say what must be achieved for efficiency objectives to be achieved
(b) service delivery targets — service delivered to customers, based on technical measures such as average waiting time
(c) market performance targets — such as share of the market, rising sales levels. These are particularly important in a competitive environment
(d) customer satisfaction targets — measures of the perceived level of service, ranging from perceptions as to punctuality of service to measures of satisfaction with the service.

These can be combined into an overall measure of quality of customer care. The virtue of a single indicator is that it makes the relative performance of staff groups clear. A single indicator also has the advantage that it prevents dominance of a single dimension (eg a very strong focus on current sales levels). This is particularly likely if:

(a) there is a direct connection between that dimension and contribution to short term financial success
(b) the dimension is easily and indisputably quantified (eg sales levels are measured through company systems and sales figures are hard to dispute).

However, combining these measures means assigning (possibly controversial) weights to the different areas. Therefore, although an overall measure of quality might be used to maintain balance and for other purposes (eg for competitions), performance according to the different standards should also be a focus of management.

Quantifying standards

All of these standards must be quantified. The old adage: "What you can't measure you can't manage" may not always be true, but it certainly applies to customer care.

Measurement against targets should not be confused with research. Research is carried out mainly to find out what policies to implement or what problems to address. Measurement is undertaken to assess performance in implementing policies. The two do not separate cleanly. However, the distinction is important because measurement dressed up as research may be incomplete and bring research into disrepute. The golden rule here is not to decide policies until the situation has been researched and not to measure until people and systems have been set up to achieve targets, and targets have been agreed and communicated.

It should go without saying that standards and their associated targets should be:

(a) *feasible*, in the sense that they relate to areas that staff can in practice control by their actions

(b) *credible*, in that staff believe that they can be achieved, that their measurement can be more or less objective, and that they really do contribute to the well-being of the organisation and its customers

(c) *focused* on the customers and on the policy areas that are most important

(d) *relevant*, ie they must cover the major service interfaces between the supplier and its customers, as revealed by the contact audit

(e) *reliable*, ie they must be part of a well considered and stable policy, which endures, so that staff know that if they help achieve them, they will not be told (now or in the future) that their performance was irrelevant

(f) *objective*, in the sense that it should be absolutely clear when and by how much the situation is improving (or deteriorating)

(g) *prioritised*, in the sense that staff know which are the most important. This is determined by the *mission* of people's jobs (see Chapter 14)

(h) clearly *beneficial* to the supplier, ie they must contribute to the mission and objectives of the company

(i) clearly *beneficial* to customers, ie they must help meet customer needs

(j) *competitive*, in the sense that they are set bearing in mind competitive offerings. As discussed earlier in this book, the decision on which areas to compete in and what standards to set relative to competition must be carefully weighed. However, as a minimum, at least some standards should lead to the creation of a significant difference — a level of care which has clearly describable advantages over that offered by competitors

(k) *progressive,* in the sense that they are not fixed but continue moving forward and changing according to changing customer needs

(l) *presentable*, ie they must not be so complicated that staff do not understand what they are or how to achieve them. There is plenty of scope for creative presentation. One of the best ideas is the Avis concept of the Customer Care Income Statement, which shows customers' repurchase intentions (and hence the likely revenue flow from them) and Customer Care Balance Sheet, which shows how satisfied customers are (and therefore indicates the value of Avis's greatest asset, its customer base).

Figure 15.1 shows the relationship between research, policy and targets.

Avoiding overstatement

The need for there to be a clear benefit cannot be overemphasised. It is easy to overstate the benefit of investment in customer care. If improvements in care fail to lead to improvements in the overall position of the supplier, then the investment must be questioned. This may be for a variety of reasons:

(a) the standards chosen are not really important to customers
(b) the measures chosen exaggerate the extent of the benefit to customers
(c) the changes being measured are too expensive to achieve
(d) the changes being made have gone beyond the point of diminishing returns. The need to avoid giving too good service which is not appreciated and may even be seen as "over-attentive" has already been discussed. General Electric, amongst others, has carried out experiments to establish where this point is. This concept should be applied to the different market segments that the supplier operates in

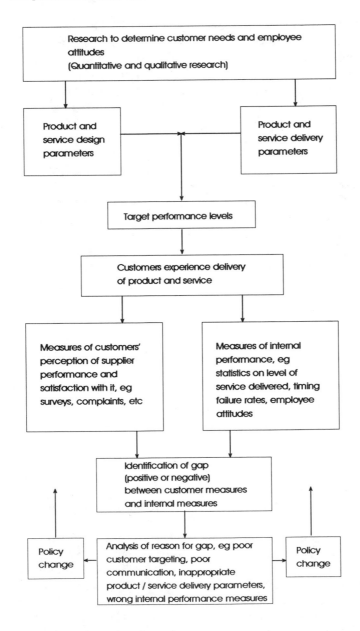

Figure 15.1 Relationship between research, policy and targets

(e) improvements in one area have been offset by deterioration in a more important area

(f) too many measures have been chosen, so that although there have been lots of small improvements, customers have not really noticed them and therefore have not responded. Meanwhile, resources have been diffused over too many policy areas.

The risks of choosing standards which do not lead to real improvements is quite high, particularly in suppliers which are new to customer care. For this reason, it is sensible to have at least some policies which are demonstrably self-funding. This means setting up clearly defined projects and associated standards and measures which are almost guaranteed to lead to improvement. This is best done after research when the highest priority areas for improvement should be self-evident. An example might be to ensure that sales leads are handled more promptly and with greater accountability. This will normally lead to customers being both more satisfied and buying more.

Measuring quality through research

The best measure of quality in marketing is repeat business. But most good marketers want to know why they are getting repeat business and why they are not. For this reason, quality questionnaires are used. Unfortunately, these are usually distributed on a "complete if you please" basis, so that results are biased towards those who feel the need to respond (perhaps because they are very satisfied or dissatisfied). For this reason, periodic random sample surveys of customers are advised. Of course, if the number of customers is low enough, then the entire customer base can be sampled.

A customer satisfaction questionnaire might ask for the following data.

(a) Name and address of customer (if required to match to a purchasing history and if the customer is prepared to give it).
(b) Details of service received (which service, when received, how much paid, how booked, etc).
(c) Perceptions of overall level of service and of specific features of the service.

(d) Suggestions as to improvements.
(e) Statement as to whether the service would be recommended to a friend (this is considered better than asking whether the consumer would buy again, as he or she may have no choice).

Examples of research studies incorporating customer satisfaction measures were given in Chapter 5.

Quality of image

Many suppliers use general corporate image surveys as a way to measure their positioning on customer care and other areas. These image surveys are valuable because there is a strong halo effect at work in customers' minds. If they think well of the supplier, they will think well of the service. Hence the importance of strong corporate branding, as discussed in Chapter 12.

Such surveys ask customers to rate a number of organisations (usually including those in parallel markets) on factors such as:

(a) whether they give good service
(b) whether they give good value for money or whether they charge too much
(c) whether they respond quickly to problems
(d) whether they are polite and/or helpful
(e) whether they use up-to-date technology
(f) whether they are doing much to become efficient
(g) whether they are good employers
(h) whether they would be recommended as a supplier to other customers.

The relationship between these measures and more specific customer care actions should always be monitored, to see whether one is affecting the other. Note that the relationship will normally be two-way.

Sources of measure

Indicators come from five main sources.

(a) Company records of staff or related activity. These are mostly input measures and include such items as:
  (i)   time to answer the telephone
  (ii)   length of telephone call
  (iii)   time to answer a letter
  (iv)   frequency and/or length of sales call
  (v)   proportion of problems resolved within a particular interval
  (vi)   time to get to customer requiring service
  (vii)   time to service a machine
  (viii) interval between need for emergency service
  (ix)   frequency of return with same complaint.
(b) Communication from customers, eg
  (i)   number of complaints received (personal, telephone calls or letters)
  (ii)   number of complimentary communications received (personal, telephone calls or letters).
(c) Customer research — either formally conducted market research or from complaint/comment forms available at point of service. This might cover:
  (i)   perceptions of and attitudes towards supplier, service and staff
  (ii)   requirements and priorities
  (iii)   satisfaction levels
  (iv)   competitive performance.
(d) Staff data — usually formal staff surveys, data arising from appraisal, staff comment or suggestion schemes, data arising from recruitment or leaving or informal feedback. Coverage includes:
  (i)   perceptions of and attitudes towards the organisation and customers
  (ii)   requirements
  (iii)   satisfaction levels
  (iv)   attrition rates (between jobs and to outside the supplier).
(e) Commercial performance — usually financial or marketing. It may include:
  (i)   sales levels (amount, frequency, type)
  (ii)   profit levels
  (iii)   customer loyalty rates (length of time customer with the supplier, proportion of business, variety of business)
  (iv)   success relative to competition.

It is a good idea to try to ensure that most of the data needed for assessing customer care performance arises from the normal information flow rather than from special research. The latter is most likely to be needed for customer and staff data of the kind mentioned under (c) and (d) above. Research is costly and should only be used where its value has been clearly demonstrated. One area where it is essential is to match the perceptions and attitudes of customers and staff with commercial performance. Many customer care problems are picked up first of all in financial figures, then in commercial surveys and traced back to staff attitudes which are the result of poor management processes. This is a long way round and rather expensive. The ideal is to pick a problem up at its point of origin (eg a change in a process) not when it has affected financial performance.

Reporting

For this reason, it is worth considering how indicators from all the above sources can best be summarised so as to draw management's attention to likely problems. Usually, this is done through finding out by experience which internal indicators are likely to be symptomatic of external problems and providing early warning reports of problems based on summaries of these internal indicators.

Only in this way can management be truly in control. When an external problem occurs, they should have been warned about it through the flow of internal data. Hence the term "no surprise". This means that although it may not be possible to prevent customers suffering, when their suffering shows up in commercial measures it should at least be anticipated, and at best action will already be in place to rectify the situation.

Experimenting with different measures is essential. It forces management to try to understand what each measure represents in terms of their area of responsibility and what they can do about it. The idea of testing different customer care approaches, with a full range of measures to see which ones best summarise what is going on in the pilot, is also a helpful aid to understanding the relative importance of different measures in different situations.

The acceptable and the ideal — tails management

In most (though not all) situations, the most damaging cases of lack of care are far more destructive to the organisation that a large number of slightly substandard cases. Hence the idea of managing tails — the tails being those in a graph of a distribution of outcomes. For example, Figure 15.2 shows how long people queue for a bed in hospital for a particular kind of non-urgent operation. If *and only if* research shows that most patients are happy to tolerate a wait of two to three months, and if medical judgement is that this kind of wait will not be damaging, then it would be appropriate to focus on ways of reducing the number of people in the right hand tail. However, if measures to do this resulted in a lengthening of the average wait to more than three months, this approach would be unsuitable.

In the case of the bank queue mentioned earlier, creating one queue reduces the size of both tails. The chance of a customer arriving and finding a very short queue is also lessened.

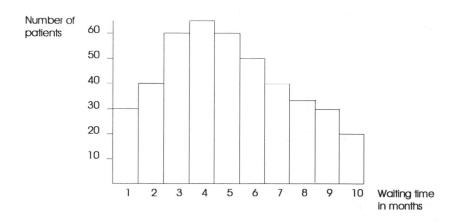

Figure 15.2 Length of queue for particular operation

Type of tail	How to manage (examples)
Wait for operation	Allocate beds to longest tail. Speed up processing of type of operations.
Retail queues	Single queue, multiple service points. Reallocate staff at peak hours.
Product reliability	Delete unreliable products. Incentives for old product trade-in.
Time for service engineer to arrive in critical situations	Rapid identification of criticality. Redeployment of staff from non-critical activities. Targeting staff on time to arrive in critical situations.
Time to answer telephone call in sales enquiry handling office	Computerised call allocations. Monitoring long calls to prevent tying up of resource.

Figure 15.3 Managing tails

Figure 15.3 shows some examples of tails and how they can be managed.

Tails management is an example of a more general policy, that of *graduated performance targets*. Most service situations are not all or nothing, for two reasons:

(a) customers measure the quality of service along a number of dimensions
(b) customers differ between each other in their judgements on service.

This means that a particular customer may be very satisfied with some aspects of a service, less so with another, but quite happy overall. Another customer might be very happy about one or two aspects of service, very unhappy about many others, and so extremely unhappy overall. Blending the responses of these two customers may give a more or less "average" picture, although the situation it represents is not at all happy. Figure 15.4 demonstrates how this arises.

Attribute	Satisfaction score		Average
	Customer A	Customer B	
Comfort of waiting room	4	5	4.5
Speed of service	5	1	3
Appropriateness of service	3	2	2.5
Treatment by service staff	4	4	4
Complaint handling	5	1	3
AVERAGE	4.2	2.6	3.4

Figure 15.4 The problem with averages

For this reason, management must approach performance measurements with care. One approach to this type of situation might be as follows.

(a) Set a floor level for average performance and raise this level each year, but only to feasible levels. One way of doing this in a company with several offices might be to set as the average level each year the level achieved by the office which just achieved better than the office in question in the previous year. A more aggressive approach might be to set as the standard the average achieved by, say, the top 10 per cent of offices.
(b) Have a separate targeting exercise for the proportion of highly dissatisfied customers and for recurring problems. This must include individual solutions for the customers.

The above is similar to NTT's approach, which distinguishes clearly between standards which are managed on an average basis and ones that are managed on an individual basis. Whatever the approach adopted, management should always consider what particular levels of performance imply for individual customers and change things so as to improve the lot of individual customers in ways that the latter appreciate.

Targeting performance by segment

The above example also suggests that setting gross, undifferentiated targets may not be wise. Some customers may be happy with one length of time of queue, others with others. For example, supermarket customers who have just dropped in to pick up a few items may be less willing to queue than those who are making a major weekly purchase, hence the idea of a quick service till for those with a small number of items. Banks have taken up this idea with special tills for quick transactions (eg paying in no more than five items or drawing money via a personal cheque) and long ones (eg foreign exchange).

These ways of segmenting are behavioural (ie by the kind of transaction the customer wishes to make). However, other methods can be psychographic. For example, customers who are impatient and prepared to pay to avoid queues or to experience a higher standard of service can be offered that higher standard, at a price. Hence first class air passengers being given special lounge and check-in facilities.

Except in the smallest suppliers, an attempt should be made to set customer care targets by segment. This will reduce costs and maximise benefits for a given investment. However, most large suppliers rightly insist on a minimum level of performance for all customers. Without this, customers experiencing poor service will spread the word.

Key performance indicators

The number of indicators that can be used to measure attempts to improve customer satisfaction or actual increased satisfaction is very great. However, it is easy not to see the wood for the trees. For this reason, managers like to identify key performance indicators — ones that are so important that achievement of target is well rewarded, and failure to achieve it a cause for immediate remedial action or even punishment. These indicators should be chosen so that they are closely related to the objectives of the supplier. It is also *essential* that they be related to what customers view as the key performance criteria.

For example, British Telecom's key performance indicator for fault clearance was set at the time of privatisation at 90 per cent of faults cleared within two days. Following research in 1986 this was changed to 90 per cent within five hours for business lines and 90 per cent within eight hours for residential lines. In 1989, further research revealed that customers were prepared to wait longer if:

(a) they were kept informed
(b) the fault was cleared first time. The 1986 target had caused too many quick fixes to take place. These led to repeat calls for the same fault.

Further investigation of British Telecom's policies demonstrated the need to segment targets further and match internal targets against (segmented) customer needs. For example, targets on time to instal a new line for a house mover needed to be not in terms of number of days wait. Customers in this situation are more concerned with keeping to appointments made, as they will often take the day off to be at home when the engineer calls. Therefore, targets were changed to measure aspects such as:

(a) the number of appointments made upon first contact
(b) the number of appointments made to the customer's satisfaction
(c) the number of appointments kept on the due date.

Here are some more examples of key performance indicators. These are not the only indicators for each company, but are chosen to give a flavour of the kind of indicator used.

American Express	Number of statement errors, number of late statements, lifetime value of customers, number of new card-members.
Hotpoint	Repeat purchases, number of complaints, number of repeat complaints.
General Electric Answer Centre	Appliances bought after calls to the Answer Centre, warranty service calls saved by calls to the Centre.
British Airways	Repeat sales, range sales (hotels, car hire).

Thomas Cook	Repeat bookings, time to answer.
Prime Computer	Number of non-technical queries answered,
Customer Action	problems not resolved on call, problems not
Line	solved on second call (Prime to customer).

Competitive performance measures

Most suppliers focus on absolute measures rather than measures relative to competition. This is for two reasons:

(a) data on competitive performance may be hard to obtain and unreliable when it is obtained
(b) it is difficult to target staff on performance relative to competition. Staff can only affect absolute performance. How well they do against competition depends on how well competitors do, not something that staff control.

Despite this, it is important, where direct or parallel competitors are important in determining the overall success of the supplier, to translate absolute performance measures into relative ones. These must take into account the agreed strategy, ie the comparison must be of areas (kinds of policy, target customers) where it has been agreed that relative performance is important.

Key performance indicators and positioning

In markets where service performance is a critical part of positioning, the key performance indicator can become part of the supplier's positioning statement. For example, J C Bamford, the earth-moving equipment company, promises same day delivery for any part for any machine they ever made. This promise is not easy to fulfil. But if such a promise is always fulfilled, then it can be promoted as a central element of positioning. Notice that such a statement bears a direct relationship to the needs of individual customer's needs. It is not a statistical statement, like "95 per cent of our flights arrive on time". This is little consolation to the passenger whose flight is so badly delayed that a connection is missed. In fact, it can worsen the situation, as the passenger may with some justice wonder why that particular flight was delayed when all the rest arrive on time.

Customer loyalty as a measure

In commercial organisations, customer retention and loyalty are amongst the most important measures. If good customer data is available, then the proportion of business coming from existing customers should be a routine measure of success. Where the supplier does not have direct access to customer buying behaviour, market research may be required to find this figure.

In a sensitive service environment, complaint levels may be an important indicator. In a public service environment, where quality of service and length of wait have become politically sensitive, length/duration of queue and complaint levels may be key indicators.

Such indicators are also useful internal communication of the success or otherwise of the supplier.

Setting targets

In summary, customer care must be underpinned by a clear framework of measurement, which shows whether customers are really being cared for. These measures must be closely related to the organisation's overall strategy, and provide a basis for setting targets for individuals and groups (staff and customers). These targets should then be adjusted in the light of experience and, ideally, improving performance. Monitoring of performance against these targets should be a prime input into appraisal of staff and their managers, and be used to control day to day policies.

Learning from results

There are many ways to measure effectiveness. In the end, the most important results are customer satisfaction and brand support, and how these are translated into financial measures, such as revenue and profit.

Intermediate criteria can be used to judge effectiveness. These are based on the *chain of productivity*, the ratios which determine the relationship between input and output. A simple example of such a chain is:

(a) profit = unit profit x number of units sold
(b) number of units sold = sales per response x number of responses
(c) number of responses = responses per customer reached x number of customers reached.

Using intermediate measures, any marketing policy could be evaluated by:

(a) the number of customers it reaches
(b) how many responses it generates (of each type)
(c) number of sales made
(d) incremental profit from the campaign
(e) how much it increases customer lifetime value

and so forth.

Building the value of customers

Long term performance should also be evaluated. This evaluation helps answer questions such as:

(a) Should a particular kind of customer be recruited?
(b) How much should the company pay to recruit new customers?
(c) What methods should be used to recruit customers?
(d) How much credit should new customers be given?
(e) What is it worth to the company to reactivate lapsed customers?
(f) Which customers are profitable now and how profitable are they?

Much statistical experience is built into such models. The more experience a supplier has using customer databases, the more easily it can develop such a model.

Valuing customers

Customers are expensive to acquire and not easy to keep. A supplier that neglects the acquisition and retention of customers will incur high marketing costs relative to any competitors that take more trouble.

The marketing information system must therefore give an accurate and up-to-date picture of acquisition and retention. The relevant management report is the *customer inventory*. This shows customer gains and losses, classified in various ways (eg by type of customer, type of product typically bought). Figure 15.5 shows an example of such an inventory.

Customer type	Total at prior year end	Added to customer base during year	Lost from customer base during year	Net change	New total
A	2600	400	250	+150	2750
B	3000	200	130	+70	3070
C	3500	150	270	−120	3380
D	2500	300	180	+120	2620
E	2000	250	140	+110	2110
F	1500	130	50	+80	1580

Figure 15.5 A customer inventory

If acquiring customers is expensive, why do it? Over the period of a customer's relationship with a company, the customer may buy many times, across all of a product range. To take this into account, the idea of *lifetime value of the customer* is used. This measures the net present value of all future contributions to overhead and profit from the customer. To estimate the lifetime value of a group of customers acquired through a particular marketing action, data is needed on:

(a) all the supplier's marketing contacts with the customer
(b) the responses and revenues that result from these contacts
(c) the costs associated with each action and response
(d) change in status of customers, eg between being a customer and not being one, or from being an intense user to an infrequent user
(e) the present value of future profits.

The concept of lifetime value can cause a supplier to reassess the way it does business. Examples of long term revenue that can be created include:

(a) warranty and service revenues on equipment and installations
(b) regular repeat purchases, sometimes with variations in the product range (eg holidays, books, domestic appliances)
(c) pension, investment and insurance schemes
(d) club subscriptions.

Consider the example of a company which sells industrial equipment. The initial sale is normally followed by sales of parts, service and consumables.

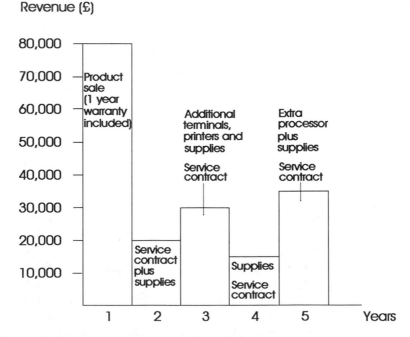

Figure 15.6 Revenue stream from typical installation

As shown in Figure 15.6, the initial sale of the product may bring immediate "after-market" revenue in the form of installation charges and an extended warranty contract. Once the initial sale is completed, there is a continuing stream after the warranty has expired. Further revenue comes from replacements, changes, upgrades, additional software, supplies, support and service contracts, post-sale consultancy and the like. The equipment sale may be preceded by consultancy services. Although such services, like the installation charges and initial guarantee costs, may be "bundled" into the initial price, they nonetheless constitute separate revenues.

On this calculation, with service and warranty charges usually around 10-15 per cent of equipment price, and installation costs up to 30 per cent of the equipment price for very complex equipment, total revenue from the product may exceed that for the initial item of equipment by a multiple of 2 or 3, even assuming no upgrade or sale of additional products. If these items are included, the multiple may be 10 or more. Given the high lifetime value relative to initial sale revenue, customer acquisition should be treated as an investment. In this example, the revenue cost profile of a group of customers might be as depicted in Figure 15.7.

Customer type, ranked by average initial contribution	Average revenue on acquisition	Average cost of acquisition	Average contribution on acquisition	Present value of future contribution	Total contribution
A	1000	600	400	500	900
B	800	550	250	540	790
C	600	500	100	490	590
D	500	500	0	400	400
E	450	500	50	300	250

Figure 15.7 Lifetime revenue / cost profiles

Getting the concept of lifetime value accepted

The concept of customer lifetime value is well established in suppliers whose customers are all identifiable and with whom a succession of financial transactions is carried out. These include mail order and financial services companies. Statistical segmentation procedures are used to find what differentiates customers with different lifetime values. The variables that account for the difference will then be used as criteria for targeting customers for new marketing actions.

Sometimes a simpler approach is best. For example, the Club Mediterrannée justifies treating customers who suffer bad flights (not its fault) with extra service by a simple calculation:

(a) each customer spends an average of over $1000 per visit
(b) each customer returns an average of four times
(c) the contribution margin is about 60 per cent
(d) therefore the average customer is worth at least $2400 ($1000 x 4 x 60%).

However, for many suppliers lifetime value is a new concept, or one that is poorly understood. In some suppliers the pressure to sell "new business" militates against use of the concept. This can distort relationships with customers and even alienate those with high lifetime values, as they may be neglected relative to their business potential. This problem can be resolved, although it may take time. One solution is as follows:

(a) first make sure that lifetime value statistics are available, at least on a sample, estimated basis
(b) carry out tests to show the benefits of taking the lifetime value approach, taking care to follow through and measure the results
(c) demonstrate the financial and customer-satisfaction benefits of the approach, being particularly careful to identify the cut-off points under different strategies
(d) propose specific changes to policy in areas where using the concept is likely to pay off best.

Valuing care actions

TARP, whose figures on the impact of customer care were quoted at the beginning of this book, have also invented the idea of a "Market Damage Simulation Model" which shows the effect of succeeding or failing with customer care. It demands a great deal of customer research

	Yr1	Yr2	Yr3	Yr4
Number of customers — year start	1000	988	979	972
Proportion GEC	.85	.85	.85	.85
Proportion PEC	.15	.15	.15	.15
Number GEC	850	840	832	826
Number PEC	150	148	147	146
Contribution per GEC ($k)	4	4	4	4
Contribution per PEC($k)	2	2	2	2
Contribution of GECs — total ($k)	3400	3359	3327	3303
Contribution of PECs — total ($k)	300	296	294	291
Total prospect pool	8000	8030	8063	8099
Number joining pool through market growth	300	300	300	300
Proportion of pool becoming customers without recommendation	.02	.02	.02	.02
Number of new customers per year without recommendation	160	161	161	162
Contribution per new unrecommended customer ($k)	2	2	2	2
Constribution of new unrecommended customers — total ($k)	320	321	323	324
Proportion of GECs recommending	.2	.2	.2	.2
Number of GECs recommending — total	170	168	166	165
Number of prospects recommended to, per GEC recommending	4	4	4	4
Number of prospects recommended to — total	680	672	665	661
Proportion of recommended prospects becoming customers	.1	.1	.1	.1
Number of recommended customers — total	68	67	67	66
Contribution per recommended customer ($k)	2.5	2.5	2.5	2.5
Contribution of recommended customers — total ($k)	170	168	166	165
Number of GECs talked to by each PEC	8	8	8	8
Number of GECs talked to by PECs — total	1200	1186	1174	1166
Proportion of those talked to leaving supplier	.2	.2	.2	.2
Number of those talked to leaving supplier — total	240	237	235	233
Number of prospects talked to by each PEC	6	6	6	6
Number of prospects talked to by PECs — total	900	889	881	874
Proportion of those talked to leaving prospect pool	.3	.3	.3	.3
Number of those talked to leaving prospect pool — total	270	267	264	262
TOTAL CONTRIBUTION	4190	4145	4110	4084

Figure 15.8 Example of customer damage modelling

327

In this example, the ratio between the number of good experience customers (GECs) and the number of poor experience customers (PECs) is critical. Because PECs are active in dissuading customers, the model is very sensitive to the ratio.

This model is relatively simple, as it assumes that there are only two types of experience — good and poor. In real life, PECs may complain, and their subsequent behaviour will be affected by how well the complaint is dealt with. The model should also take into account the purchasing frequency. More specifically, additional rows should be added to allow for:

(a) proportion and number of customers complaining

(b) proportion and number of customers whose complaints are handled well or poorly

(c) buying and recommending behaviour of those whose complaints are handled well or poorly

(d) the rebuying frequency of all categories of customers, from those who are completely satisfied to those whose complaints are handled poorly.

to quantify the impact, but once this research has been done it is easy to simulate the results of changes in level of care. Nowadays, the widespread use of spreadsheet modelling makes such an approach more comprehensible. Figure 15.8 provides an example of such a model.

Conclusion

Customer lifetime value underlies not only measurement but the whole concept of customer care. Suppliers should care for customers if customers are valuable to them. This value extends beyond the current business year, usually for many years into the future. Therefore, managing relationships with customers should be seen as a long term programme but one which starts to bring benefits immediately. Though in some cases the costs may outweigh the benefits in the short run, in the long run, as many successful companies have demonstrated, the benefits outweigh the costs.

Index

329